Abram Pocz...
(516) 686-7708

THE
BOOK OF
STRATAGEMS

THE
BOOK OF
STRATAGEMS

Tactics for Triumph and Survival

HARRO VON SENGER

Edited and translated by
Myron B. Gubitz

VIKING

VIKING
Published by the Penguin Group
Viking Penguin, a division of Penguin Books USA Inc.,
375 Hudson Street, New York, New York 10014, U.S.A.
Penguin Books Ltd, 27 Wrights Lane,
London W8 5TZ, England
Penguin Books Australia Ltd, Ringwood,
Victoria, Australia
Penguin Books Canada Ltd, 10 Alcorn Avenue, Suite 300,
Toronto, Ontario, Canada M4V 3B2
Penguin Books (N.Z.) Ltd, 182–190 Wairau Road,
Auckland 10, New Zealand

Penguin Books Ltd, Registered Offices:
Harmondsworth, Middlesex, England

First published in 1991 by Viking Penguin,
a division of Penguin Books USA Inc.

1 3 5 7 9 10 8 6 4 2

Translation copyright © Viking Penguin,
a division of Penguin Books USA Inc., 1991
All rights reserved

Originally published in Switzerland
as Strategeme by Scherz Verlag.
© 1988 Scherz Verlag, Bern, Munchen, Wien.

LIBRARY OF CONGRESS CATALOGING IN PUBLICATION DATA
Senger, Harro von.
[Strategeme. English]
The book of stratagems/Harro von Senger; edited and translated
by Myron B. Gubitz.
p.   cm.
Translation of: Strategeme.
Includes bibliographical references and index.
ISBN 0-670-83962-0
1. Strategy.   I. Gubitz, Myron B.   II. Title.
U162.S4313   1991
355.4—dc20   91–50174

Printed in the United States of America
Set in Sabon
Designed by Ruth Kolbert

TRANSLATOR'S ACKNOWLEDGMENTS

In a project such as this, there are always a few people who play a crucial role. I would like to offer special thanks to Dr. Susan Cherniak, professor of Chinese at Smith College, Massachusetts, who served as our "resident expert" on Chinese language, history, and literature; Paul DeAngelis, an outstanding editor who started the ball rolling; and last, but far from least, my wife, Carole, my toughest and most discerning editor and proofreader.   —M.B.G.

CONTENTS

A PROLOGUE
IN TWO TALES

THE OPEN CITY GATES

Accompanied by 5,000 troops, Prime Minister Zhuge Liang of the kingdom of Shu went to the city of Xicheng to oversee the transfer of supplies from there to Hanzhong. Suddenly a succession of messengers arrived on swift horses. They reported that General Sima Yi, of the hostile kingdom of Wei, was marching on Xicheng with a vast army of 150,000 men. At that point Zhuge Liang did not have a single general with him, only a staff of civil officials. Half of his 5,000 troops had already left Xicheng bearing supplies; only 2,500 soldiers remained in the city. When the officials in his entourage heard the news, they grew pale with fright. Zhuge Liang went up on the city walls to reconnoiter. Sure enough, along the horizon huge dust clouds were swirling toward the heavens as wave upon wave of General Sima Yi's troops advanced.

Zhuge Liang gave these orders: "Take all flags and banners down from the city walls and hide them. Every soldier to his post! Anyone leaving his post without orders will be beheaded. Open the four city gates wide. At each gate twenty soldiers, disguised as commoners, are to be set sweeping the streets. When

Sima Yi's army approaches, no one is to take any independent action. I have a particular stratagem in mind."

Thereupon Zhuge Liang shrouded himself in a cloak of crane feathers, placed a jaunty silk hat on his head, took up a zither, and, accompanied by two pages, went out onto the city wall again. There he sat down on an observation tower up front near the parapet, lit a few sticks of incense, and began to play the zither.

When General Sima Yi's advance scouts reached the city walls and saw all this, they hurried back to report to their commander. Sima Yi laughed in disbelief. He ordered his troops to halt their advance, then mounted a swift horse and rode on to take a closer look at the city. Sure enough, there was Zhuge Liang seated atop the observation tower, a cheerful smile on his face, playing the zither as wisps of smoke rose from the joss sticks. To his left was a young page grasping a precious sword with both hands, to his right another page holding a fan. Near the entrance to the city's main gate, twenty commoners were calmly sweeping the streets, their heads bowed over their brooms.

Seeing all this, Sima Yi began to have grave misgivings. He returned to his troops, ordered his vanguard and rear guard to reverse their positions, and marched his men back toward the mountains north of the city. Along the way, his son Sima Zhao said, "Father, why are you pulling our troops back? Zhuge Liang probably set up this scene because he has no soldiers."

Sima Yi replied, "Zhuge Liang is usually cautious and deliberate in his actions. He has never done anything daring. The gates to the city were wide open today. That is a sure sign of a trap. If my troops had entered the city, they would certainly have fallen prey to some stratagem. Believe me! A quick retreat was the most appropriate move."

So Sima Yi's entire army moved off. Prime Minister Zhuge Liang saw the enemy troops disappear in the distance, and he clapped his hands and laughed with delight. The officials in his party were amazed and said, "Sima Yi is a famous general of the kingdom of Wei. Today he came here at the head of 150,000 crack troops. Yet when he saw you, O Minister of Shu, he beat a hasty retreat. Why?"

Zhuge Liang answered, "He based his thinking on the fact that I am usually cautious and deliberate and never make bold moves. When he saw this scene, he assumed that our troops had set an ambush. So he withdrew. Normally I do avoid risky undertakings, but this time I resorted to a daring ploy because there was no other choice."

The officials bowed their heads in awe and exclaimed, "The stratagems of our Prime Minister would fool even the spirits of our ancestors. Had we had our way, we would have abandoned the city and fled."

Zhuge Liang said, "I only had 2,500 soldiers. If we had abandoned the city and fled, we would not have gotten very far. Sima Yi would surely have captured us."

In a later period, this third-century event was celebrated in a poem:

> A three-foot zither, inlaid with jade, overcame the elite troops, back when Zhuge Liang got the enemy to retreat from Xicheng. To this day the locals still point to the spot: "Here 150,000 men turned their horses around."

SURVEYING THE LAND AND WINNING A CONCUBINE

A clever young boy lost both his parents and came to live with his aunt and uncle. One day he noticed his uncle's sad expression and asked him what was wrong. His uncle replied that he was unhappy because he had no son. He would have liked to take a concubine into the house to insure himself a male heir, but his wife forbade it. This is what was troubling him.

The young boy thought for a while and then said, "Don't worry, Uncle. I see a way to get Auntie to agree."

The older man was incredulous. "There's nothing you can do," he replied.

Early the next morning the boy took a tailor's rule and began to measure the ground in front of the entrance to his uncle's house. He made his actions very ostentatious, so that his aunt would be lured outside.

"What are you doing here?" she inquired.

"I'm surveying the property," the boy responded coolly, and continued his measurements.

"What? Surveying?" asked his aunt. "What has our property got to do with you?"

With a self-confident air, the lad replied, "It has a great deal to do with me, Auntie. I'm making preparations for the future. You and Uncle are no longer so young. And you have no son. So one day this house will surely be mine. I'm taking measurements now, because when that day comes I'll want to make some changes here."

At this, his aunt trembled with fury. Saying not another word, she ran into the house, woke her husband, and urged him to take a concubine as quickly as he could.

THE
BOOK OF
STRATAGEMS

Introduction

Stratagems are used everywhere, by people in all walks of life. But Western civilization has never produced anything remotely resembling the highly condensed catalog of devious tactics known as the "36 Stratagems." The entire catalog consists of a mere 138 Chinese characters. Yet into these terse 36 Stratagems the Chinese have compressed much of their thousands of years of experience in dealing with enemies (both internal and external) and overcoming difficult and dangerous situations.

The Oxford English Dictionary (vol. 10, Oxford, 1933) defines the word *stratagem* as follows:

1. *a.* An operation or act of generalship; usually an artifice or trick designed to outwit or surprise the enemy.
1. *b.* In generalized sense: Military artifice.
2. *a.* Any artifice or trick; a device or scheme for obtaining an advantage.
2. *b.* In generalized sense: Skill in devising expedients; artifice, cunning.

The Chinese language, in which individual written characters may have several meanings depending on the context in which they appear, has several characters which have been used from ancient times to modern days to designate the concept of stratagem:

着 —modern Mandarin pronunciation *zhāo*

策 —modern Mandarin pronunciation *móu*

謀 —modern Mandarin pronunciation *cè*

計 —modern Mandarin pronunciation *jì*

There are others as well. But the most commonly used is the last of those listed: *ji*. The written character—XX—is built up of two parts:

言 —pronounced *yán* in Mandarin, with the meaning of "to speak, say, tell," and

十 —pronounced *shí,* and standing for "ten."

Taken together, the two parts mean "count to ten," or in a more generalized sense, "to count, to calculate" (in both meanings of the English word), and as a noun, "calculation, plan." In certain contexts, *ji* and the other characters have two very distinct and closely related meanings:

1. a tactic or ruse of war;
2. artifice in political and/or private life.

There is one more written character worthy of special mention: the one that appears as the decorative element on the dust jacket and title page of this volume. It is pronounced *zhì*. In most Western dictionaries of the Chinese language it is rendered as "wisdom, knowledge," etc. But in many Chinese texts, both old and new, it is frequently used in the sense of "trick"—or, in a more value-neutral formulation, "stratagem," typical of the manner in which wisdom and cunning are integrated in Chinese.

The first mention of the 36 Stratagems appears in the *Nan Qi shu* (History of the Southern Qi). The Southern Qi Dynasty lasted from A.D. 479 to 502; its history was compiled soon after by Xiao Zixian (A.D. 489–537). Included in the chronicle is a biography of the political figure Wang Jingze, who is reported to have once mentioned the "36 stratagems [*sanshiliu ce*] of Master Tan."

This Master Tan was the renowned General Tan Daoji (d. A.D. 436), who served the Southern Song Dynasty. The "Biography of Tan Daoji" contained in chapter 15 of the *Nan shi* (History of the Southern Dynasties) includes the following episode:

> As commander of the [Song] expeditionary force, Tan Daoji marched northward and fought his way to the Ji River. [But] the Wei army was very powerful, [so] he subsequently took [the city of] Huatai [instead of standing to fight at the Ji River]. He fought more than thirty battles against the forces of Wei and won most of them. When his army reached Licheng, its supply lines were cut and he ordered a retreat. From defectors, the enemy learned of the Song army's shortage of supplies, of the unrest in its ranks and its declining morale. One night Tan Daoji had his soldiers weigh sand, call out the weighed quantities, and sprinkle the little remaining rice over the [piles of sand]. In the dawn's light the Wei troops thought that Tan Daoji's army had an ample supply of rice after all and halted their pursuit. Thinking the defectors were liars, [the Wei soldiers] beheaded them. But panic broke out among Tan Daoji's troops, who were numerically inferior to their enemy and also profoundly exhausted. So Tan Daoji ordered his soldiers to put on their armor. And he slowly rode around his camp in a battle chariot. When the Wei troops saw this, they feared an ambush, did not dare approach [the Song

encampment], and withdrew. Although Tan Daoji had not succeeded in conquering the region south of the Yellow River, he returned home with his army unscathed. His fame as a hero spread everywhere, and the state of Wei feared him greatly.

This report makes it clear that Tan Daoji succeeded in saving his army from destruction through the use of various tactical devices. Whether he actually had at his disposal a catalog of 36 stratagems is not revealed by the chronicles in question. But "36" need not be taken literally, since the Chinese have a penchant for using numerical expressions in a figurative sense. In mentioning the "36 stratagems of Master Tan," Wang Jingze may have used the figure simply to mean "numerous," just as *trente-six* is sometimes used in French colloquial speech to mean an indefinite high number.

In the oldest known document on the 36 Stratagems (about which more shortly), the number 36 is interpreted on the basis of the *I Ching* (Book of Changes), a volume of oracles the central content of which dates from between the tenth and eighth centuries B.C. [Note: The Pinyin system of transcription generally used in this present work, *The Book of Stratagems,* would ordinarily require that the Chinese title of the *Book of Changes* be rendered *Yijing,* but since the form *I Ching* is more familiar to American readers, it will be used throughout.—ED.] According to the oldest commentary on the *I Ching,* which dates from about the middle of the first millennium B.C., the underlying concept of the work is the dualism of *yin* and *yang,* two opposing forces. In broad terms, *yang* might be said to represent the "masculine" principle, rationality, clarity, brightness, while *yin* is seen as the "feminine" principle, emotion, ambiguity, shadow. By extension, *yin* also embraces that which is neither sharp nor straight, deviousness, hence tricks. According to the *I Ching,* the principle of *yin* is represented numerically by 6. Thus 36 may be seen as the *yin* element squared, symbolizing a plenitude of tricks or stratagems.

The meaning ascribed to *ji*—or "stratagem," in the Chinese

sense—ranges from a simple trick or a spontaneous action based on sheer presence of mind to complex, carefully planned behavior that may be schematically outlined as follows:

- a situation is perceived as precarious, but it precludes direct action;
- the situation involves another party, an "enemy" or opponent;
- the other party is drawn in, tricked, deceived in some fashion;
- the deception is secretly sponsored and/or perpetrated by the beneficiary of the stratagem, though it is sometimes staged to make it look as if the sponsor or perpetrator were not involved;
- the stratagem is used to achieve a specific goal or purpose, which always seems "good" or positive to its sponsor;
- that goal may be, but is not necessarily, negative for the other party.

Among the chief general goals of stratagems are: masking something which is true, pretending something which is untrue, gaining the initiative or advantage, gaining a prize, encirclement, enticement, and flight.

As has already been noted, the stratagems are permeated with the spirit of the ancient Chinese concept of *yin* and *yang* as complementary polarities, interacting cosmic principles. This can be most readily seen as the ever-present tension between the "bright" or visible (*yang*) and that which is planned and acted out in the shadow of secrecy (*yin*). Some stratagems are rooted in Daoist concepts, such as *wu wei,* or nonintervention. Others bear the spiritual legacy of the ancient School of Legalism, which preached to Chinese rulers the importance of *shu* (the techniques of power), *fa* (the primacy of the law as an instrument of rule), and *shi* (personal position as the foundation of power and influence). Many instances of applied stratagems also demonstrate the School of Legalism's insistence on "reasons of state," the priority of state interests over Confucian ethical norms.

A CRYSTALLIZATION OF MILLENNIA

The Chinese word *ji,* which I translate in this work as "stratagem," appears in the world's oldest treatise on military theory, *The Art of War,* by Sunzi, a contemporary of Confucius. [Note: In contemporary American usage the name Sunzi is more commonly written as Sun Tzu, which is the form that shall be used hereafter in this book.—ED.] The word *ji* is part of the title of chapter 1, in which the art of war is characterized as "the art of deception." And in chapter 3, the title of which has been translated by British sinologist Lionel Giles as "Attack by Stratagem," the following passage appears: "Therefore one who is good at martial arts overcomes others' forces without battle, conquers others' cities without siege. . . ." According to Sun Tzu, military victory over the enemy ranks merely third in the value scale of the martial arts. Second place is given to victory by diplomatic means, and first place to victory by stratagem.

Clearly, stratagems have been considered significant in China since ancient times. Over the course of centuries, there gradually crystallized a body of idiomatic expressions, colorful metaphoric phrases that describe a whole range of stratagems. These idioms were fashioned in part by popular speech and in part by military theorists, philosophers, historians, and literary figures. Among the stratagem-metaphors, some expressions refer to historic events of two thousand years ago and earlier; others are rooted in popular folktales; some phrases merely allude to tactics, others indicate the specific steps to be taken in carrying out a particular stratagem. In terms of style, the catalog of the 36 Stratagems is for the most part a list of maxims.

The verbal dress in which the stratagems are clad is very scanty. The entire list, as has been noted, consists of only 138 Chinese characters; most of the idioms are expressed by 4 written characters, some by only 3. But this linguistic spareness leaves a great deal of latitude for interpretation and illustration. Indeed, interpretation and illustration are essential, since the maxims by themselves would be largely incomprehensible as stratagems without explanation and example.

Until relatively recently, the catalog of 36 Stratagems, taken as a whole, was treated as a more or less esoteric body of knowledge—though many of the individual idioms were familiar to most Chinese from childhood on. The great popularity of the stratagems is due largely to Chinese popular literature. The classic novels and novellas known to almost every Chinese frequently include tales involving stratagems. Prominent among them is the historical novel *Sanguo yanyi* (The Romance of the Three Kingdoms), which might almost be characterized as a stratagem textbook. There is hardly a trick of war the planning and execution of which is not described in its pages, sometimes in great detail. There is even an old Chinese saying: "He who has read *The Romance of the Three Kingdoms* knows how to apply stratagems."

Today, China's mass media help keep familiarity with the stratagems alive. The aphoristic formulas crop up in reports on domestic political developments (e.g., editorial comments on behavior of officials considered "harmful to the people") and analyses of foreign developments of which China's leaders do not approve. Comic strips also help to popularize the stratagems. Typical examples are the six-part series titled *The 36 Stratagems*, published in 1981 in Jilin Province, with a print run of close to 1.15 million, and the twelve-part comic-strip series *A Collection on the Art of War Based on the 36 Stratagems*, published in 1982 in Guangxi with a print run of 400,000.

THE BLOSSOMING OF STRATAGEM LITERATURE IN CHINA

The Hongmen Secret Society was founded around A.D. 1674 to break the rule of the Manchurian Qing Dynasty (1644–1911) and restore the native Chinese Ming Dynasty (1368–1644) to the throne. Until a few years ago it was generally believed that the Hongmen Society had been the first to collate assorted materials into a coherent guidebook on the artifices of war. Entitled *Hongmen zhexue* (Hongmen Philosophy), this work was thought to be the source of all versions of the 36 Stratagems now in circulation. But in 1941 a somewhat older source text was discovered.

In 1962 the Archive of the Political Institute of the People's Liberation Army issued, for internal use and without comment, a treatise of apparently unknown origin dealing with the 36 Stratagems. This proved to be a reprint of an older document which had been purchased by chance in 1941 at a roadside bookstall in Chengdu, the capital of Sichuan Province, by a man named Shu He. On its cover, this older publication bore in large characters the title "The 36 Stratagems," and next to it in smaller letters, "Secret Book of the Art of War" (in Chinese, *Sanshiliu ji miben bingfa*). Published by Xinghua Press of Chengdu and printed on handmade paper, the pamphlet contained a note identifying the source of the text as a manuscript which had been discovered that same year in a bookstore in Binzhou, Shaanxi Province.

The treatise discovered in 1941 was made available to the general public for the first time in 1979, in an edition published in Jilin; a new, illustrated edition was issued in March 1987, a second printing of which appeared in March 1989. In the Jilin version, the original (1941) treatise was reprinted in classical Chinese, with a modern Chinese translation accompanied by notes and explanations.

The foreword to the 1979 Jilin edition contains speculations on the manuscript's origin. According to the editors, its many references to the *I Ching* indicate that the treatise's author may have been influenced by Zhao Benxue or one of his disciples. (Zhao Benxue, a military theorist of the Ming period, lived from 1465 to 1557 and was the first to systematically analyze warfare in terms of the *I Ching*. Applying the idea of the constant interplay of *yin* and *yang* to the dialectics of warfare, he examined such pairs of opposites as reality and appearance, superior and inferior numbers, strength and weakness, frontal attack and ambush, unconventional and conventional methods, and advance and retreat.) The Jilin editors conclude that the manuscript discovered in 1941 may date from the late Ming or early Qing period and thus may predate the Hongmen Secret Society's compilation.

Another monograph on the 36 Stratagems was published in 1981 by the Soldiers' Press (*Zhanshi Chubanshe*) in Beijing (which changed its name in the mid-1980s to the People's Liberation Army Press—*Jiefangjun Chubanshe*). This work was titled *The 36 Stratagems: A Modern Version.* Based on the older stratagem treatise, it also incorporates modern examples of stratagem application, some from other countries as well as China (the ninth printing of this book appeared in March 1991, with a printing of more than 1.5 million copies).

In recent years, numerous monographs on the stratagems have appeared elsewhere in the Far East. In Taiwan, *The Secret Book of the 36 Stratagems, with Explanations* was first issued in 1982, based largely on the 1979 Jilin treatise. A booklet titled *Wisdom in Struggle,* with the subtitle *The 36 Stratagems,* went into nineteen editions in Taiwan between 1976 and 1985. Its contents are virtually identical to those of a Hong Kong book published in 1969 under the title *The 36 Stratagems, with Examples from Times Past and Present.* (For the original titles and other bibliographic information on these Chinese-language works, see the book list in Appendix B.)

While traveling in September 1987, I purchased three Korean books about the Chinese stratagems in Seoul and five Japanese works on the same subject in Tokyo, the earliest of the latter dating from 1981. As to the present work, to my knowledge its original German-language version (1988) was the first book to appear on this subject in a Western language.

THE WORLD OF THE STRATAGEMS

When Chinese-language publications about the 36 Stratagems are compared, it becomes evident that the emphasis in the People's Republic is on their application to foreign affairs and military matters. The books from Taiwan and Hong Kong, on the other hand, supplement the military dimension by highlighting how the stratagems may be applied in civilian life.

The following passage appears in the foreword to the seventh edition (1989) of *The 36 Stratagems: A Modern Version:*

> This publication arises from the need to know and use stratagems in military conflict. The traditional material [of the stratagems] has been subjected to appropriate review in the light of Marxist military theory and is used [in this book] as the basis for developing modern military applications. . . . [The] theory of stratagems is an important component of military theory. If a military commander wants to take the initiative, much will depend on whether he can . . . prove himself superior to his opponent through the skillful use of stratagems. This enables him to transform an unfavorable situation into a favorable one, to defeat a superior force with a small number of troops, indeed, sometimes even to bring his opponent down without using military force at all. . . . With scientific and technological progress, the stratagems must sometimes be applied by new means and sometimes imbued with new content, yet their fundamental contours remain relatively stable.

The foreword to the Jilin editions of the 36 Stratagems (1979, 1987, 1989) likewise emphasizes their military character:

> The treatise on the 36 Stratagems belongs to the realm of so-called unorthodox (or unconventional) warfare. It is an encyclopedia of what Chinese military theorists since Sunzi [Sun Tzu] have characterized as *guidao* (the way of deceiving the enemy).

The literature from the People's Republic also contains some cautionary remarks, such as this from the Jilin edition:

> Reactionary feudalistic chaff also lies rotting beneath the 36 Stratagems, specifically in those which aim at gaining booty. A critical attitude is therefore necessary.

Taiwanese and Hong Kong publications take a somewhat broader view of the stratagems, as indicated by these lines from the foreword to the nineteenth edition of *Tricks in Combat: The 36 Stratagems* (Taipei, 1985):

> The stratagems are like invisible knives, which are hidden in the mind of man and flash out only when they are put to use. They are used by the military, but also by politicians, businessmen and academics. He who is versed in the application of stratagems can plunge an orderly world into chaos or bring order to a chaotic world; he can produce thunder and lightning from a clear sky, can transform poverty into riches, insignificance into prestige, the most hopeless situation into a promising one. Human life is struggle, and in struggle one needs stratagems. Everyone stands in the line of combat: a brief moment of inattention, and someone may grab something of yours. But he who understands how to use stratagems will always hold the initiative in his own hand. Whether in palaces or shanties, stratagems are applicable everywhere.

In the Chinese view, the stratagems do not serve only to help "evil" outwit the "good." There are many situations in which a "good" person, pursuing an honorable goal but finding himself or herself in a weak position, can achieve that goal only through the use of stratagems. This was notably true in classical China, where laws were not designed to protect the individual and there was no independent judiciary to safeguard the individual's rights. In such circumstances, practical knowledge of the artifices and tricks which could help one survive in life's struggle was essential.

Nonetheless, there is an inevitable question of the relation between stratagems and traditional Chinese ethics, particularly the norms of Confucianism. The stratagem books published in the People's Republic do not deal with this matter. But the volume published in Hong Kong in 1969 has something to say about it:

> Stratagems are the exact opposite of "Confucian" humanity and virtue. But he who treats his enemy with humanity and virtue only harms himself. . . . Using the rhetoric of virtue to maintain a pretense to others . . . is acceptable. But you must not fool yourself [with such rhetoric], at least not when engaged in combat, whether with the weapons of reason or of force . . . Our age boasts of being civilized. Yet the more civilized a society, the more rampant are lies and deception. In such an environment, the 36 Stratagems are the perfect means of offense and defense. They constitute a body of practical knowledge which is far more valuable than empty moralistic phrases.

For Westerners, knowledge of the 36 Stratagems can provide a key to much of Chinese thinking. But sinology, the study of Chinese culture, is not just a narrow academic field of interest only to a few specialists; it is also of global significance, providing new insights into human nature in general. Hence, study of the stratagems can also be invaluable in illuminating many aspects of Western life and culture. Of the traditional catalog of 36 Stratagems, 18 are fully documented in this volume, with the remainder to follow in Volume 2.

One last thought: when immersing oneself in the world of the stratagems, it is well to bear in mind the admonition of Chinese sage Hong Zicheng: "A heart hostile to others is inexcusable. But a heart wary of others is indispensable." Or, in the words of the Gospel, "Be wary as serpents, innocent as doves."

Fool the Emperor and Cross the Sea

The Chinese characters	瞞	天	过	海
Modern Mandarin pronunciation	*mán*	*tiān*	*guò*	*hǎi*
Meaning of each character	fool (or deceive)	Emperor (or Heaven)	cross	sea
Interpretation with reference to the oldest known case	Trick the Emperor into sailing across the sea by inviting him into a seaside house which is, in reality, a camouflaged ship.			
Applications	Conceal the real objective; disguise the course being pursued; camouflage the real purpose. The *coram publico* stratagem.			

The history of this stratagem goes back to a military campaign mounted by the seventh-century Tang Emperor Taizong against Koguryō, across the Yellow Sea on the Korean Peninsula. There are two known versions of the story. But before we examine them, it might be helpful to explain how I first got on the trail of the stratagems.

For purposes of study and research, I spent 1971–73 in Taipei, 1973–75 in Tokyo, and 1975–77 in Beijing. At the Mandarin Training Center of Normal Taiwan University in Taipei, I first heard Professor Bai Zhengshi make passing mention of the "36 Stratagems." As it turned out, he knew little about them. So I asked my fellow students—and soon I had a list of 36 rather cryptic-seeming phrases. Surprisingly, even my Chinese colleagues found some of them puzzling. But my interest had been kindled, and from then on it never wavered.

First I tried to figure out the meaning of the key phrases, which consist sometimes of three, but usually of four written characters. It was no simple undertaking. Initially neither my professors nor my fellow students could explain the deeper significance of Stratagem No. 1, for example. They all translated the second character with its obvious meaning of "Heaven" rather than that of "Emperor." The result was a rendition— still the more widely accepted one in the People's Republic and Taiwan—which states, "Fool the Heavens and cross the sea." In 1976 a professor at Beijing University told me of the earliest known case history and its source: the biography of General Xue Rengui (A.D. 614–683) in the *Encyclopedia of the Yongle Reign* [A.D. 1403–24], one of the world's oldest and largest encyclopedias. Some years later I found confirmation for this in *The 36 Stratagems: Secret Book of the Art of War,* published in Jilin, and *The Secret Book of the 36 Stratagems, with Explanations,* issued in Taipei.

So much for the first version (given below in Section 1.1, "Crossing the Sea in a House"). It took me a long time to track down the second version (Section 1.2, "The Wooden City in the Sea") after finding a reference to it in an article in a social science journal.[1] The author of the article, Wu Gu, cited a sentence involving Stratagem No. 1 in the fantastic historical novel *Shuo Tang* (Tales from the Tang Period). But I could not trace the quote in any editions of the novel currently available in Taiwan or the People's Republic, all of which are based on a bowdlerized and abridged version dating from the nineteenth century.

Finally, in 1986, I located a 1736 edition of the novel in a Beijing library. And there I found the second version of the case history, which I have shortened slightly and recounted in Section 1.2. The stratagem is cited verbatim in the title of the relevant chapter of the novel: *Man tian ji Taizong guo hai* (The Stratagem of Fooling the Emperor Brings Emperor Taizong Across the Sea).

1.1 CROSSING THE SEA IN A HOUSE

Arriving at the shore of the Yellow Sea with an army of 300,000 men, the Emperor hesitates. Water, nothing but endless water. Koguryŏ is a thousand miles away. Why has he not listened to those advisers who warned him against undertaking this campaign? Plagued by doubt, he turns to his military commanders for suggestions as to the next step. His generals ask for time to consider.

Fearing that the Emperor might decide to pull his forces back, the military leaders ask the advice of the resourceful General Xue Rengui, who proposes a clever way to get the Emperor and all his men swiftly across the waters. "How would it be," he asks, "if the Emperor could embark as calmly as if he were on dry land?" The General undertakes to make all the necessary arrangements.

The next day the military men inform the Emperor that a wealthy farmer, who lives directly on the waterfront, has volunteered to provide the food supplies for the overseas journey and would like to speak with His Majesty. Delighted, the Emperor leads his entourage down to the shore. But he gets no glimpse of the sea itself, because a clever arrangement of 10,000 canvases hides it from his view.

The wealthy farmer respectfully invites the Emperor into his house. Colorful tapestries cover the walls, and the floors are thick with precious carpets. The Emperor and his advisers are seated and drink some wine. After a while it seems to the monarch as if the wind is whistling on every side and there is a sound like the pounding of waves; beakers and candelabra sway back and forth. Astonished, the Emperor orders an official to open the curtains—and sees the black, endless sea. "Where are we?" he roars. One of his advisers explains, "We and the entire army are on the open sea, heading for Koguryō." Faced with this fait accompli, the Emperor regains his decisiveness and bravely sails on for the eastern shore.

1.2 THE WOODEN CITY IN THE SEA

According to the second version of the story, the Emperor does not hesitate but embarks directly, without the assistance of a camouflaged ship. His entire army of 100,000 warriors, horses, and riders is accommodated on a fleet of 1,300 craft, with the Emperor and his closest advisers sailing on the dragon flagship.

After three days on the water, a great storm comes up. The waves rise monstrously into the air, many fathoms high. The Emperor is so frightened that his face turns ashen. Soldiers and warhorses are tossed about wildly and regain their footing only to be dashed down again. Even the Emperor, the Son of Heaven himself, is thrown to the deck. Everyone is seasick. Finally the frightened Emperor groans, "Gentlemen, I shall not continue this campaign to the east. Let our enemy come and attack us!"

And so, despite warnings by some advisers that the Koreans will attack China unless the crossing is continued, the imperial fleet turns and sails back to Dengzhou (in Shandong), landing there three days later. The Emperor and his entourage enter the port city, where his adviser Xu Maogong addresses him. "The campaign against the Eastern Kingdom is an affair of state. How can Your Majesty return to the imperial capital?"

The Emperor replies, "The storm at sea is frightful. Rather than sail on, I prefer to return to our capital at Chang'an."

Xu Maogong responds, "Do not worry, Majesty. After a few days the storm will play itself out. In the period of calm that follows, we can cross the sea to subjugate the Eastern Kingdom."

"If that is the case," says the Emperor, "let us wait."

That night Xu Maogong goes to the army camp. "What brings you here in the middle of the night?" asks General Jingde.

"It seems that His Majesty is losing his taste for this campaign," replies the imperial adviser. "We shall conquer the Eastern Kingdom only if we find a stratagem with which to fool the Emperor into crossing the sea. Go to Zhang Huan and demand that he work out such a stratagem for us."

Jingde goes to Zhang Huan and says, "The Emperor fears wind and wave. He is unwilling to reembark. Find us a stratagem by which we can fool the Emperor into making the crossing. His Majesty must not feel the mighty power of the sea. He must reach the eastern coast in a state of calm." And the General adds, "I'm going to have a ditch dug. If you fail to come up with an appropriate stratagem by morning, I'll have you put down into it one fathom deep. If you cannot produce the stratagem by noon, two fathoms deep you'll go, and if not by evening, three fathoms. After that, if you cannot produce a stratagem, I'll have you buried alive."

With a few companions, Zhang Huan hatches this plan: Several hundred huge tree trunks are to be purchased and carpenters hired to create a floating wooden "city." A few houses are to be built before and behind the city wall. The ground near the houses is to be covered with sand and earth, and flowers and grass planted there. Streets must also be laid down. Soldiers are to masquerade as well-disciplined townsmen. In the midst of the city, the three-story Pavilion of Calm is to be built to accommodate the Emperor, and in it Buddhist monks are to be set praying. This wooden city is to be launched into the sea first. When a storm comes up, it will be "discovered" and serve the Emperor as a refuge from the forces of nature. The Emperor will step "ashore," rest himself in the Pavilion of Calm, see the storm and the waves no more, and no longer vacillate about the Korean campaign. Once the storm has passed, the Emperor can be encouraged to return to his flagship.

Zhang Huan's stratagem is approved and carried out. After three months, the wooden city is declared seaworthy and it is launched. Soon it sails beyond the horizon. Three days later Xu Maogong says to the Emperor, "Your Majesty, I have calculated the play of *yin-yang* forces for the time ahead. During the next half year the wind will drop. Would this not be a favorable time to board our ships and cross the sea?"

The Emperor agrees and gives the command to embark. After three days the fleet begins to sway perilously once more. The Emperor says, "That is the sign of an approaching storm. I prefer to sail back to Shandong again."

Says Xu Maogong, "Majesty, do not concern yourself. There is a place up ahead where we can drop anchor."

General Jingde pretends to peer long and hard into the distance. Suddenly he says, "Majesty, I see a city. We can anchor there and find protection from the storm."

The Emperor asks, "What city is that? Is it under my rule?"

Xu Maogong replies, "Majesty, I have checked the map. It is a citadel built for shelter from the storm. And it is under your imperial jurisdiction. Your Majesty can go ashore there and thus avoid the storm and the waves."

"Very well," says the Emperor.

So the dragon flagship and the rest of the fleet drop anchor off the wooden island. The Emperor and his entourage disembark. The "townsmen" make their obeisance before the Son of Heaven and welcome him to their city. The Emperor asks, "Is there a place here where one can enjoy peace and quiet for a while?"

The well-prepared inhabitants of the floating island lead the Emperor to the Pavilion of Calm, where he finds a perfect setting for rest and relaxation that helps him forget the stress of his overseas endeavor.

In this way the Emperor is fooled and manipulated into crossing the sea.

1.3   THE MARRIAGE VOW

In "The Open City Gates" as related in our Prologue, we found Zhuge Liang (A.D. 181–234) seated on a city wall, using a stratagem to trick the approaching enemy into retreating while playing his zither.

At twenty-six, Zhuge Liang was still unmarried—an advanced age for bachelorhood in those days. Each day he studied hard and spent some time playing the zither. Though he thoroughly enjoyed his life, his elder brother and his sister-in-law kept trying to find a wife for him. But Zhuge Liang had already rejected seven candidates.

One day his sister-in-law made a scene about it. Zhuge Liang attempted to calm her. "I'm afraid to sleep in the same bed with another person but to dream different dreams," he said. His sister-in-law insisted, "Marriage is a heavenly dispensation. You cannot be as choosy about it as you are when buying an ass or a horse. Really! I have already proposed seven maidens, each as lovely as a fairy. But you've turned them all down. Do you really want to wait until the 'Right One' is born for your benefit?"

Zhuge Liang knew how much his brother and sister-in-law wanted him to start a family. So he was obliged to say, "Wife of My Brother, please keep looking."

She replied, "I'm thinking of the eighth daughter of the Zhu family, who live near the eastern gate of the city."

"What are her ideals and her talents?" asked Zhuge Liang.

"Ideals? Talents?" responded his sister-in-law harshly. "It is a virtue when a woman is without education!" Seeing Zhuge Liang shake his head wearily, she added, "This time I'll arrange everything. No more excuses. And you won't leave this room until you agree."

"If only My Brother's Wife would not place a beautiful face above everything else," said Zhuge Liang.

His sister-in-law replied, "There's an old saying: 'Capable man, beautiful wife.' You are a man of great talent. All the more reason for you to have a beautiful wife. Or would you prefer an ugly one?"

"She doesn't necessarily have to be ugly. But . . . as a matter of fact, someone does come to mind."

His sister-in-law wanted to know immediately of whom he was thinking. Zhuge Liang said, "My old teacher Huang Chengyan has a daughter. Her name is Huang Zhengying. I have heard that she is extremely knowledgeable and noble-minded . . ."

His brother's wife interrupted. "What? Huang Zhengying? Her nickname is 'Ugly.' She's looked terrible since she was a baby. Her skin is as dark as a mudfish. I haven't seen her in years. She's probably grown even nastier-looking in the meantime."

Zhuge Liang listened to this tirade with a smile, but said nothing at first. Then he commented, "As a maiden matures, she changes eighteen times. Perhaps . . ."

Again his sister-in-law interrupted him. "That one? The more she's changed, the uglier she's probably become."

Zhuge Liang replied, "Brother's Wife, the ear is less reliable than the eye. I have read her poems. Truly, she would be right for me. Please, do go and see her."

Huang Zhengying was indeed no beauty. But she was intelligent and energetic. Each day, after her sewing, she would devote herself entirely to study. She was already twenty-four years old, and no one had ever asked for her hand in marriage. This was a source of considerable worry to her father, a circumstance which had not escaped her.

Zhuge Liang's sister-in-law made her appearance. With a sanctimonious smile she said to Father Huang, "I have heard that the flowers in your garden bloom with a special splendor. May I see them?" The ingenuous Huang led her out into his garden, where his homely daughter happened to be spending some time with her pretty maid. The sister-in-law saw the two young women from a distance, thought the pretty one was Huang's daughter, and was secretly delighted at how she had changed. She now revealed to Father Huang the true purpose of her visit. His daughter, who had overheard their conversation from behind a hedge, called out, "If your brother-in-law really wants me as his wife, let him come here himself and see who I am. The sooner the better!"

Still under an erroneous impression, the sister-in-law now urged Zhuge Liang to leave his hut in the Longzhong Mountains as soon as possible and pay a visit to the Huang family in Xingliang. She went with him, whipping the horses to make them hurry. As they approached the Huang family home, they heard the daughter playing the zither within. The melody bespoke a noble sensibility which would not be defeated by adversity. "What beautiful playing," declared Zhuge Liang. Father Huang, recognizing his former pupil's voice, hurried out of the house and conducted his visitors into the reception chamber.

Now Zhuge Liang wanted to meet the daughter. She was sent for, but kept the others waiting a long time. Actually, she had observed Zhuge Liang through the curtains. His expressive face and imposing stature gladdened her heart. To test his nature, she quickly wrote a poem and had it brought to him by her maid. Zhuge Liang received it and read these lines:

> *Through the curtains I saw his face*
> *But as yet I do not know his heart.*
> *In the room of the four treasures*
> *Would I gladly speak with him.*

The four treasures refer to the four traditional implements of the scholar: ink stone, ink, paper, and writing brush. Zhuge Liang knew immediately that he had been summoned to the study. There the two women awaited him, one pretty, the other homely. They asked him to be seated.

First the pretty one asked his name, his age, and other mundane details. Then the homely one said, "You are a man of great abilities. How is it that, at your age, you have not yet started a family?" Zhuge Liang replied courteously, "In these restless times it is difficult to start a family. I am constantly worried about the state of the empire and have not been able to think a great deal about marriage."

The homely woman said, "From your answer, I gather that you have high ambitions."

Zhuge Liang was astonished. How could she know of his far-reaching plans? If the homely one had made that clever assumption, then she, and not the pretty one, must be the daughter of the house. "My brother's wife has made a mistake," he said to himself.

Without any hesitation, he said, "Liu Bei, the Emperor's uncle, wants me to come down from the mountains and enter his service, so that I can help in maintaining our threatened Han Dynasty."

Huang Zhengying asked, "Are you still undecided?" This question surprised Zhuge Liang once again. He replied, "Yes, that is why I seek the advice of your father, my old teacher."

"What is your inclination?" Huang Zhengying inquired.

"These days the empire is torn," said Zhuge Liang. "Local

warlords have carved it up. Perhaps it is best to worry only about oneself, to cultivate one's own field and enjoy a peaceful life to the end."

The pretty maid seemed delighted with this and said, "Yes, that's it! Start a family and lead a peaceful, unobtrusive life, without being drawn down from the mountains to the world below."

Zhuge Liang turned to the homely girl and asked for her opinion.

She replied, "You are a man of uncommon abilities, already known far and wide. The resurgence of the Han Dynasty—that is what our people dream of. Liu Bei is able to recognize capable men. He has already visited you in your thatched hut twice. I assume he will come a third time." [See Section 16.13, "Three Visits to the Thatched Hut."]

This estimate of the situation accorded exactly with Zhuge Liang's own. The homely girl continued, "You have already acquired a knowledge of literature and military science to help you rescue our empire and its people. Now you should take Jiang Taigong as your model. [See Section 17.7, "Angling for a King."] He served the founder of the Zhou Dynasty. Under no circumstance should shining pearls remain hidden in the darkness of the earth."

Hearing these words, Zhuge Liang felt his admiration for the homely girl increase. There and then he decided to come down from the mountains to the world and prepared to return home immediately. The pretty maid, however, held him back, saying, "You came here to seek a bride!"

"I know my bride now," said Zhuge Liang. "She is the one who spoke with me so nobly."

Huang Zhengying heard this with great joy. But she said, "Think it over three times. Your sister-in-law . . ."

Zhuge Liang understood what she meant. He interrupted her and said, "Do not worry. Brother's Wife only wants the best for me."

"Are you not worried that people will talk?" she continued to press him.

"Everyone is free to say what he will. My heart will not be moved."

Now, at last, Huang Zhengying accepted his suit. Deeply moved, she said, "It is Fate that our two hearts should be linked from now on."

At that moment Zhuge Liang's sister-in-law stormed into the room. She still thought that the pretty maid was Huang Zhengying, pulled her near, and asked Zhuge Liang if he had made up his mind. Embarrassed, the maid said, "Mistress . . ."

"Mistress!" said the other. "Just call me Brother's Wife."

Then she saw how the homely girl looked at her, blushing, and she realized the truth. In distress she said loudly, "Has a decision been made?" Huang Zhengying hung her head and kept silent. The sister-in-law looked at Huang Zhengying and then at Zhuge Liang. She thought, "Really! They are not at all a good match!" Then she pulled Zhuge Liang abruptly from his seat and pushed him out of the room, muttering, "My foolish young brother-in-law!"

Once back in the Longzhong Mountains, Zhuge Liang's sister-in-law urged him to change his mind. But he said neither yes nor no, merely smiling slyly, which drove her almost frantic.

One day Zhuge Liang's close friend Meng Gongwei came for a visit, and the sister-in-law asked him to have a serious talk with Zhuge Liang. But the latter refused to be drawn into a discussion. The sister-in-law was desperate, fearing for her own good reputation. People would blame her if her brother-in-law chose such an ugly woman for his wife. So she gave Zhuge Liang an ultimatum: "Unless you annul your betrothal, we are no longer related and I want nothing more to do with you!"

Meng Gongwei said to his orphaned friend, "Your elder brother's wife is like a mother to you. You should listen to what she says."

What could Zhuge Liang do? He did not wish to alter his decision. On the other hand, neither did he wish to bring adversity down upon his sister-in-law. Suddenly he had an idea. He immediately took up a brush and drafted a document. This he handed to Meng Gongwei, who found that it contained the following poem:

> *Your face makes people laugh. How could you be a wife*
>   *of mine?*
> *Yesterday I hoped to woo you. Today my heart is filled*
>   *with another decision!*
> *Forgive me! Realize how inconstant Life is!*
> *After all, what promise of marriage, merely uttered by the*
>   *lips, is irrevocable?*

Pleased and satisfied by this declaration, Zhuge Liang's friend placed the document in his sleeve, and the sister-in-law laughed with relief. Meng Gongwei was prepared to act on his friend's behalf and deliver the painful missive to the Huang family. When Father Huang read the poem, he was overcome with sadness. He immediately called his daughter to him. Though she did not want to believe what her father told her, tears came to her eyes. Meng Gongwei handed her the paper. But when she had read the poem, her tears quickly gave way to a cheerful laugh. Meng Gongwei stared at her in amazement. Had she lost her mind?

Since writing that document, Zhuge Liang seemed a changed man. Whenever his sister-in-law would sing the praises of a new prospective wife, he would visit her immediately—insisting, however, that he go alone. Each time he returned home his verdict was negative, but it was delivered with a radiant smile. His sister-in-law was on tenterhooks, but she held her peace. Suspicious, she asked her maid if her brother-in-law actually visited each of the women she had recommended. "Yes," came the reply, "but he hasn't liked any of them."

Patience is always rewarded, however. One day Zhuge Liang announced to his sister-in-law that he had found the right woman and would marry her in three days. His sister-in-law was overjoyed, and said to herself, "Whomever he's chosen, she's bound to be better than that ugly Huang." Preparations for the wedding were begun immediately.

On the wedding day the flower wagon arrived bearing the veiled bride. An expectant crowd stood at the house door to greet her. When she had been conducted into the festively decorated parlor, she slowly lifted her veil. It was the homely Huang Zhengying! Zhuge Liang's sister-in-law and Meng Gongwei were thunderstruck. The sister-in-law said in a biting voice, "Didn't you deliver the message annulling the betrothal?" Meng Gongwei looked imploringly at Zhuge Liang, who asked him, "Can you still recall the poem I wrote?" Meng Gongwei repeated it by heart:

> *Your face makes people laugh. How could you be a wife of mine?*
> *Yesterday I hoped to woo you. Today my heart is filled with another decision!*
> *Forgive me! Realize how inconstant life is!*
> *After all, what promise of marriage, merely uttered by the lips, is irrevocable?*

Having recited these lines, he suddenly shouted, "Hah! I fell into your trap!"

The sister-in-law was utterly bewildered. Meng Gongwei said to her, "Don't you see? The poem is an acrostic."

"What's that?" asked the woman.

"The last characters of each line of verse, taken together, form a new sentence. The sentence reads: 'My decision is irrevocable.'"

Now Huang Zhengying faced the task of reconciling her infuriated sister-in-law to the facts. She spoke kindly to her, emphasized her deep bond with Zhuge Liang, and finally said, "He used the stratagem known as 'Fool the emperor and cross the sea.' Oh, my sister-in-law! Be generous now, and do not stand in our way."

The pleading of Zhuge Liang and his bride finally had its effect, and the sister-in-law was won over.[2]

How did Zhuge Liang apply Stratagem No. 1 in this incident? By composing the poem, which was read by all parties concerned, he was able to spread two contradictory messages: that he was dissolving his engagement and that he was determined to stick to it. The second sense of it, of course, was understood only by his clever fiancée, whom he also visited each time he went out to inspect one of his sister-in-law's chosen candidates. Together they made plans for the wedding day. While Zhuge Liang never deviated from the pursuit of his initial marriage goal, his sister-in-law and friend were deluded into thinking that he was acceding to their wishes. He succeeded in making his wedding plans under their very noses, and they never caught on until it was too late.

Zhuge Liang "fooled the emperor"—in this case, the people closest to him, particularly his sister-in-law as an authority figure—and at the same time he "crossed the sea"—i.e., he managed to navigate the difficult time until his objective had been achieved.

1.4 TARGET PRACTICE AT THE CITY GATE

In the second century A.D., a certain city was surrounded by enemy troops. How could outside relief be called in? Commander Kong Rong turned to a certain Tai Shici for help. The next day, to the astonishment of the enemy troops encamped a short distance away, Tai and three other men rode out of the encircled city's main gate. Tai Shici dismounted, set up a target in front of the city wall, and he and his men proceeded to engage in archery practice. When their arrows had all been shot, the four men mounted their horses and rode back through the gate into the city. The next day the target practice outside the city wall was repeated. This time only a few enemy soldiers got up to watch; the others remained at their ease, paying no attention. When the procedure was repeated on the third day, no enemy troops found the archery practice worthy of any notice. On the fourth day, in the middle of the target practice, Tai Shici leaped onto his horse, whipped it up, rode out like an arrow, and broke through the enemy lines. By the time the enemy soldiers had recovered from their surprise, he was well out of sight and on his way to bring help.[3]

1.5 GENERAL HE RUOBI'S TROOP MOVEMENTS

In A.D. 589 the Sui ruler wanted to conquer the opposing state of Chen, situated south of the Yangtze River. Before the start of hostilities the Sui commander, General He Ruobi, shifted the position of his troops three times. At the first movement, the Chen commanders thought the enemy was about to attack and placed their troops in a state of maximum alert. The second time they took the enemy troop movements a little less seriously. By the third time, the alertness of the Chen troops had diminished so much that a sudden Sui attack met hardly any resistance and ended in a complete victory.[4]

1.6 BENEATH THE COLORFUL CLOAK

In "Crossing the Sea in a House" (Section 1.1), the older of the two original source tales given above, the Emperor is made to think that he is being ushered into a house, although his steps are actually taking him to a very different destination: a ship. In the tale "Target Practice at the City Gate" (Section 1.4), enemy soldiers are lulled into inattention by an apparently harmless training exercise. The hidden intent behind that spectacle is to break through the enemy lines and spread the alarm to friendly forces that will help to lift the siege of the city.

When Stratagem No. 1 is divested of its colorful cloak of imagery, its general purpose becomes clear: to camouflage a goal, a method, or a course of action. The true purpose is disguised to look like something else, in extreme cases like its exact opposite.

As the following few examples illustrate, Stratagem No. 1

has repeatedly provided leaders in the People's Republic of China with a perspective from which to view political developments, both domestic and foreign.

When he fell into disfavor in the mid-1970s, Deng Xiaoping was accused of using Stratagem No. 1 in the sense of masking his real purpose. The press at that time offered comments such as this:

> In order to realize his revisionist program, Deng Xiaoping fabricated three poisonous documents: "On the General Work Program of the Party and the Entire Nation," "Some Questions Concerning Scientific and Technical Work," and "Some Questions Concerning the Acceleration of Industrial Development." Common to all those poisonous weeds is the large number of quotes from the writings of our revolutionary teachers. . . . This is typical of the technique of paying lip service to Marxism while in reality deviating from it.

In the late 1970s, reports in the Chinese press accused the Gang of Four of having formulated policies designed to mask their pursuit of purely personal ambitions. In a report dated February 26, 1978, Hua Guofeng, then chairman of the Chinese Communist Party, characterized them in the following terms:

> The Gang of Four is a clique of . . . the worst sort of hypocrites, who were clever at disguising themselves. They constantly waved the red flag in order to fight against the red flag, carried the banner of the struggle against capitalist restoration with the intent of restoring capitalism, and loudly proclaimed antirevisionist slogans in order to divert attention from their revisionist practices. Their "revolutionary" behavior was meant to cloak their true nature.

What had previously been seen as proof of their passionate dedication to Mao was reinterpreted in the light of Stratagem No. 1 after their fall from favor. All the actions and statements which formerly had been considered beyond reproach were now damned as mere tricks to disguise policies aimed against genuine socialism. Some press commentaries on the situation carried explicit references to Stratagem No. 1. More frequently, however, the Chinese mass media used colorful, modern equivalents of the stratagem, such as "wearing a red hat but having a black heart" or the previously mentioned phrase "waving the red flag in order to fight against the red flag."

In the foreign policy arena, Chinese press analyses based on Stratagem No. 1 are common. During the long years of Sino-Soviet estrangement, for example, Moscow was often accused of using its loudly trumpeted antiracism to mask its desire for the acquisition of strategic materials (notably in South Africa), while its support for Third World liberation movements was berated as mere camouflage for its true objective: securing a strategic seaway as part of its encirclement of Europe. The following observations and phrases are drawn from Chinese press comments during the years 1978–80:

> Aggressors busily preparing to launch new attacks generally blow the pipes of peace and disarmament very loudly. . . . The music of peace [is meant to] drown out the thunder of cannon. . . . Moscow's "support for the struggle of other peoples to achieve freedom and progress" is in fact [according to Chinese commentators] another way of saying that the Soviet Union reserves the right to intervene anywhere in the world. [In this view of things] the Conference on Security and Cooperation in Europe was really a "conference on insecurity in Europe" which the Kremlin used to lull the West into a false sense of security.

It is not only the Soviets who have been viewed through the lens of Stratagem No. 1. In 1982 both superpowers, the USSR and the U.S., were accused by the Chinese of "waving the peace banner" while in reality engaging in an unprecedented arms race. And in July 1983 the official Communist Party newspaper *Renmin Ribao* (People's Daily) stated that Vietnam had raised the specter of an alleged Chinese threat in order to mask its own aggression against Cambodia.

Cartoons on foreign affairs also provide insight into how

deeply Stratagem No. 1 is rooted in Chinese thought. The following examples are taken from the *People's Daily* in 1978–82: In one cartoon, the Soviet Union is pictured as a greedy alligator, its fang-filled maw camouflaged by a cloth on which are printed the words "Strictly Vegetarian." In another cartoon, the USSR is represented as a shark whose gaping jaws, hidden beneath the surface of the water, gobble one small fish after another; the part of the shark's body which is above the waterline is disguised as a black ship bearing the words "Peaceful Cooperation." A third cartoon shows Soviet soldiers in a ditch, digging their way from Afghanistan to the oil-rich countries of the Middle East, with their operation masked by a protective screen on which two doves of peace are painted.

The 1991 edition of *The 36 Stratagems: A Modern Version* points up two twentieth-century applications of Stratagem No. 1:

> *a.* Early in World War II, the Germans postponed the start of their French campaign twenty-nine times, dulling France's vigilance so much that, when the actual attack finally came, the French did not initially recognize it for what it was.
>
> *b.* The Arabs made similar preparations for the Yom Kippur War of 1973. After their defeat in the Six Day War of 1967, they held annual military maneuvers which involved troop concentrations at the Suez Canal. Behind what seemed like an annual exercise, they prepared for the real attack that launched the Yom Kippur War.

A suitable close to our comments on Stratagem No. 1 is provided by a quotation from *The 36 Stratagems: Secret Book of the Art of War:*

> That which seems fully open to public scrutiny too often masks the deepest secrets.

Besiege Wei to Rescue Zhao

The Chinese characters	围	魏	救	赵
Modern Mandarin pronunciation	*wéi*	Wèi	*jiù*	Zhào
Meaning of each character	besiege	Wei	rescue	Zhao

Interpretation with reference to the oldest known case	Rescue the state of Zhao by besieging the state of Wei, whose troops are attacking Zhao.
Application	Subdue the enemy indirectly by threatening one of his unprotected weak spots. The "thrust into the void" or "Achilles' heel" stratagem.

2.1 WITH THE ARMY INTO THE VOID

The oldest recorded instance of this stratagem is an incident recounted by the famous historian Sima Qian (second century B.C.) in his work *Shi ji* (Records of the Historian), the first of China's twenty-four dynastic histories. The tale is still told to Chinese children today.[1]

Sima Qian takes us back to pre-imperial China, to the period between the fifth and third centuries B.C. At that time a great many small states were jockeying for position, and wars were the order of the day. In 354 B.C., the state of Wei attacked the state of Zhao and laid siege to its capital, Handan. The ruler of Zhao requested assistance from the state of Qi. In 353 B.C., the King of Qi dispatched an army of eighty thousand men under the command of General Tian Ji, with Sun Bin as his adviser.

How was the Qi army to mount its attack? Tian Ji wanted to launch his troops directly into Zhao for a head-on clash with the Wei army. But Sun Bin was opposed to such a plan. He said, "You do not untie a knot by forcibly pulling and tearing at it. You do not separate fighting cocks from one another by stepping between them yourself. If you wish to end the siege, it is best to avoid the area of fullness [that is, the region where the enemy troops are massed] and to advance instead into the emptiness [the region left unprotected by the enemy]. All of Wei's finest troops are in the state of Zhao. Wei itself is without military guard. Therefore I propose that we attack Daliang, the most important city in Wei. If we do so, the Wei army will immediately break off its siege of Handan and hurry back to protect its own territory."

Tian Ji followed Sun Bin's advice. As soon as news of the Qi army's attack against Wei had spread, the Wei army halted its siege of Zhao and began a forced march back to Wei. In the meantime, the Qi army had laid an ambush at a carefully selected spot near Guiling, which the Wei army would have to pass. There the Qi troops waited at their ease until the time came to inflict a bitter defeat on the army of Wei, which was actually much stronger but now exhausted by its hurried march homeward. Thus the state of Zhao was saved. (For a more detailed look at Sun Bin's tactics in this ambush, see Section 11.10, "General Tian Ji's Battle Plan.") Offered here in a rather free translation, this incident was written down by Sima Qian more than two thousand years ago. But the earliest known source to actually use the four-character phrase *wéi Wèi jiù Zhào* is the famous Ming-period novel *The Romance of the Three Kingdoms* by Luo Guanzhong. In chapter 30 of that work, there is a reference to "the stratagem of Sun Bin: Besiege Wei to rescue Zhao."

The Sun Bin who planned that campaign was a descendant of Sun Tzu [Sunzi], the author of the world's oldest military treatise, *The Art of War*.[2] So it is hardly surprising that Sun Bin too composed a military treatise. Lost for nearly two thousand years, that document was rediscovered in 1972, written on 232 small bamboo tablets which were dug up by archeologists in Shandong Province and published under the title *Sun Bin bingfa* (Sun Bin's Art of War).

2.2 OF FULLNESS AND EMPTINESS

This stratagem may be expressed somewhat abstractly by the phrases "avoid the fullness" (that is, the area occupied by the enemy) and "advance into the emptiness" (i.e., the area vacated by the enemy). "Emptiness" and "fullness" are two fundamental concepts of traditional Chinese military theory mentioned in Sun Tzu's *The Art of War*. In the sixth chapter of that work, which deals with concepts of *xu* and *shi* (translated as "emptiness" and "fullness" by Thomas Cleary, and as "weak points and strong" in the James Clavell rendition), Sun Tzu writes:

> Appear where they cannot go, head for where they least expect you. . . . When you want to do battle, even if the opponent is deeply entrenched in a defensive position, he will be unable to avoid fighting if you attack where he will surely go to the rescue.[3]

In a 1983 work titled *Military Phraseology,* this stratagem is explained as follows:

> Instead of directly rescuing a region threatened by the enemy, attack bases in the enemy's rear. In this way the enemy is forced to withdraw his troops and rescue his own hinterland. The threatened region is thus relieved.[4]

Stratagem No. 2 is also examined in *A Selection of Philosophical Parables and Tales from Ancient China,* as follows:

> All things are linked one to another. This is also true of the mutual relationship between fullness and emptiness. If one puts that linkage to good use, one can bring about a fundamental shift in the balance of power with one's enemy, transform a precarious situation into a favorable one, and achieve victory.[5]

In his treatise *Strategic Problems of the Partisan War Against the Japanese Aggression,* dating from May 1938, Mao Zedong cites Stratagem No. 2 as follows:

> If the enemy entrenches himself on our base territory, we should leave part of our forces here to encircle the enemy. At the same time we should use our main force to launch an attack in the region from which the enemy has come; there, we should step up our activities in order to force the enemy to withdraw from our base territory and attack our main forces. This is the technique of "Besiege Wei to rescue Zhao."[6]

2.3 FROM PRE-CONFUCIAN TIMES

The classic Confucian work *Zuo zhuan* (Zuo Commentary), one of the oldest Chinese historical writings from the pre–Christian era, contains accounts of the application of Stratagem No. 2. The following two examples date from a period even before the struggle between Zhao and Wei which provided the traditional formulation of the tactic.

In the year 623 B.C., troops from the state of Chu besieged the state of Jiang. An army from the state of Jin then invaded Chu in order to relieve Jiang.

In 632 B.C., the state of Chu attacked the state of Song, which requested aid from the state of Jin. But Duke Wen, ruler of Jin, owed a debt of gratitude to the monarch of Chu, who had helped him during his nineteen-year exile. How could he now make a direct move against Chu? Hu Yan, one of the duke's advisers, suggested a way out: Jin should attack Cao and Wei, two states which had treated Duke Wen discourteously during his exile and were allied to Chu through inheritance and marriage. Chu would then withdraw its troops from Song and hasten to rescue Cao and Wei. And that is precisely what happened.[7]

2.4   DENG XIAOPING'S TROOPS

The following incident is recounted in *The 36 Stratagems: A Modern Version,*[8] as an illustration of Stratagem No. 2:

In August 1947, when Chinese Nationalist leader Chiang Kai-shek was preparing a major offensive against the territory then held by the Chinese Communist Party, troops commanded by Deng Xiaoping and Liu Bocheng left their own base territory and hastened in forced marches more than one thousand miles to the Dabie Mountains on the other side of the Yellow River, inside the territory still dominated by Chiang Kai-shek. Chiang was thus faced with an immediate threat to his power base. He was compelled to defend it against a possible attack by the People's Army and so was unable to launch his offensive against the Red-held areas. This single stroke altered the entire course of the war.

2.5   MODERN TAIWANESE ANALYSES OF STRATAGEM NO. 2

The Secret Book of the 36 Stratagems, with Explanations,[9] by Shu Han, gives some contemporary illustrations of Stratagem No. 2. According to this source, when the People's Republic of China invaded Vietnam in the spring of 1979, it was operating on the principle of "Besiege Wei to rescue Zhao." By invading Vietnam, the Chinese hoped to force the Vietnamese to withdraw their troops from Cambodia in order to protect their own territory. In this case, however, the trick did not work, because the Chinese threat to Vietnam was not great enough. China, says the author of *The Secret Book,* should have besieged Hanoi; had it done so, the stratagem would have been successful.

Three further examples from this Taiwanese work on the stratagems show how broadly No. 2 can be interpreted. According to Shu Han, the aircraft hijackings by terrorists that repeatedly plague the free world are applications of this tactic, as was the taking of American hostages in Teheran, which enabled Iran to play with the world's mightiest power as if it were a toy. The same may be said about Washington's grain embargo against the Soviet Union, imposed after the Kremlin's invasion of Afghanistan.

Wherever the stratagems are studied, the following words of Sun Tzu are considered of special relevance to No. 2:

> Military formation is like water—the form of water is to avoid the high and go to the low, the form of a military force is to avoid the full and attack the empty. . . . Water has no constant shape . . . so a military force has no constant formation: the ability to gain victory by changing and adapting according to the opponent is called genius.[10]

Kill with a Borrowed Knife

The Chinese characters	借	刀	杀	人
Modern Mandarin pronunciation	*jiè*	*dāo*	*shā*	*rén*
Meaning of each character	borrow	knife	kill	person

Applications	Eliminate an opponent using an outside agency (the "strawman" stratagem); harm someone else indirectly without exposing oneself ("alibi" or "substitute" stratagem).

There is no original source tale to which the four written characters of Stratagem No. 3 refer. The characters present the stratagem directly and graphically.

3.1   WITH THE SWORD OF THE AMMONITES

The Old Testament contains a striking example of Stratagem No. 3, but with a distinctly Biblical moral twist. The story is related in chapters 11–12 of the Second Book of Samuel:

> At the turn of the year, when kings take the field, David sent Joab out with his other officers and all the Israelite forces, and they ravaged Ammon and laid siege to Rabbah, while David remained in Jerusalem. One evening David got up from his couch and, as he walked about on the roof of the palace, he saw from there a woman bathing, and she was very beautiful. He sent to inquire who she was, and the answer came, "It must be Bathsheba daughter of Eliam and wife of Uriah the Hittite." . . .

David wrote a letter to Joab and sent Uriah with it. He wrote in the letter: "Put Uriah opposite the enemy where the fighting is fiercest and then fall back, and leave him to meet his death." Joab . . . stationed Uriah at a point where he knew they would put up a stout fight. The men of the city sallied out and engaged Joab, and some of David's guards fell; Uriah the Hittite was also killed. Joab sent David a dispatch with all the news of the battle. . . .

When Uriah's wife heard that her husband was dead, she mourned for him; and when the period of mourning was over, David sent for her and brought her into his house. She became his wife and bore him a son.[1]

What is striking about the Old Testament tale is God's disapproval and punishment of this application of Stratagem No. 3. Chapter 11 ends with the words: "But what David had done was wrong in the eyes of the Lord." In Chapter 12 God uses the prophet Nathan to level the accusation and pronounce the punishment:

> You have struck down Uriah the Hittite with the sword of the Ammonites; the man himself you murdered by the sword of the Ammonites, and you have stolen his wife. . . . Because in this you have shown your contempt for the Lord, the boy that will be born to you shall die.

And indeed David and Bathsheba's son dies.

The idea of divine retribution for unethical application of a stratagem is rather alien to Chinese culture. However, in works of Chinese literature, those who use stratagems with evil intent often come to a bad end. Not infrequently, they are also left with a bad name, a foul reputation passed down through generations in works of literature or art, and such a negative legacy was the most painful punishment for a Chinese of ancient times. (See Section 7.12, "The Alleged Crime of Yue Fei," and Section 18.9, "Posthumous Fame through Brush and Ink.")

3.2 Loki's Missile in Hother's Hand

The Norse god Balder was good and beautiful, shedding radiance wherever he went. The son of the great god Odin and the goddess Frigg, he was a favorite of the gods. The story of his death is told in the Prose Edda and is recounted in Frazer's *The Golden Bough* as follows:

> Once on a time Balder dreamed heavy dreams which seemed to forebode his death. Thereupon the gods held a council and resolved to make him secure against every danger. So the goddess Frigg took an oath from fire and water, iron and all metals, stones and earth, from trees, sicknesses and poisons, and from all four-footed beasts, birds, and creeping things, that they would not hurt Balder. When this was done Balder was deemed invulnerable; so the gods amused themselves by setting him in their midst, while some shot at him, others hewed at him, and others threw stones at him. But whatever they did, nothing could hurt him; and at this they were all glad. Only Loki, the mischief-maker, was displeased, and he went in the guise of an old woman to Frigg, who told him that the weapons of the gods could not wound Balder, since she had made them all swear not to hurt him. Then Loki asked, "Have all things sworn to spare Balder?" She answered, "East of Walhalla grows a plant called mistletoe; it seemed to me too young to swear." So Loki went and pulled the mistletoe and took it to the assembly of the gods. There he found the blind god Hother standing at the outside of the circle. Loki asked him, "Why do you not shoot at Balder?" Hother answered, "Because I do not see where he stands; besides I have no weapon." Then said Loki, "Do like the rest and show Balder honor, as they all do. I will show you where he stands, and do you shoot at him with this twig." Hother took the mistletoe and threw it at Balder, as Loki directed him. The mistletoe struck Balder and pierced him through and through, and he fell down dead.[2]

In this famous myth, Loki borrowed Hother's hand as the "knife" with which to kill Balder.

3.3 TWO PEACHES KILL THREE KNIGHTS

In the Spring and Autumn Period (722–468 B.C.), three bold warriors served Duke Jing of the state of Qi: Gongsun Jie, Tian Kaijiang, and Gu Yezi. No one was able to withstand their daring and courage. Their strength enabled them to catch a tiger with their bare hands.

One day Yanzi, Chief Minister of Qi, met the three knights. None of the fighters rose from his seat in deference to the official. Yanzi was furious at this violation of the ritual of respect. He went to the Duke and reported the incident, which he regarded as dangerous to the state. "Those three failed to pay proper respect to their superior. Can we count on them to help put down domestic unrest, if needed, or to take steps against our external enemies? No! Hence I propose that the sooner they are eliminated, the better."

Duke Jing sighed in embarrassment. "Those three are heroes. We are unlikely to be able to capture or kill them. What should we do?"

Yanzi thought for a while. Then he said, "I have an idea. Send a messenger to the three men, bearing two peaches, with this message: 'He who has performed the greatest deeds may take a peach.' "

Duke Jing sent the peaches. And the three knights began to measure their deeds one against the other. Gongsun Jie spoke first. "Once I killed a wild boar with my bare hands, and another time I caught a tiger the same way. My deeds entitle me to a peach." And he took one of the fruits.

Tian Kaijiang was the next to speak. "Twice I have routed a whole army with nothing but my naked sword in my hand. That deed certainly entitles me to a peach." And he too took a fruit.

When Gu Yezi saw that no peach was left for him, he said bitterly, "Once, when I was crossing the Yellow River in my lord's entourage, a giant turtle grabbed my horse and disappeared with it into the rushing waters. I dived to the bottom and ran a hundred steps upstream and nine miles downstream.

Finally I found the turtle, killed it, and rescued my horse. When I returned to the surface with the horse's tail in my left hand and the turtle's head in my right, the people along the bank thought I was a river god. That deed is surely worthy of a peach. Well, will neither of you give me his peach?"

With that, he drew his sword and rose up. When Gongsun Jie and Tian Kaijiang saw the fury of their comrade, they were overcome with a sense of guilt and they said, "Our bravery does not equal yours, and our deeds do not match yours. By taking the peaches ourselves and leaving none for you, we showed excessive greed. It would be cowardly not to pay for such behavior with our lives." Both of them returned the peaches, drew their swords, and slit their own throats.

Faced with the two corpses, Gu Yezi began to feel qualms of conscience. He said, "It is monstrous that my two comrades have died and I alone remain alive. It is a violation of duty to shame others with one's words and boast of one's own prowess. And it is cowardly to feel disgust at one's own deeds and not to die. On the other hand, if only my two comrades had shared a peach between them, they would have had what was coming to them. And I would have been able to take the peach I deserved."

With that, he dropped his peach and likewise cut his own throat. The messenger returned to the palace and reported to the Duke, "They are all three dead." Whereupon the ruler had the men buried in accordance with knightly ritual.

> *I entered the city gate of Qi*
> *and saw Tangyinli in the distance,*
> *and in its midst three burial mounds,*
> *one next to the other, like triplets.*
> *I asked: Whose graves are those?*
> *And was told in reply: Those of*
> *Gongsun Jie, Tian Kaijiang*
> *and Gu Yezi!*
> *Their strength could move mountains,*
> *and their distinction was incomparable.*

But one morning they were defamed.
Then two peaches killed the three knights.
Who was capable of such a stratagem?
The Minister of Qi—Yanzi.[3]

3.4   THE BRAVE LITTLE TAILOR

In the wondrous storehouse of fairy tales collected by the Brothers Grimm, there are many that could be cited as examples of stratagem application. Particularly apt for Stratagem No. 3 is the story known as "The Brave Little Tailor" (or sometimes as "Seven at a Blow"). It tells of a clever little tailor who, irritated by a bunch of flies landing on his jam, kills seven of the insects with a single blow. Impressed with his own prowess, he decides that the world must know of it too. He makes himself a girdle embroidered with the words "Seven at a Blow" and goes out into the world to seek his fortune. His first adventure involves a giant, against whose great strength the tailor matches his own guile—and emerges victorious, thanks to a combination of wit, trickiness, and good luck. In the version given in *The Blue Fairy Book,* the tale goes on:

> The little tailor continued to follow his nose, and after he had wandered about for a long time he came to the courtyard of a royal palace, and feeling tired he lay down on the grass and fell asleep. While he lay there the people came, and looking him all over read on his girdle: "Seven at a Blow." "Oh!" they said, "what can this great hero of a hundred fights want in our peaceful land? He must indeed be a mighty man of valor." They went and told the King about him, and said what a weighty and useful man he'd be in time of war, and that it would be well to secure him at any price. This counsel pleased the King, and he sent one of his courtiers down to the little tailor to offer him, when he awoke, a commission in their army. . . . "That's the very thing I came here for," he answered. "I am quite ready to enter the King's service." So he was received with

all honor, and given a special house of his own to live in.

But the other officers resented the success of the little tailor, and wished him a thousand miles away. . . . So they resolved to go in a body to the King, and all to send in their papers. "We are not made," they said, "to hold out against a man who kills seven at a blow." The King was grieved at the thought of losing all his faithful servants for the sake of one man, and he wished heartily that he had never set eyes on him, or that he could get rid of him. But he didn't dare to send him away, for he feared he might kill him along with his people, and place himself on the throne. He pondered long and deeply over the matter, and finally came to a conclusion. He sent to the tailor and told him that, seeing what a great and warlike hero he was, he was about to make him an offer. In a certain wood of his kingdom there dwelt two giants who did much harm by the way they robbed, murdered, burned, and plundered everything about them. "No one could approach them without endangering his life. But if he could overcome and kill these two giants he should have his only daughter for a wife, and half his kingdom into the bargain; he might have a hundred horsemen too, to back him up." "That's the very thing for a man like me," thought the little tailor; "one doesn't get the offer of a beautiful princess and half a kingdom every day." "Done with you," he answered. "I'll soon put an end to the giants. But I haven't the smallest need of your hundred horsemen; a fellow who can slay seven at a blow need not be afraid of two."

The little tailor set out, and the hundred horsemen followed him. When he came to the outskirts of the wood he said to his followers, "You wait here, I'll manage the giants by myself." And he went on into the wood, casting his sharp little eyes right and left about him. After a while he spied the two giants lying asleep under a tree, and snoring till the very boughs bent with the breeze. The little tailor lost no time in filling his wallet with stones, and then climbed up the tree under which they lay. When he got to about the middle of it he slipped along a branch till he sat just above the sleepers, when he threw down one stone after the other on the nearest giant. The giant felt nothing for a long time, but at last he woke up, and pinching his companion said, "What did you strike me for?" "I didn't strike you," said the other, "you must be dreaming." They both lay down to sleep again, and the tailor threw down a stone on the second giant, who sprang up and cried, "What's that for? Why did you throw something at me?" "I didn't throw anything," growled the first one. They wrangled on for a time, till, as both were tired, they made up the matter and fell asleep again. The little tailor began his game once more, and flung the largest stone he could find in his wallet with all his force, and hit the first giant on the chest. "This is too much of a good thing!" he yelled, and springing up like a madman, he knocked his companion against the tree till he trembled. He gave, however, as good as he got, and they both became so enraged that they tore up trees and beat each other with them, till they both fell dead at once on the ground.[4]

In this tale it is the King who first tries to apply Stratagem No. 3, wanting to be rid of the valiant little tailor but not daring to confront him directly. Hoping that the giants will serve as his "knife," the monarch masks his deadly intent as a seemingly honorable commission with a princely reward attached to it.

The tailor also uses Stratagem No. 3. Throwing the stones, he sows discord between the sleepy giants and gets them so worked up that they do one another in. The tailor uses the giants' own strength as the "knife" with which to kill them.

3.5   DUKE HUAN'S BURIED DOCUMENT

In the late eighth century B.C., Duke Huan of the state of Zheng wanted to conquer the state of Kuai. He had a document drawn up, listing the names of all the capable ministers and generals in Kuai, and proclaiming:

> Should the state of Kuai fall, all ministers and generals of the state of Kuai herein listed will be given official positions in the state of Zheng. Moreover, all the land of the state of Kuai will be divided among them.

As a second step, Duke Huan had a great altar built outside the city walls and the document buried there. Finally, he ordered that chickens and pigs be slaughtered and held a solemn ceremony in which he swore to Heaven that he would keep his promise to the dignitaries of Kuai. When the ruler of Kuai heard about all this, he suspected his civilian and military leaders of treason; in an outburst of fury, he had them executed to the last man. In this way Duke Huan used the ruler of Kuai as the "knife" with which to eliminate the elite of Kuai—after which it was an easy matter for him to conquer it.[5]

3.6 CONFUCIUS SAVES HIS HOMELAND

Even Confucius is said to have resorted to Stratagem No. 3. It was at the time when the powerful state of Qi was preparing to attack Confucius's homeland, the weak state of Lu. To prevent this, Confucius sent his rhetorically gifted disciple Zigong to the surrounding states. Zigong first persuaded the military leaders of Qi to attack the state of Wu instead of attacking Lu. He then went on to Wu and persuaded its ruler to attack Qi in order to protect Lu. Once war had broken out between Qi and Wu, Zigong hurried to the state of Jin and persuaded its ruler to declare war against Wu. In this way, Confucius succeeded in saving his home state of Lu.

In this instance, the other states served as the "borrowed knife" by which the danger to Lu was averted.

3.7 OLD GENERAL LIAN PO AND THE HOTHEAD ZHAO KUO

After conquering the Han state in the year 260 B.C., the state of Qin (which was destined to unify all of China in 221 B.C.) decided to attack the state of Zhao. The King of Zhao assigned the elderly General Lian Po to conduct the defense. An experienced warrior, Lian Po chose to entrench his forces in Changping. The Qin troops attacked repeatedly, but Lian Po held the line, refusing to be drawn into a direct clash with the strong Qin army.

Now there lived in Zhao one Zhao Kuo, son of a deceased general. This young man had a good deal of theoretical but little practical military knowledge. Nonetheless he had risen high in the ranks of Zhao's army. He was uncomfortable with Lian Po's defensive tactics and accused him before the King of cowardice. The ruler then commanded General Lian Po to move aggressively against the Qin army. But the old General refused.

Qin spies learned of the differences of opinion causing friction between the King of Zhao, Zhao Kuo, and Lian Po. Qin agents bribed residents of the Zhao capital to spread the rumor that Qin feared Zhao Kuo might be appointed general, and that Lian Po was preparing to capitulate. The King of Zhao heard of this rumor. He demoted Lian Po and appointed Zhao Kuo his successor. The new general took the first opportunity to engage the superior Qin army in direct combat, whereupon the Qin forces immediately encircled the Zhao army and wiped it out. The young General Zhao Kuo was among those who fell.

This was the beginning of the end for the state of Zhao, which was annexed by Qin in 228 B.C.

3.8   STALIN AND THE NAZIS: "BORROWED KNIVES"

According to the 1989 edition of *The 36 Stratagems: A Modern Version*,[6] the Germans forged documents in 1936 which made Soviet Marshal Tukhachevski, whom they greatly feared, appear to be a traitor. The documents were leaked to the Soviet secret police. Stalin was convinced of their authenticity, and he had Tukhachevski executed—thus playing the role of the "borrowed knife."[7]

A Hong Kong book on the stratagems[8] notes, however, that

in every other respect Stalin was unexcelled in the use of Stratagem No. 3. In 1944, say the Hong Kong authors, the forty-thousand-man Polish underground army in Warsaw wanted to exploit the Germans' difficult predicament following Stalingrad and the Allied landing in Normandy, to prevent Warsaw from becoming a battleground between the Germans and the Russians. On July 31, 1944, a forward Soviet tank unit reached the outskirts of Warsaw, and the Polish underground army thought the time ripe for an attack against the Germans in the city. The offensive was planned for August 1. But as soon as the people of Warsaw had begun their armed uprising against the German army, the Soviet advance suddenly ground to a halt and the Soviets began pulling back. The Germans, seeing that there was no longer any immediate threat from the Soviets, turned their full force against the Polish underground organizations in Warsaw. Roosevelt and Churchill repeatedly cabled Stalin, asking him to resume the Soviet advance and save Warsaw. But Stalin refused; indeed, he even protested against American and British air support for Warsaw, claiming that it violated Soviet airspace.

It was only on September 10, 1944, in the sixth week of the Warsaw uprising, that the Soviet Union resumed its military operations. Under protection of the Red Army, troops of the Polish Communist Party penetrated the Warsaw suburbs. On September 15 the Soviet forces again halted their advance, and the Germans continued mopping up all nests of resistance, virtually turning Warsaw into a ghost city. Only when the Polish underground army had been virtually exterminated did the Red Army choose to march into Warsaw.

The authors of the Hong Kong book on the stratagems, Ma Senliang and Zhang Laiping, regard that incident as an application of Strategy No. 3 by Stalin, who saw the Polish underground in Warsaw as an obstacle to a Communist takeover and "borrowed" the German army to eliminate the Polish enemy.

3.9 WANG XIFENG AND THE TWO CONCUBINES

The novel *Hongloumeng* (Dream of the Red Chamber), by Cao Xueqin (d. ca. 1763), is one of the most famous literary works of classical China. Chapter 69 of the work bears the title: "A clever person kills with a borrowed sword, another feels compelled to commit suicide by swallowing molten gold." The story leading up to those events is as follows:

Jia Lian, the husband of Wang Xifeng, had long been fed up with his wife, not only because she had failed to give him a male heir but also because she had often been sick. He fell in love with the beautiful Lady You, secretly took her as his concubine, and set her up in a little house near the family compound. Through a servant, Wang Xifeng learned about her husband's mistress. One day, when he was on a journey, she visited Lady You, pretending great sympathy, and invited her to move into the compound. During the move, Wang Xifeng managed to get rid of Lady You's old servant and instead gave her one of her own women, who had been primed with special instructions.

From that time on, Wang Xifeng directed unceasing harassment against Lady You. Outwardly, she was friendliness and warmth personified when she visited with Lady You once each week. Lady You thus had no idea that, in the background, Wang Xifeng was doing everything possible to make her life miserable.

In the meantime Jia Lian returned from his travels, and his father gave him seventeen-year-old Qiu Tong as a gift. Jia Lian now spent whole days and nights with his younger concubine. Naturally enough, Wang Xifeng hated the young newcomer no less than she hated the older one, but Qiu Tong served her as a welcome tool for the elimination of Lady You. She was now able to apply the stratagem "Kill with a borrowed knife" and look on serenely from the heights as the two concubines fought one another. Once Lady You had been dispatched by the seventeen-year-old, Wang Xifeng said to herself, she would find it easy enough to get rid of the girl.

And so Wang Xifeng constantly goaded Qiu Tong on against

Lady You. "You are young and inexperienced, and do not know the danger you are in," she would whisper to the girl. "She holds his heart in her hand. Even I must bow down before her. But be careful. You'll destroy yourself if you are openly hostile to her."

"I have no intention of bowing before her!" said Qiu Tong rebelliously. "It's easy to see where your weakness and caution have led—your authority has evaporated. Just let me be! I'll deal with that whore. She'll learn who I am!"

Qiu Tong deliberately spoke those words loudly enough so that Lady You could not fail to hear. Beside herself at such malice, Lady You spent the rest of the day weeping and could not eat a bite.

Finally, with the aid of a bribed fortune-teller, Wang Xifeng incited the younger concubine to such an extent that the girl became bold enough to stand beneath the window of a nearby pavilion in which Lady You was staying and let loose a stream of invective against her. The unhappy Lady You broke down utterly, and that night she committed suicide by swallowing molten gold.[9]

3.10 THE CASE OF DÜRRENMATT

Friedrich Dürrenmatt's *The Judge and His Hangman* is perhaps the most popular work of modern Swiss literature in the People's Republic of China. Millions of copies have been printed in comic-strip form. The following plot summary, taken from a Dürrenmatt picture book published in Guizhou Province, seems to hint that the novel's popularity in China may be partly due to its relevance to Stratagem No. 3:

> The elderly Swiss police commissioner Bärlach is an honest, incorruptible man. But in a capitalist society he can apply the law only to commonplace, petty crimes. He is unable to bring a serious criminal like Gastmann before the bar

of justice, though Gastmann has every manner of evil deed on his conscience. Bärlach has gathered proof of Gastmann's crimes. But because Gastmann is in cahoots with the political elite, with powerful capitalists and a foreign ruling clique, it is extremely difficult to subject him to the full force of the law. So Bärlach must forgo legal prosecution. Instead, he manipulates the mind of a murderer who is trying to blame someone else (i.e., Gastmann) for his own crime, and he lets Gastmann be killed by the murderer.

3.11 THE HAN DRUMMER

Toward the end of the Han period there lived a certain Mi Heng, a man who was articulate and literate, skilled not only in poetry but also in music, especially in playing the drums. But he had a proud and unyielding nature. One time Cao Cao, founder of the Wei Dynasty, one of the three realms depicted in *The Romance of the Three Kingdoms,* wanted to meet Mi Heng. But Mi Heng refused. So Cao Cao had him conscripted into his army as a drummer. Later, Cao Cao held a great banquet on an island in the Yangtze River, at which he hoped to humiliate Mi Heng before all the guests. But Mi Heng turned the tables on him, exposing Cao Cao to ridicule by writing a poem about the parrots which the banquet guests had given as gifts to Cao Cao. From then on, the place became known as Parrot Island.

Said Cao Cao to Kong Rong, "Mi Heng has dared to ridicule me. Yet he is a very capable man, and widely known. If I were to kill him, I would be accused of small-mindedness. Now, Commandant Liu Biao is a vicious and irritable fellow. I'll have Mi Heng transferred to his command. Liu Biao will surely find him unbearable and get rid of him in short order." So Cao Cao had Mi Heng transferred to Liu Biao's service. And indeed, before long the latter's lieutenant, Huang Zu, had killed Mi Heng, who was only twenty-five years old.

The death of the youthful Mi Heng, a victim of Stratagem No. 3, was still mourned in China almost fifteen hundred years later. Visiting Mi Heng's grave on Parrot Island, the poet Song Xiang (1756–1826) composed a poem describing the drummer's tomb, comparing it to the unknown graves of Cao Cao and Huang Zu:

> *For two days the ship has been anchored off Parrot Island. Day after day the waves flow over buildings sunk beneath the waters. Mi Heng's tragic drumbeat floats on the wondrous wind, and the perfume of a sad parrot poem streams from the sweet-smelling grass on the grave.*
> *I visit your autumnal burial place. Do not reject my humble offer of sacrificial wine. Who knows any longer where Cao and Huang are buried, and who thinks of them?*

3.12 CONCLUSION

According to the 1989 edition of the Beijing book on the stratagems,[10] No. 3 was originally used in the continual power struggles of officials in the thoroughly decadent feudal bureaucracy of ancient China; to that extent it is to be condemned.

But in military matters, states the same work, it is important to understand how to use the strength of others. You may, for example, incite and exploit conflict in the enemy camp, using such conflict as the "borrowed knife." The borrowed "object" may be any one of many things: You may borrow the enemy's strength by leading him on to exhaust his energies, while you yourself remain rested and finally overwhelm him (see Stratagem No. 4). You may "borrow" the enemy's generals by inciting conflict among them, so that they begin to fight one another. You can also borrow the enemy's stratagems, learning his intentions and turning them against him.

According to a Taiwanese book on the stratagems,[11] military theoreticians of ancient China felt that it was inglorious to rely on the help of allies. The supreme art of war consisted, they believed, in borrowing the military, economic, and intellectual forces of *enemies* to defeat enemies. As it is stated in the Chinese tract *Bingfa yuanji* (The Core of the Art of War):

> If you are limited in your own strength, then borrow the strength of the enemy. If you cannot neutralize an enemy, borrow an enemy's knife to do so. If you have no generals, borrow those of the enemy. In this way you need not be active yourself, but can remain at rest. What you cannot achieve yourself, you can achieve with the hand of the enemy.

Await the Exhausted Enemy at Your Ease

The Chinese characters	以	逸	待	劳
Modern Mandarin pronunciation	*yǐ*	*yì*	*dài*	*láo*
Meaning of each character	in	ease	await	exhausted
Application	Preserve your own strength while maneuvering the enemy into exhausting himself.			

The short formula for Stratagem No. 4 appears for the first time in chapter 7 of the famous 2,500-year-old treatise by Sun Tzu, *The Art of War*:

> Standing your ground, awaiting those far away, awaiting the weary in comfort, awaiting the hungry with full stomachs, is mastering strength.[1]

In chapter 6 of the same work, the following passage appears:

> Those who are first on the battlefield and await [their] opponents are at ease; those who are last on the battlefield and head into battle get worn out. . . . Therefore good warriors cause others to come to them, and do not go to others.[2]

4.1 THE TRAP AT GUILING

As a situation evolves, especially in war, circumstances constantly change. Accordingly, the use of one stratagem alone may not suffice. In such a case, two or even three stratagems may be required as the situation changes.

For example, in the fourth century B.C., Sun Bin first applied Stratagem No. 2, besieging Wei to rescue Zhao; he then applied No. 4 by ambushing the Wei army, which had exhausted itself in a forced march from Zhao, and defeating it. (See Section 2.1, "With the Army into the Void.")

To "await the enemy" is not always to be construed in a passive sense, according to Chinese sources, but frequently as an active undertaking. Some action is often necessary to deliberately exhaust the enemy or to steer him in the desired direction, in any case to "lure him into the depths of your own territory" (yòu dí shēn rù), then take advantage of a favorable time to engage in battle. Here the important thing is literally to lead the enemy around by the nose and not permit him to set the pace.

4.2   THE AMBUSH AT MALING

In 342 B.C., twelve years after Zhao was saved through the siege of Wei, the state of Wei attacked the Han state. The Han ruler called on the state of Qi for help. Tian Ji and Sun Bin, commanding the Qi army, immediately led it in an attack against the Wei capital. As soon as he heard about this, Pang Juan, commander of the Wei troops, pulled them back out of Han territory. Sun Bin knew of General Pang Juan's arrogance and his low opinion of the Qi troops. Faced with an advancing Wei army, Sun Bin began an apparent retreat. On the first day his troops left behind traces of 100,000 campfires; on the second day 50,000, and on the third day only 30,000. Pang Juan, eager for victory, concluded that the Qi army had been seriously weakened by mass desertions. So he left the bulk of his infantry behind and set out in pursuit with some lightly equipped troops. He covered two days' worth of ground in a single day's march. Sun Bin had calculated that Pang Juan would reach Maling at dusk.

He set an ambush there and waited. As planned, the Wei troops arrived exhausted from their forced march, and Sun Bin's army demolished them. General Pang Juan committed suicide on the battlefield.[3]

4.3 MAO'S SIXTEEN CHARACTERS— A FORMULA FOR GUERRILLA WARFARE

In his essay *Strategic Problems of the Revolutionary War in China,* dated December 1936,[4] Mao Zedong wrote:

> If an attacking opponent is superior to our army in numbers and firepower, we can alter the balance of power only when the enemy has penetrated deep into the interior of our base territory and there has drained the cup of bitterness to the lees, so that "the fat grow lean and the lean exhaust themselves to death." At that point the enemy army, though still strong, has been substantially weakened; its soldiers are tired out and demoralized, and many of the enemy's weaknesses are revealed. The Red Army is still weak, but it has been preserving its strength, storing its energies, and awaiting the exhausted enemy at its ease. At this point it is possible, as a rule, to strike a certain balance in the strength of the two sides or to transform the enemy's absolute superiority into a merely relative superiority—sometimes it is even possible for us to gain the upper hand.

And in a telegram dated April 1947, detailing the course of operations in the northwestern theater, Mao declared:

> Our course is . . . to harry . . . the enemy in this area for some time yet, and then, when [his] exhaustion and [his] food shortages have reached an extreme, to seek an opportunity to destroy him. . . . Unless we fully weaken and starve out the enemy, we cannot attain the final victory. This method may be termed the exhaustion tactic: You tire the enemy until he is totally exhausted, and then destroy him.

Loot a Burning House

The Chinese characters	趁	火	打	刦
Modern Mandarin pronunciation	*chèn*	*huǒ*	*dǎ*	*jié*
Meaning of each character	exploit	confla-gration	commit	robbery

Applications	"Exploit a fire to commit a robbery"—exploit another's troubles or crisis for your own advantage; attack the enemy when he is in a state of chaos. The "vulture" stratagem.

The basic concept of Stratagem No. 5 is to be found in Sun Tzu's *The Art of War*: "When the enemy is confused, you can use this opportunity to take them."[1]

5.1   THE RADIANT ROBE

One of the oldest appearances of the short formula for this stratagem is in the sixteenth-century novel *Journey to the West*, by Wu Cheng'en.[2] The book recounts the adventures of the monk Tripitaka and his companions as they travel westward from the empire of the Tang Dynasty in search of sacred Buddhist scriptures which they are to bring back to China. On this odyssey, Tripitaka is accompanied by Sun Wukong, the divine Monkey King who is a master of magical arts, as well as Sha the Sand Monk (nicknamed "Sandy" in some translations), and Zhu Bajie, a pig ("Pigsy"). On their way, they encounter all manner of threats—demons, monsters, false priests, fiends— and must overcome a constant succession of dangers.

One evening during their travels, Tripitaka and the Monkey King reach a temple in which there are more than seventy rooms and 200 monks. There they ask permission to spend the night. While they are being given tea from an elegant tea service, they are asked by the abbot of the monastery whether Tripitaka has in his possession any precious object which he could show him. The Monkey King reminds Tripitaka of a certain robe in their luggage. The monks laugh, pointing out that they own hundreds of robes of the finest silk and splendid embroidery. The abbot has these robes shown to his two guests. The Monkey King is unimpressed and asks if he may show the robe they have brought. Even as he unpacks it, a radiance shines through the two layers of oiled paper in which it is wrapped. When Monkey takes it out, a red radiance and a fragrant scent fill the room. What a magnificent robe!

The abbot immediately begins to think evil thoughts. He kneels before Tripitaka, complains that he cannot see the robe in detail because of his poor eyesight, and asks to take it with him to his cell so that he can examine it carefully overnight. The robe is handed over. That night the abbot takes counsel with his monks to determine how he can gain possession of the splendid garment. A young monk by the name of Great Stratagem suggests that the Zen hall be set afire and the two guests sleeping in it burned to death. Quickly the monks heap firewood around the Zen hall. But the Monkey King is not asleep; with half-closed eyes he is doing breathing exercises. He hears the sound of running feet outside the hall and the creaking of firewood in the wind. Suspicious, he gets up. In order not to wake the sleeping Tripitaka he changes himself into a bee, flies out, and sees the firewood. He decides to catch the monks in their own trap. Changed back into his usual form, he quickly flies up to the southern gate of Heaven, where he obtains a firefighting blanket from Devaraja, King of Heaven. He brings the blanket back to the Zen hall and wraps Tripitaka in it, so that he is safe. From the ridge of the roof he watches the monks lighting the wood. He speaks a magic incantation and then blows out mightily. A strong wind comes up and fans the flames, which gradually envelop the entire monastery. Only the Zen hall with Tripitaka in it remains unharmed. So the monks suffer the fate they had planned for their guests.

All the animals and demons in the surrounding mountains awaken, including the Mountain Demon in the Cave of the Black Wind, twenty miles south of the monastery. Hastening to help the monks, the Mountain Demon flies on a cloud and sees that the front and back halls of the monastery are completely empty, while the fire rages through the corridors on both sides. The demon runs into the hall, and in the abbot's room it sees something wrapped in blue, from which a multicolored radiance emanates. It opens the package and discovers the precious robe, a rare Buddhist treasure. Forgetting all its good intentions, the demon wraps up the robe, exploiting the fire to commit a robbery, and quickly flies back to its mountain cave with its booty.

5.2 QI HOLDS BACK

At the start of the Warring States period (475–221 B.C.), there were about twenty separate states on Chinese territory. Among them were Chu, Han, Qi, Qin, Wei, Yan, and Zhao.

Qi and Han were allies. They wanted to conquer Yan but did not dare invade because of Zhao and Chu. Suddenly Qin and its ally Wei attacked the state of Han. The ruler of Qi was eager to help his Han ally, but his adviser Tian Chensi warned, "The destruction of Han would threaten the very existence of Zhao and Chu. So those two will give aid to Han as quickly as possible."

As a result, Qi did not intervene in the fighting. But Zhao and Chu behaved exactly as Tian Chensi had predicted. Suddenly Qin, Wei, Zhao, and Chu were all embroiled in a war over Han. The seemingly neutral state of Qi took advantage of that moment, when war was raging on every side, to mount an attack against the state of Yan, which had also kept out of the fighting. In the year 270 B.C., Qi conquered Yan.

5.3   UNEQUAL TREATIES AND LOST TERRITORY

In more recent times, foreign powers have often taken advantage of China's backwardness, in conjunction with dire conditions in the country, to apply Stratagem No. 5.

After losing the First Opium War (1840–42), China was exhausted and demoralized. Britain and the USA exploited the situation to conclude one-sided agreements favorable to them (present-day Chinese refer to these as the "unequal treaties"). The French, rubbing their hands with glee, so to speak, saw an opportunity for great profit. In August 1844, "exploiting a fire to commit a robbery," the French government, which had maintained hardly any relations with the Middle Kingdom prior to the Opium War, sent Marie Melchior Joseph Théodore de Lagrené as a special emissary to China. Within weeks he concluded the Treaty of Huangpu, which could not have been more favorable to France.[3]

Another historical gloss was offered by the *Beijing Daily* on November 14, 1981. The typically verbose title of the article was "Czarist Russia exploits a fire to commit a robbery, in order to slice off a piece of our territory." The article commemorated the Sino-Russian Treaty of Beijing signed 120 years earlier. When British and French troops attacked Beijing in 1860, plundering and burning the Summer Palace, Czarist Russia took the opportunity to exploit China's weakness and applied massive pressure to get the government to sign the Treaty of Beijing which, according to the *Beijing Daily* article, enabled Russia to "annex some 400,000 square kilometers of Chinese territory east of the Ussuri."

5.4   ESAU EXHAUSTED

The first major episode in the Biblical saga of Jacob and Esau is told in Genesis 25:29–34:

> One day Jacob prepared a broth and when Esau came in
> from the country, exhausted, he said to Jacob, "I am ex-
> hausted; let me swallow some of that red broth." . . . Jacob
> said, "Not till you sell me your rights as the firstborn."
> Esau replied, "I am at death's door; what use is my birth-
> right to me?" Jacob said, "Not till you swear!"; so he swore
> an oath and sold his birthright to Jacob. Then Jacob gave
> Esau bread and the lentil broth, and he ate and drank and
> went away without more ado.[4]

The Bible adds one more sentence to this brief episode: "Thus
Esau showed how little he valued his birthright." From the
standpoint of Chinese stratagem mentality, however, something
is still missing: an evaluation of Jacob's behavior. It might read
like this: "With great presence of mind he took advantage of
his brother Esau's exhausted state and maneuvered him into
relinquishing his birthright as the firstborn for a dish of lentil
broth."

5.5   THE ILLITERATE KOREAN

Korea, about 1930: Honest and industrious, filled with respect
for his parents, loving kindness for his wife, and deep concern
for his siblings, the peasant Ho Tal-su works hard every day.
But he is consumed by one worry: His only child, his daughter
Phoenix, has gone off to North China to search for her husband,
who was abducted by the invading Japanese. Many months have
passed since her departure, and there has been no news of her.
Eventually an itinerant kerosene peddler brings a letter from
Phoenix. Ho Tal-su is not at home when the peddler comes, so
the man leaves the letter in front of the door and moves on.
Returning home, the illiterate peasant thinks that the letter is
just some piece of paper the peddler has thrown away. He tears
a piece of it off and uses it to roll himself a cigarette. With the
rest he plugs a hole in his window.
A few days later news spreads about a catastrophic flood in

the part of China to which Ho's daughter has gone. The peasant's family is troubled and they decide to borrow money from their landlord so that Ho's wife can go in search of their daughter. Just as she is about to depart on her journey, the peddler happens by again and asks Ho Tal-su whether he had received his daughter's letter. Ho recalls that he had plugged the window with it. With the torn letter in hand, Ho and his wife run in every direction, searching for someone who can read it to them. Desperate, they meet a young man who pretends that he can read. When he stares at the scrap of paper helplessly, Ho and his wife assume that the letter contains bad news about their daughter. That night the family members cry bitterly. But finally the peasant finds someone who really can read, his own niece. She brings her teacher along, just to be sure. The fragment of the letter reveals that their daughter Phoenix is well; in fact, she has given birth to a son. Ho Tal-su's tears of grief are changed into tears of joy. But a shock follows. His two readers also reveal to him the contents of the document which the landlord had drawn up before lending Ho money, and to which Ho had affixed his thumbprint. It states that the peasant has sold his niece to the landowner for a mere twenty won!

This is a rough plot summary of *The Daughter's Letter,* a play performed in 1987 by the National Theater Troupe of North Korea. According to the Beijing newspaper *Guangming Daily,* it was a new production of a play which "Comrade Kim Il-sung wrote in the Chinese province of Jilin during the war of resistance against Japan, and in the original performance of which he played a role." The play's passionate message, wrote Chinese theater critic Zhu Kechuan, is that "knowledge is power." Every viewer leaves this play, remarked Zhu, realizing that "the backward attitude that education and literacy are useless to the working farmer does enormous harm."

In the context of stratagems, it is worth noting the behavior of the landlord, which leads to the play's dramatic climax. He exploits the peasant's difficulty (the "fire") to commit a "robbery," tricking the ignorant farmer into selling him his niece for a ridiculously small sum of money.

Clamor in the East, Attack in the West

The Chinese characters	声	東	击	西
Modern Mandarin pronunciation	*shēng*	*dōng*	*jī*	*xī*
Meaning of each character	make noise	East	attack	West

Applications	Announce an attack to the east but carry it out to the west; feint eastward but attack westward. Diversionary maneuver to mask the real direction of an attack.

The short formula above goes back to the Tang historian and government official Du You (A.D. 735–812), who wrote:

> One announces an attack in the east, in order to really mount an attack in the west.[1]

The basic concept of Stratagem No. 6 is formulated in Sun Tzu's *The Art of War* as:

> Attack where there is no defense. . . . If they are alert on their eastern flank, strike on their western flank.[2]

And in the work titled *Huainanzi,* composed under the aegis of Prince Liu An of Huainan (179–122 B.C.), the following passage appears:

> A bird wishing to peck something bends its head and thus hides its beak. . . . The tiger and the leopard do not show their claws. . . . The art of war thus consists in pretending to be soft and weak, but when fighting breaks out, meeting the enemy with hardness and strength, and in

pretending to pull in defensively, but at the appropriate moment breaking loose. . . .

The 1989 edition of the Beijing book on the stratagems explains No. 6 this way:

> The goal is to disguise the direction of an attack. Through agile operations you show your forces sometimes in the west, then again in the east; strike suddenly, only to withdraw with equal suddenness; pretend that an attack is imminent, but then do not carry it out; pretend peaceable intent, when you really intend to attack; begin a course of action which seems to imply a certain logical sequence, but then suddenly break it off; let something happen seemingly at random which in reality is quite deliberate; pretend to be ready for action, when you are really incapable of it, and vice versa. On the basis of what he perceives as comprehensible phenomena, the enemy draws hasty conclusions and makes the wrong preparations, only to find himself attacked and defeated at a place he had not anticipated.

6.1 THE SIMULATED ALLIANCE

In the Warring States period, the states of Qi, Han, and Wei attacked the state of Yan. To assist Yan, Jing Yang pretended to lead an army from the state of Chu on a northward route, but then mounted a surprise attack against an important city in Wei, whereupon Qi, Han, and Wei broke off their attack against Yan.

Having attained its goal of saving Yan, the Chu army wanted to withdraw from the Wei city it had conquered. But the western side of the city was suddenly besieged by the Han army and the eastern side by the Qi army. The Chu forces were caught in a pincers movement. What could be done?

Jing Yang decided to open the city's western gate, letting chariots and soldiers ride in and out by day and keeping the lamps burning at night. In this way he simulated lively traffic between the Chu and Han armies. As expected, suspicion grew in the ranks of the Qi forces that Han and Chu might be forming an alliance for an attack on Qi. So the Qi army withdrew. Left to itself, the Han army feared an attack by the much stronger forces of Chu. One dark and stormy night the Han troops departed, and the army of Chu was able to return home in peace.

6.2   THE UNEXPECTED RIVER CROSSING

Having destroyed China's first centralized imperial government in the year 206 B.C., Liu Bang, founder of the Han Dynasty, had to continue fighting for years against local warlords who had come to power during the years of the Qin Dynasty's decline. One of Liu's opponents was Prince Bao of Wei.

To defend himself against an attack by the Han army, Prince Bao ordered General Bo Zhi to use all the Wei forces in an ambush on the eastern bank of the Yellow River, near Puban. Bo Zhi blocked the crossing over the Yellow River, along with all shipping on the river; he also had all the peasants' boats hidden and set a mobile unit to constantly patrol the riverbank. Convinced that the Han army had no other way to cross the Yellow River except at Puban, he took only these precautions.

Han Xin, commander of the Han army, realized that a direct attack at Puban would be unlikely to succeed. Nevertheless he had the Han army's main camp set up opposite that of the Wei army near Puban and saw to it that many flags were raised and all the ships at his disposal anchored there. By day the Han troops raised a racket and beat their drums, and at night torches burned throughout the camp, where there was much lively activity. Everything created the impression that a river crossing by the Han forces was imminent. Believing this, Bo Zhi paid no attention at all to the upper reaches of the Yellow River.

In the meantime Han Xin secretly transferred his main fighting force northward, where it crossed the Yellow River at Xiayang. That move heralded the final defeat of Prince Bao of Wei.[3]

6.3 CONFUSING THE "YELLOW TURBANS"

Toward the end of the Eastern Han period (A.D. 25–220), Zhu Jun besieged the city of Yuan, in which the "Yellow Turban" rebels had entrenched themselves. To better scout the enemy positions, he had an earth wall piled up outside the city walls. He then had the war drums beaten and mounted a feint attack against the western side of the city. When, watching from the top of the earth wall, he saw that all the Yellow Turbans were hurrying to defend the western side, he mounted a lightning strike with his main force on the northeastern side—and easily gained entry into the city.

6.4 THE TRUMPETS OF JERICHO

"Jericho was bolted and barred against the Israelites; no one went out, no one came in," says the Bible in chapter 6 of the Book of Joshua. At God's command, Joshua tells the people his plan for conquest. The Old Testament tale continues:

> When Joshua had spoken to the army, the seven priests carrying the seven trumpets of ram's horn before the Lord passed on and blew the trumpets, with the Ark of the Covenant of the Lord following them. The drafted men marched in front of the priests who blew the trumpets, and the rearguard followed the Ark. . . . Thus [the Ark of the Lord went] round the city, making the circuit of it once, and then they went back to the camp and spent the night there. . . . This they did for six days. But on the seventh day they rose at dawn and marched seven times round the city in the same way. . . . The seventh time the priests blew

ZHU DE'S SURPRISE MOVE

927, troops stationed in Nanchang, in Jiangxi
ed against the Guomindang regime recently
ng Kai-shek. These troops formed the nucleus
ed Army. Under pressure from the Guomindang
the rebel units marched southward. There, with
n Mountains as a base, eleven Communist base
blished by the year 1930, including one near the
. When Guomindang troops attacked Yongxin,
ommandant of the fourth Revolutionary Peasant
d Gaolong in Hunan Province to the west, to
ression that the Red forces were invading Hunan.
the Red Army was then quickly withdrawn from
covering 130 miles in a forced march, wiped out
ment in Caoshi and captured Yongxin. According
's Daily of August 2, 1982, Zhu De's operation
application of the principle "Clamor in the east,
west."

.7 CAMBODIA INSTEAD OF CHINA

the north, but attack in the west" was the headline,
ratagem No. 6, that appeared over an article in the
e People's Daily dated October 26, 1978. According
le, Vietnam at that time was constantly fuming about
threat from the north and an imminent Chinese war
etnam. In reality, wrote the Chinese correspondent,
mese regime was simply trying to divert the attention
people from the problems created by the Vietnamese
ms buildup and to divert the world's attention from
mminent invasion of Cambodia.

the trum
Lord has
the trump
fell the wa
straight ah

A student of m
commentary:

For six days
seventh, a seg
raelites concen
suggested elsew
to cover the nois
the city's fortific
way. And this ur
segment of wall

If this assumption is
peters may be seen as a
in keeping with Stratag

6.5 THE

Under the Han Emperor
feudal lords jointly rose
troops who were firmly en
manded by General Zhou Y
the southeastern corner of
mand to reinforce the guarc
of the city. Shortly thereafter
main force to the northwest
failed to make a breakthroug

6.

On August 1, 1
Province, rebell
formed by Chia
of the Chinese F
forces, some of
the Jinggangsh
areas were esta
city of Yongxi
Zhu De, then
Army, attacke
create the imp
About half of
Gaolong and,
an enemy reg
to the *People*
was a skillfu
attack in the

"Clamor in
based on S
edition of t
to the artic
a Chinese
against Vi
the Vietna
of its own
army's ar
Hanoi's i

6.8 CLAMOR IN THE EAST, CLAMOR IN THE WEST

In the famous novel *Shuihu zhuan* (Water Margin)[6], there is an episode in which Stratagem No. 6 is combined with No. 4, in order to gradually wear the enemy out. The tactic is used by a band of robbers whose mountain headquarters were located on the summit of the Mountain of Cool Winds. These robbers were joined by some honorable men who had fled the authorities because they had been falsely accused of various crimes and could get no justice under ancient China's corrupt judicial system. As the episode begins, the hotheaded General Qin Ming, who has been ordered to destroy the robbers' nest, leads his men in an attempt to storm the mountaintop.[7]

> With wild battle cries, the troops stormed up the mountainside, foot soldiers in the lead. The path took them up and down steep ravines, across dangerous rocky outcroppings. Finally the vanguard of forty or fifty men neared the crest and looked upward. Suddenly, with a noise like thunder, huge blocks of wood and stone came crashing down from the boulders above, and the men were drenched in veritable floods of hot lime and stinking slops. There could be no retreat. They threw themselves on the ground and lay there helpless. The units behind them quickly turned tail and ran for safety.
>
> Beside himself with fury, Qin Ming gathered about him those troops who had managed to return and marched them eastward along the foot of the mountain, looking for another way up. Suddenly, from the western slope, there came the sound of drums, and a group of robbers carrying red flags came out of the dense woods. Hastily Qin Ming led his infantry and cavalry westward—but then the drums stopped and there were no more red flags to be seen. When he took a closer look at the path on which the robbers had come and gone, he found that it was no proper path at all, merely a narrow track such as those used by firewood gatherers—and it had been blocked with branches.
>
> The soldiers had begun clearing the track, when a scout reported that drums had been heard and red flags seen on

the eastern slope. Swift as the wind, Qin Ming gathered his troops and hurried them eastward. But when they arrived, the drums were silent, the flags had disappeared, and the few paths leading upward had been blocked with felled trees and tangled undergrowth.

Again a scout came running up: He had heard drums and seen red flags on the western slope. Qin Ming galloped back—the same foolishness!

He gnashed his teeth in fury, as if to grind them into dust. The troops that had hurried after him now stood about exhausted. But listen! From the east came drawn-out drumbeats. . . . About-face—ride—nothing to hear, nothing to see. . . .

In this way General Qin Ming's forces were worn down so that his defeat was inevitable.

6.9 SKY-HIGH PING-PONG BALLS

In 1977, Chinese table tennis players successfully used Stratagem No. 6 in a major tournament. When it was their service, they would throw the ball very high in the air; their opponents followed the ball with their eyes and were thus diverted from the opposing players' preparations for the stroke. In this case, of course, it was not a matter of "east" and "west" but of up and down. The east-west axis mentioned in the short formula should, in any case, be understood figuratively rather than literally.

Create Something from Nothing

The Chinese characters	無	中	生	有
Modern Mandarin pronunciation	*wú*	*zhōng*	*shēng*	*yǒu*
Meaning of each character	non-existent	in the midst of	create	existent

Applications	The "creator" stratagem:
	a. An apparition or illusion is deliberately created in such a way that the enemy sees it for what it is; his vigilance is thus lulled, so that later he mistakes a real danger for the illusion and falls victim to it without resistance.
	b. Gain an advantage, or create a change of opinion or of reality, by conjuring an illusion.
	c. Make something up out of whole cloth; present a falsehood as fact; fabricate rumors, campaigns of lies and slander; make a mountain out of a molehill. The stratagem of disinformation.

The short formula given above is rooted in chapter 40 of the *Daodejing* (or *Tao-te-ching*), the basic Daoist scripture ascribed to sixth century B.C. Chinese philosopher Laozi (Lao-tze). The relevant passage in that work reads:

> Things in the world arise from Existence, and Existence arises from Non-Existence.

That is to say, each thing before it came into existence was nonexistent, and thus arises from Nothingness.

This is not the appropriate place for an excursion into Daoism. But it is worth noting that, from the times of the Tang Dynasty (A.D. 618–907) to the present, the *Daodejing*, which in the West is generally treated as a profoundly philosophical work, has often been regarded in China as a military tract. The justification for this view is that about twenty of its eighty-one chapters treat military issues in disguised, philosophical form, and that the other chapters also show clear signs of a militarily oriented, tactical, and strategic mentality. An edition of Laozi's writings published in Shanghai in 1977 takes the position, some-what controversial even in China, that the *Daodejing* "is a mil-itary tract which generalizes from the wartime experiences of the Spring and Autumn period and the Warring States period. . . . It applies military philosophy to every aspect of nature and society."

From a military perspective, Stratagem No. 7 is about linking fiction and reality, and letting reality suddenly emerge from fiction. The "Nothing" in this case is an illusion designed to confuse the enemy; the "Something" is the true intent which is hidden behind the illusion and suddenly emerges from it at a moment when the enemy still believes he is confronted by an illusion.

As indicated at the head of this chapter, Stratagem No. 7 can be applied on three different levels.

7.1   STRAW DUMMIES INSTEAD OF SOLDIERS

During the Tang Dynasty, in the year A.D. 755, the military governor An Lushan rebelled. Among the rebels was General Ling Huchao, who besieged the city of Yongqiu. Loyalist Gen-eral Zhang Xun, who had to defend the city with only a small number of troops and weapons, commanded his soldiers to make about a thousand man-sized straw dummies dressed in black clothing, to fasten them to lines and let them slide down the outside of the city walls during the oncoming night. The rebel soldiers besieging the city thought that opposing troops were clambering down the city walls and let loose a hail of arrows against them. Zhang Xun had the straw dolls drawn up again and "captured" several thousand arrows.

A bit later General Zhang Xun had real soldiers climb down the city walls. Ling Huchao and his troops thought that the enemy was hoping to harvest more arrows with straw dummies. So this time they laughed scornfully and made no preparations for battle. Zhang Xun's five hundred volunteers mounted a lightning strike against Ling Huchao's camp, set fire to its tents, killed some of the besieging rebels, and scattered the rest to the four winds.

7.2 FROM THE KOREAN WAR

The 1987 edition of *The 36 Stratagems: A Modern Version*[1] offers the following example of No. 7:

During the Korean War, the battle on Sanggamryong Mountain raged from October 8 to November 25, 1952. In a combat zone of only 3.7 square kilometers (1.3 square miles), the Americans used about sixty thousand troops and dropped thousands of bombs, the explosive force of which reduced the height of the mountain by 2 meters (6.6 feet). Finally, the Chinese troops holding the peak were forced to pull back into tunnels, from which the Americans tried to smoke them out and destroy them.

One night a company of Chinese soldiers exploited the Americans' fatigue. They threw empty cans and other noisy objects in the direction in which they planned to attack. At first the U.S. troops reacted alertly to every sound, immediately shooting at the spot from which each noise came. The Chinese repeated this tactic three times in a row. Finally the Americans' alertness wore down. At that point a small Chinese unit quickly emerged from the tunnel and blew up the American bunker located only about 20 meters from the tunnel's mouth. By the time the Americans realized what was happening, the Chinese soldiers had withdrawn back into their tunnel.

7.3 THE ARMY OF ZURICH WOMEN

On another level, Stratagem No. 7 can be used to actually "create" something from the "nothing" of an illusion. This is illustrated by the following examples.

In the summer of 1292, Duke Albrecht of the Hapsburgs, having dealt the people of Canton Zurich a serious defeat at

Winterthur, lay siege to the city of Zurich. (At stake was the status of the Hapsburgs in the rebellious Swiss lands.) After a serious attack against a major fortification, Zurich's capitulation seemed only a matter of time. Suddenly the women of the city sprang into the breach. Armed, they marched to the Lindenhof[2] "with drum and fife" and took up positions to make it look as though there were thousands of them. Albrecht, who had been anticipating an easy victory over the seriously decimated Zurchers, was readily deceived and broke off his siege.

By cleverly positioning themselves on the Lindenhof, the city's women created the illusion of tremendous defensive preparedness. From this "nothing"—i.e., this illusion—they created a "something," namely, the enemy withdrawal. The story may be too good to be true, but *se non è vero, è ben trovato!*[3]

7.4   HANNIBAL, ROMMEL AND THE SOVIETS

When Hannibal found himself drawn into an ambush in a deep valley by the Roman General Fabius in 217 B.C., he broke out by employing a fiery stratagem. In the night he had bundles of brushwood tied to the horns of two thousand oxen and set alight. The animals were driven toward the Roman troops, who thought that the entire Carthaginian army was marching against them. In the ensuing confusion, Hannibal and his troops were able to get out of the trap.[4]

More than two thousand years later, during the fighting in North Africa in World War II, Germany's Field Marshal Rommel fooled his opponents by mounting dummy tanks on Volkswagens and having a few vehicles drag heavy objects through the desert sand to raise huge dust clouds, creating the illusion that large mechanized forces were on the move.

During the Second World War a unit of Soviet engineers commanded by a Captain Gozeridse was ordered to quickly mine a road along which a strong enemy unit was being supplied. There were no mines left in the Soviet battalion at the time, and to wait until some could be delivered would be to ignore the need for haste.

Gozeridse ordered signs to be painted with the German message *Achtung, Minen!* (Caution, mines!). During the night, the Soviet engineers crept through the enemy lines and planted the signs along the road. In the morning, Soviet observers watched as the Nazis halted their vehicles, nervously read the signs, and seemed clearly afraid to proceed. Traffic ground to a halt, and a line of German vehicles backed up on the road. Then the Soviet gunners, with whom Gozeridse had arranged everything in advance, opened fire on the startled Nazis and inflicted heavy losses on them.

Near Staraya Russiya, the main Soviet battle line ran along the edge of a wood. In order to observe the enemy, Soviet soldiers had to climb up into the pine trees. Because of the added weight the pines began to sway back and forth, which made them conspicuous against the background of stationary trees. The Germans saw this, realized what was happening, and opened fire on the moving pines. The Red soldiers tried to avoid shaking the trees, but it was impossible. So the squadron commander decided to fool the enemy. He ordered his men to fasten lines to the tips of the pines at night, with the other ends of the lines down in their trenches. The next morning the soldiers pulled on the ropes and shook the trees. The Nazi troops fired machine guns at the swaying pines. As soon as the fire would slacken, the Soviet soldiers pulled on their lines again, and the German fire resumed. This continued until midday. Only then did the Nazis realize that they had been deceived and held their fire. From then on the Soviet observers could use the pines without danger, since the German soldiers no longer fired at them.

7.5 VIETNAM'S FLOATING LEAFLETS

The signal for Vietnam's ten-year war of resistance (A.D. 1418–28) against Ming rule was the uprising at Lam Son, headed by Lê-Loi. His most important adviser was Nguyên Trai, whose battle tract, *Binh Ngô dai-cáo* (Great Proclamation on the Defeat of the Ngo [*Ngo* was a derogatory term for the Chinese]), shows him to be an outstanding expert on ancient Chinese tactical and strategic thinking. He regarded "winning the hearts and minds" of the Vietnamese people as of equal importance with conquering enemy positions, and ascribed great value to propaganda and political agitation. Among his repertoire of tactics was Stratagem No. 7, as the following anecdote shows:

Nguyên Trai ordered that the prophecy "Lê-Loi shall be king, and Nguyên Trai his minister" be inscribed, in delicate strokes, on the leaves of trees. To convey this message required only a few of the Chinese characters then in common use in Vietnam. These were written on the leaves not with ink but with lard. Ants gnawed at the fat-covered parts of the leaves, so that the message was eaten out of their surface. The leaves were then set floating in all directions on brooks and streams. When the Vietnamese people found these inscribed leaves floating in the water, they took the message for a heavenly sign of victory and fought with heightened morale against the foreign occupying troops, who were finally driven out in the year A.D. 1428.[5]

7.6 THE JOURNEY TO JIN

During the Warring States period there were numerous peripatetic politicians, who traveled from state to state in China declaiming their wisdom and looking for a ruler who would take them into his service. Among those political pundits was Zhang Yi, originally from the state of Wei. During his wanderings he came to the state of Chu, where he lived for a while in great poverty. During that time his followers grew angry and threatened to leave him. Zhang Yi said, "Wait till I've spoken to the King." The ruler granted him an audience but did not prove to be very gracious. At Zhang Yi's request, the King permitted him to travel on to Jin.

Zhang Yi asked, "Does His Majesty wish anything from Jin?"

"There is gold, pearls, and ivory enough in Chu. I wish nothing."

"Does His Majesty not like beautiful women?"

"How so?"

"Because the women there are as lovely as goddesses."

"Chu is a remote land. I have never seen its beautiful women. But how could I not be interested?"

Requesting that Zhang Yi acquire a few such women for him, the monarch gave him gifts of pearls and jade.

The King's two favorite wives learned of this (with Zhang Yi's help, according to the Hong Kong book *The 36 Stratagems, with Examples from Times Past and Present*), grew frightened, and paid him a large quantity of gold in the hope that they would be spared the ignominy of being supplanted by foreign women.

Before his departure Zhang Yi requested permission to drink a final farewell toast to his ruler. The King granted permission and gave the politician his drink. After a while Zhang Yi requested that those with whom the ruler normally ate be likewise called in, so that he could drink a farewell toast to them as well. The King then had his two favorite wives summoned. When Zhang Yi saw them, he threw himself to the ground before the King and cried, "I lied to you and deserve to die."

"How so?" inquired the monarch.

"I have traveled throughout the kingdom and nowhere have I seen women as beautiful as these. Thus, when I promised to bring Your Majesty the most beautiful women of all, I lied."

"You are forgiven," said the King. "I have always been convinced that these two women are the most beautiful under the dome of Heaven."[6]

Zhang Yi's projected journey to Jin and his pledge to acquire divinely beautiful women there are empty promises; they are the "nothing." The gifts of gold and jewels and the king's favor are the "something" created out of that "nothing."

7.7 KILLING THE DOG: A LESSON FOR A HUSBAND[7]

Incited by two drinking companions against his younger brother Sun Rong, Court Councillor Sun Hua chases his brother out of his house. Sun Rong, an honorable man who lives only for his studies, goes to live in a hut near an abandoned brickworks and earns a miserable livelihood as a beggar. All the pleas of Sun Hua's wife and their aged servant fail to persuade the official that his brother is merely an innocent victim of slander by the two tipplers.

Sun Hua's wife resorts to Stratagem No. 7. A neighbor woman has leased a piece of land from Sun Hua. Overcoming the neighbor's strong reluctance, the councillor's wife persuades the woman to kill her dog. The two women dress the bloody cadaver in men's clothing and, that night, place the body in the doorway of the councillor's house. Coming home tipsy from a drinking bout with his two malicious drinking companions, Sun Hua finds the bloody corpse in the dark. In his drunken state he thinks it is a human body and is afraid that he will be accused of murder. He immediately seeks out his two comrades, who have sworn to stand by him under any and all circumstances, and asks them to help drag the corpse away and bury it. But the two tipplers make excuses, one claiming heart trouble and the other a painful hip, and they slam the door in the face of their pleading friend.

Returning home, the hapless Sun Hua is persuaded by his wife to appeal to his younger brother for help. The couple go to him together, and Sun Rong agrees to help. He drags the presumed corpse out of the city in the middle of the night and buries it in the sand of the riverbank. The councillor now realizes the kind of men his drinking buddies are. He has a reconciliation with his brother and invites him back into his house. When his drinking companions try to win their way back into his favor, Sun Hua rejects them, telling one he has a bad heart, the other he has a painful hip. Furious, the two men accuse the councillor and his brother of murder and of hiding the corpse. During the trial Sun Hua's wife appears as witness for the defense. The presumed body is exhumed and the defendants' innocence thus proven. But the two accusers are punished. The case is brought to the attention of the throne, and Sun Rong is rewarded for his fraternal loyalty with a government post.

7.8 MATRICIDE: A LESSON FOR A WIFE[8]

In the Qingshan production brigade there lived a family of four: Mother Wang, her son Mr. Wang, his wife Cassia Blossom, and their little son. Mr. Wang worked in the district's farm machine factory. The relationship between Mother Wang and her daughter-in-law was like that between a positive and negative electrical charge in the sky. As soon as they would meet, thunder roared, lightning struck, and rain poured down. There were repeated confrontations, daily fights. It looked as though they would continue to butt heads even after death.

One day the little boy fell to the ground and began to scream. Grandma Wang wanted to pick him up. She stretched out her arms—but then stopped. She recalled that, only a few days before in a similar situation, Cassia Blossom had accused her of pushing the child down. As Grandma Wang hesitated, unsure what to do, Cassia Blossom appeared and barked, "The child has fallen down and hurt himself, and you just stand there. You'll only be happy when he kills himself!"

As soon as the daughter-in-law opened her mouth, the mother-in-law responded in her own less-than-shy manner. And things took their usual course. Lips became rifles, tongues turned into swords, and everything came spewing out like rotten cabbage and spoiled turnips.

wildly, her face felt as if it were burning, she felt cold sweat all over her body, and her legs were so weak that she almost collapsed.

Mother Wang, for her part, thought she was dreaming. It was only the second time since her son's marriage that she had been called "Mama" by Cassia Blossom. The more usual forms of address were "Old Lady" and "Crazy Old Woman." And bringing her a treat besides! Yesterday she had been like a storm witch; today she was more like Guanyin, the Buddhist goddess of mercy. Had she merely put honey on her lips but kept arsenic in her heart? Could she have poisoned the chicken soup? Was she trying to kill her with it?

At first Mother Wang thought she would give the soup to the dog. But after a while she said to herself, "I'm sixty-six years old. Better to die right now than go on leading this miserable life." So she swallowed the soup in one gulp and lay down on the bed, dressed in her best clothes, waiting for stomach pains and death.

She waited in vain. In fact, to her surprise she began feeling a good deal better. Then Cassia Blossom returned, again greeted her gently, using the word "Mama," and brought her a bowl of rice porridge. Without hesitation, Mother Wang sat up, took the food, ate it, and lay down again. She lay there the entire morning with no pain, no attacks of dizziness. On the contrary, she felt steadily better, more lively. And she began to wonder.

At noon Mother Wang got up and went into the kitchen. She was astonished to see that her little cook stove had disappeared. But freshly cooked rice and vegetables steamed temptingly on the table. Cassia Blossom came in and said, "Mama, until now I haven't been good to you. I made you angry all the time. From now on, let's be good to one another." So saying, she drew Mother Wang down to the freshly set table.

And from then on it was "Mama" this and "Mama" that. Cassia Blossom's mouth was sweet, and her hands were quick and skillful in seeing to the comfort of her mother-in-law, whose heart soon softened. To Cassia Blossom it was all a game. But Mother Wang took it very seriously. She thought, "If my daughter-in-law treats me well, I'll be good to her too."

Now, when Cassia Blossom came home from her production unit, the meals were all cooked, her little son was in fine fettle, and the pigs had been fed. As a rule Cassia Blossom had to get up at four-thirty every morning to take care of her many household chores before going to work, and even then she was often late. One evening Mother Wang secretly took the one alarm clock in the house from Cassia Blossom's room and put it in her own. The next morning, when Cassia Blossom awoke, the sky was much lighter than usual and breakfast was already on the table in the kitchen. Now it was her heart that softened, and tears filled her eyes. This time when she called the older woman "Mama" it really was sincere.

Late one night Cassia Blossom suddenly developed a high fever. Mother Wang heard her groaning and quickly ran to her room. First she took her grandson and made him comfortable in her own bedroom, then she took care of Cassia Blossom, and early the next morning she sent for the doctor. Thanks to his treatment and Mother Wang's tender care, Cassia Blossom soon recovered. But she still felt very weak. Mother Wang took the pound of lichee nuts which someone had given her as a New Year's gift and brought them to her daughter-in-law. But Cassia Blossom refused to eat them, saying over and over, "I've never bought you anything to eat. How could I have the effrontery to eat your fruit now?"

Mother Wang replied, "What does 'mine' and 'yours' matter? We're all family. Eat the fruit, it'll give you strength." Whereupon she sat down beside Cassia Blossom's bed, opened one lichee nut after another, and placed them in Cassia Blossom's mouth. As she ate the fruit, the younger woman felt a succession of emotions bombard her: sweet, sour, bitter, fiery. Involuntarily, tears came to her eyes. As soon as she had fully recovered, she bought her mother-in-law a pound of lichee nuts and also gave her coupons for five kilos of rice, along with five yuan, and earnestly requested that she buy for herself whatever she wanted to eat. Now it was Mother Wang's turn to be so deeply touched that the tears came. She dried her eyes with the corner of her skirt.

Daughter-in-law and mother-in-law proceeded to live together in harmony. After two months Mr. Wang returned home. Seeing the altered situation, he lost no time. After dinner he took a vial from his jacket pocket, shook it, poured its contents into a glass, mixed it with warm water, and brought it to his mother's room. Cassia Blossom, who was knitting a woolen dress, had hardly paid any attention to what was going on. When Mr. Wang came back, she asked him, "What did you bring to your mother's room?"

"Poison!"

Cassia Blossom cried out, and her whole body shook. The woolen dress fell to the floor. Mr. Wang clamped his hand over her mouth and said, "Have you lost your senses? What's all the noise about?"

As soon as he released Cassia Blossom, she tried to run out and get a doctor. But Mr. Wang quickly blocked the door. "What did we decide two months ago?" he demanded. "On the way home I heard from the neighbors that you'd been getting along beautifully with my mother. You've played the game well. Now everything is ripe for poisoning my mother. No one will suspect us."

Hearing this, Cassia Blossom began to cry, kneeled before her husband, and implored him, "Please, please call the doctor quickly. Your mother mustn't die. I was wrong. Your mother is a good person."

"Then why were things so terrible before?" asked Mr. Wang.

"I was stubborn," replied his wife, "and she was stubborn, and we became more and more pigheaded. Then I was good to her, and she became good too, and things got better and better. Then, I don't know what happened, but suddenly I felt good about her. And now I understand that having an older person in the house all the time is something precious."

When Mr. Wang heard this, he helped his wife to stand up and began to laugh. Then he revealed to Cassia Blossom that he had really brought his mother some medicine. His murder plan had only been a ruse, a stratagem he had devised to change his wife's attitude toward his mother. He had hoped that, if Cassia Blossom would be good to his mother, his mother would also be good to her and that Cassia Blossom's simulated goodness would be transformed into the real thing.

Cassia Blossom felt as if she had awakened from a dream. She pounded on her husband's shoulders and said, "You . . . you scoundrel. You tricked me!"

"No, I didn't trick you," said Mr. Wang. "I taught you a lesson. But my method was a little unorthodox."

They looked at each other and laughed.

In this example, the pretended matricide plan was the "nothing" from which "something" arose—the improved relationship between a young wife and her mother-in-law.

7.9 DENG XIAOPING'S CLOTH SHOES FOR BAREFOOT DOCTORS

The third level of application of Stratagem No. 7 involves disinformation, the invention of lies, defamation, misleading rumors, etc. In 1955 Mao Zedong condemned this use of the stratagem by "representatives of all exploiter classes." During the time of the Gang of Four, former Defense Minister Lin Biao (Mao's designated successor, who, according to the official Chinese version, was killed in an air crash in September 1971) was also attacked for using No. 7. In 1982 the Gang of Four was in turn charged[9] with having invented lies, crimes, and accusations—in short, of having made a great deal out of nothing.

One of those affected was Deng Xiaoping. In October 1974, during a conversation with a medical delegation from a Third World country, Deng spoke of China's "barefoot doctors" (roughly, what the West would call paramedics). He praised their value, and then remarked that the barefoot doctors spent some of their time healing people and some doing manual labor. At the outset, he said, they had little specialized knowledge and could treat only the simplest ailments. A few years later, however, they were already able "to buy straw sandals"—i.e., they had improved their medical knowledge. In a few years, Deng added, they would be able to wear "cloth shoes."

A year later, while the Cultural Revolution was still raging, these remarks were turned against Deng. He was accused of wishing that the barefoot doctors would no longer have to go barefoot. An anti-Deng pamphlet continued in these words:

> The incorrigible advocate of the capitalist path boldly suggests that the barefoot doctors "wear straw shoes," or even "cloth shoes." That means nothing less than that they put on capitalist shoes and walk down the revisionist path. Such hysterical and confused talk, aimed at revolt, is typical of the restorers [of capitalism].

A commentary published after the Cultural Revolution, however, set the record straight. It pointed out that Deng's talk of "straw sandals" and "cloth shoes" was meant to be understood figuratively, as a metaphor for the growing medical knowledge of the barefoot doctors.

Explicitly referring to Stratagem No. 7, the *People's Daily* of December 25, 1976, pointed out how the Gang of Four had created and disseminated "black material" (i.e., half-true, out-of-context, or totally fabricated excerpts from conversations, writings, and speeches) about Central Committee members and high regional functionaries who had fallen into disfavor.

7.10   TROUBLE IN YUNNAN

According to subsequent revelations, during the Cultural Revolution grisly events were repeatedly fabricated "out of nothing" and then were used as a basis on which to fatally accuse certain party officials of being renegades, agents of capitalism, counterrevolutionaries, etc.

In January 1968 there were armed clashes between large groups of people in Yunnan Province, causing injuries and deaths. One of the groups involved in the fighting was termed the "West Yunnan Storm Brigade" by a local supporter of Lin Biao. The group was accused of various crimes, branded as counterrevolutionary, and its members ruthlessly persecuted. During one military operation, eleven hundred members of the group were killed. This action enabled the Lin Biao supporter to achieve a certain position of power in Yunnan, which he then further exploited to persecute so-called "supporters of the West Yunnan Storm Brigade" in fifty-four districts of the province.

In a parallel case, Jiang Qing, wife of Mao Zedong, was reported in January 1968 to have said to a party secretary of Yunnan Province, "I have read the plan of the Yunnan network of Guomindang agents, and also watched all your actions carefully. You have carried out that Guomindang plan." Lin Biao's representative in Yunnan used that statement by Jiang Qing as the basis on which to brand the Yunnan party secretary as a renegade and "executor of the plan of the Yunnan network of Guomindang agents" and subject him to merciless political persecution. All supporters of that party secretary were also subjected to the same treatment.

After the Cultural Revolution, the case was investigated. According to the *People's Daily* of September 26, 1978, no West Yunnan Storm Brigade ever existed, and none of the crimes ascribed to it ever actually took place. The "plan of the Yunnan network of Guomindang agents" was something fabricated entirely out of thin air, and the persecuted party secretary was neither a renegade nor an agent. The accusations were launched solely on the basis of Jiang Qing's statement.

7.11 CHINA AND THE PAKISTANI ATOMIC BOMB

The Chinese press sometimes uses Stratagem No. 7 as an aid to the interpretation of international events. *Renmin Ribao* (People's Daily) has pointed out, "The Soviet Union in particular takes every opportunity to create something out of nothing against China." The following examples of Soviet statements that, according to the Chinese, were pure fabrication are drawn from issues of the *People's Daily* between 1978 and 1984:

- China and Pakistan are planning a joint intervention in Afghanistan.
- China is working with Pakistan on developing nuclear weapons.
- There are Afghan rebel camps in Xinjiang.
- Two Israeli officials visited China, which is about to forge an alliance with Israel.
- Chinese helicopters have penetrated Indian airspace.
- Lee Harvey Oswald, who assassinated President John F. Kennedy, maintained contacts with China.
- China maintains contacts with the Italian terrorist group Red Brigades.

7.12   THE ALLEGED CRIME OF YUE FEI

Few heroes in Chinese history have enjoyed as much popularity as the twelfth-century General Yue Fei. His loyalty to his nation was considered exemplary. Favorite tales about him revolve around his humble origins, the discipline of his troops, and his concern for the common folk. Plays, operas, and a novel have been written about him, and he has even been elevated to the rank of a Daoist divinity.

Yue Fei's fame rests on his energetic defense of the Southern Song Dynasty's territory. But he was made immortal by his death in A.D. 1142, which was caused by the imperial court he had so bravely defended.

The Jurchen, Tungus tribes from the far north, had overrun Chinese territory north of the Yangtze River, and the Jin Dynasty which they had founded (A.D. 1115–1234) was pushing steadily farther south toward where the Chinese emperor had fled. Yue Fei, who had worked for a landowner and risen to be his bodyguard, volunteered for military service and quickly developed into a capable officer. He formed a peasant army which was renowned for its discipline. His words of instruction to his troops became famous: "Do not tear houses down because you need firewood, even if you are freezing; do not steal from the people, even if you are hungry."

The Chinese army soon reconquered large areas from the interlopers, and in the fall of the year 1140, Yue Fei's troops dealt a serious defeat to the Jin forces in Henan Province. The next task was to drive the Jurchen army back to its base headquarters in the northeast. Suddenly, Yue Fei and the other generals intent on liberating their country received imperial orders to fall back.

According to the version most commonly accepted in China today, the events leading up to Yue Fei's death were as follows: The ruler of the Jin Dynasty, who regarded Yue Fei as an unbeatable opponent, interpreted the orders commanding the Chinese forces to pull back as a sign that the party favoring appeasement of the invaders was gaining influence at China's imperial court. He immediately had a letter delivered to Chief Councillor Qin Kui, in which he demanded the elimination of Yue Fei as a precondition for peace negotiations. Councillor Qin Kui was among the wealthiest landowners of his time, and his lands lay in the area of Nanking, which was a major deployment zone, as well as the region from which most of the soldiers for the battle against the Jin forces had been conscripted. Having a vested interest in a swift peace settlement, he undertook to fulfill the enemy's stipulated condition—with the aid of Stratagem No. 7.

First, Qin Kui fabricated a false accusation against Yue Fei's subordinate, General Zhang Xian, to the effect that he had planned a rebellion against the imperial throne. Then he claimed that Yue Fei and his son Yue Yun had written subversive letters to Zhang Xian urging him to revolt. Based on this false accusation, Qin Kui had Zhang Xian and Yue Yun imprisoned. Then he ordered Yue Fei to come to Lin'an, the provisional capital, on the pretext of wanting to question him. Unsuspecting, Yue

Fei complied with the order, and immediately on his arrival in the capital he was arrested and thrown in prison.

Qin Kui insisted on his story that Yue Fei, Yue Yun, and Zhang Xian had been jointly planning a coup. According to the official *History of the Song Dynasty* written in A.D. 1343–45, he was challenged by General Han Shizhong. In response to the challenge, Qin Kui gave an answer which has become notorious in Chinese lore: The letters proving his assertion had been burned, said the chief councillor, so that it was no longer possible to examine their contents—but the criminal act itself had "presumably occurred" (*mo xu you*).

(The phrase *mo xu you* is often used by the press in the People's Republic as a euphemism for the application of Stratagem No. 7 by malicious slanderers, who are trying to brand an innocent party as a villain through the assertion of an alleged crime.)

Following a trial based on the false accusation, Yue Fei and his two codefendants were executed in the Fengbo Pavilion in Lin'an, on the eve of the Chinese New Year's celebration in the year A.D. 1142. Yue Fei was only thirty-nine years old.

Because of his enormous popularity, Yue Fei's fate aroused a wave of indignation throughout the realm. Twenty years later a new emperor ascended the throne. To gain popular favor he had the remains of the three executed men exhumed and those of Yue Fei and his son Yue Yun ceremonially cremated on the shore of Lin'an's West Lake. In the year 1221 a temple was built on that spot to honor them. The structure still stands today.

During the Cultural Revolution (1966–76), Yue Fei's tomb was destroyed, but it has since been reconstructed and decorated with a new statue of the folk hero. On the tomb, four cast-iron figures are shown kneeling before Yue Fei, as if to beg his pardon. One of the figures represents Chief Councillor Qin Kui, another his wife, and the remaining two are other accomplices in the plot against Yue Fei. The statues clearly express the popular disgust at their evil deed.

7.13   THREE MEN MAKE A TIGER

During the Warring States period, the states of Wei and Zhao concluded a treaty of friendship, part of which was an agreement that the Prince of Wei would be sent to Zhao as a hostage. The King of Wei entrusted his closest adviser, Minister Pang Cong, with the task of escorting the Prince. Pang Cong foresaw that during his absence certain courtiers would slander him to the monarch. Before his departure he asked his ruler, "Your Majesty, if someone were to report to you that a tiger is roaming the streets of your capital, would you believe him?"

"No. How could such a thing be possible?"

"But if a second person came with the same report, would Your Majesty then credit it?"

After a moment's thought the ruler said, "No, even two people could not convince me."

"But if a third person came and reported that he had seen a tiger in the streets, would Your Majesty believe it?"

"Of course I would believe it," replied the ruler. "If three people say the same thing, it must be true."

To which Pang Cong responded, "I shall shortly depart for the distant state of Zhao to escort our Prince there. During my absence, surely more than three people will come and slander me. I hope that Your Majesty will consider carefully before coming to any conclusions."

The King nodded and said, "I know what you mean. You may go."

Many courtiers indeed sought audience with the monarch and slandered Pang Cong. At first the King paid no attention. But as a steady stream of voices was raised to condemn Pang Cong, the ruler grew suspicious, until he became convinced of his adviser's wicked character. Upon his return Pang Cong quickly saw that he had lost his ruler's favor—simply because rumors, repeated often enough, had come to be regarded as truth.

7.14   FOUR STAGES OF RUMOR

According to Chen Xiaochuan, there are four stages in the escalation of rumor against someone one wishes to harm or eliminate. If the individual in question is in fact blameless, the first step is to try and blacken his name politically. If that does not work, the second step is to attack him in the financial realm and accuse him of dishonest dealings. If the person is still regarded as honorable, the next target should be his allegedly immoral way of life. If that shot also misses its mark, his character should be blackened and he should be accused of such traits as excessive pride. The damage begins when the person's superiors start to believe the rumors.

In the Hong Kong publication *The 36 Stratagems, with Examples from Times Past and Present,* the following passage appears:

> Rumors are among the most fearsome things. With just a few words, a hero can be made to lay down his weapons, a man can even be made to take his own life. It is not important how long the rumor has been in circulation, for by the time its accuracy can be properly checked, its effects have often become irreversible.

7.15   THE END OF RUMOR

When Confucius was asked about the essence of clear vision, the Master replied, "He who remains unimpressed by a long and steady barrage of slander may be characterized as clear-sighted."

And in the book ascribed to the philosopher Xunzi it is written:

> A rolling ball stops rolling when it falls into a hole. A circulating rumor stops circulating when it comes up against a wise man.

Openly Repair the Walkway, Secretly March to Chencang

The Chinese characters	暗	渡	陳	倉
Modern Mandarin pronunciation	*àn*	*dù*	*Chén*	*Cāng*
Meaning of each character	secretly	march	Chencang	

[Eight-character alternate version]

The Chinese characters	明修 栈道，暗渡陈仓			
Modern Mandarin pronunciation	*míng xiū*	*zhàn dào,*	*àn dù*	*Chén Cāng*
Meaning of each character	visibly repair	wooden path,	secretly march	Chencang

Interpretation with reference to earliest known case	Openly (i.e., visibly) set to work repairing the burned-out wooden pathway from Hanzhong to Guanzhong. But before the repairs are finished, secretly march troops to Guanzhong by way of Chencang.

Applications

a. The stratagem of the hidden route march, or secret detour.

b. Hide your sophisticated intent behind an apparently innocuous action; the "normalcy"; stratagem—i.e., mask an uncommon (unorthodox, unconventional, abnormal) intention behind commonplace (orthodox, conventional, normal) deeds or words.

8.1 THE BURNED-OUT WOODEN PATH

In the year 207 B.C., Xiang Yu scored a decisive victory over the Qin Dynasty in the battle of Yulu. This was followed by a power struggle between him and other rebel leaders, notably Liu Bang (also known as Peigong). In 206, Xiang Yu led 400,000 troops into Guanzhong, the fertile and strategically well-secured Qin heartland, in order to attack its capital at Xianyang. Arriving in the area, he discovered that Liu Bang, at the head of 100,000 men, had already conquered the city and claimed the title King of Guanzhong. This was in accord with the wishes of King Huai of Chu (see Section 14.2, "The Shepherd Xin Becomes King of Chu"), who in that transitional period was acknowledged as the supreme authority—though sometimes only for the sake of appearances—by the most influential of the rebel leaders. King Huai had promised that the first rebel leader to capture the city of Xianyang would be named ruler of Guanzhong.

Xiang Yu was furious at Liu Bang's success. He marched his

forces into Guanzhong, set up camp near Hongmen, and declared that he would destroy Liu Bang. Far weaker militarily, Liu could not have stood up to Xiang Yu at that time. So he hastened to Hongmen to mollify the more powerful rebel leader. Xiang Yu invited him to a feast, and Fan Zeng, Xiang Yu's adviser, proposed that Xiang's brother, Xiang Zhuang, perform a sword dance after the meal and kill Liu Bang during the performance, since Fan Zeng contended that Liu Bang constituted a long-term threat to Xiang Yu. But Liu Bang managed to escape before the meal was over, leaving the table with the excuse of having to relieve himself. To this day the phrase "the Hongmen feast" (*Hongmen yan*) is known to educated Chinese, as is the expression *Xiang Zhuang wu jian, yi zai Peigong*, meaning "Xiang Zhuang dances with a sword, but his attention is concentrated on Peigong [the other name for Liu Bang]."

Liu Bang subsequently ceded Xianyang and the territory of Guanzhong to Xiang Yu, who in 206 B.C. assumed the title "Hegemon of Western Chu." As his personal realm he selected parts of what are today the provinces of Jiangsu, Anhui, Shandong, and Henan, with the capital at Pengcheng. In the rest of China he established eighteen fiefdoms with a prince at the head of each. Wishing to keep Liu Bang as far away as possible, he rewarded him with Hanzhong, consisting of territories in the eastern and western sections of what is now Sichuan Province, along with southern and western segments of today's Shaanxi and Hubei provinces. He also appointed Liu Bang ruler of Han—from which the name and founding date of the Han Dynasty are derived. To keep Liu Bang in his place, however, Xiang Yu divided Guanzhong (which borders on Hanzhong) into three parts, which he awarded as fiefdoms to three generals from the now-defunct Qin empire who had gone over to his side. Liu Bang's closest neighbor was the former Qin General Zhang Dan, who now ruled in Chencang.

Having ceded Guanzhong to his victorious rival Xiang Yu, Liu Bang was forced to leave the territory and march his troops to Hanzhong, which had been assigned as his realm. En route, he ordered that the wooden walkways and bridges through several hundred miles of mountain gorges be burned. This had

8.2 SEEING THE OBVIOUS

example is from the Period of the Three Kingdoms (A.D. 280). The three mutually contentious realms at that time Wei, Wu, and Shu. Wei's General Deng Ai and his troops set up their camp on the northern bank of the White River. ee days later, the Shu General Jiang Wei commanded his ordinate Liao Hua to position his troops on the southern k of the river, opposite Deng Ai's camp.

At this point General Deng Ai said to his commander, "Since r forces are much weaker than his, if Jiang Wei had mounted surprise attack he would certainly have beaten us in the normal ourse of things. But now there's no movement on his side of he river. I assume that Jiang is trying to cut off our rear, and that he had Liao Hua take up a position on the opposite bank merely to pin us down. I'm sure that Jiang Wei will march eastward with a large army to take our main base at Taocheng."

That same night Deng Ai ordered part of his forces to march to Taocheng via a back route. They arrived just as Jiang Wei was about to cross the river and occupy the city. But Deng Ai prevented it, and Taocheng remained in his hands.

This is a case of an unsuccessful application of Stratagem No. 8. Deng Ai saw through the tactic, because Jiang Wei's deviation from normal military procedure—which in this case dictated an immediate attack against Deng Ai's much weaker forces across the river—was too obvious, and aroused Deng's suspicion.

8.3 NORMANDY INSTEAD OF CALAIS

According to the 1989 edition of the Beijing book *The 36 Stratagems: A Modern Version,* the Allied landing in Normandy in June 1944 may be regarded as a "secret march to Chencang" with the aid of modern military technology. The natural circumstances, geography, and factors of transport and air support

two purposes: first, to protect hin
from Guanzhong and especially fr
Zhang Dan; second, to establish tl
had no intention of ever returning e

A little later, but still in the year 2
had not been awarded any territory b
rebellion against him in what had fort
of the state of Qi. At that point Liu Ba
Han Xin (d. 196 B.C.) to prepare for an
confuse the enemy, Han Xin sent a few t
work on the burned wooden walkways in
cang, General Zhang Dan laughed at this, th
take such a handful of workers many years t
ways and bridges. But General Han Xin neve
that route. Shortly after the repair work had l
Bang's main force on a secret march via a di
Chencang. General Zhang Dan was taken by sur
defeated, after which he committed suicide. For
secret march to Chencang was the start of a victori
against Xiang Yu, which ended in 202 B.C. with th
establishment of the Han Dynasty.

This
220-
wer
had
Th
sul
ba

o
a
c
t

This popular episode in Chinese history has often be
For example, in the prologue to a play of the Yuan peri
Bang as the Han Emperor declaims at great length, rev
the events we have just examined, explaining how Xia
was unjustly crowned king of Guanzhong and how he ¿
sinated King Huai, who had crowned him, and finally declai

> I used Han Xin's stratagem, "Openly Repair the Wooden
> Path, Secretly March to Chencang." I conquered the ter-
> ritories of the three rebel Qin generals, and finally took
> Pengcheng, Xiang Yu's capital.

Another play, this one from the Ming period, bears the title
Supreme Commander Han Marches Secretly to Chencang.

would have made an operation from southeastern England to the area around Calais more logical than a landing in Normandy launched from southern England. The Germans were also of that opinion, believing that the Allies would choose the shorter route over the longer. They consequently concentrated their main defenses around Calais. The Allies used a variety of deceptive maneuvers to strengthen the Germans' mistaken belief. In eastern England, across the Channel from Calais, the presence of a First U.S. Army Group, ostensibly commanded by General Patton, was faked; in southern English ports and along the Thames, fleets of dummy landing craft were set afloat. At the same time, the Allies intensified their bombing raids over the Calais area, while Normandy was subjected to only routine bombardment. All of this reinforced the German belief that the Allied landing was planned for Calais.

This Chinese view of the Normandy invasion is confirmed by Western reports. The *Great Atlas of World War II,* published in Munich in 1974, states:

> The entire operation was coupled with the most perfect diversionary maneuver of the entire war. The Allies made every effort to persuade the Germans that the actual landing would take place along the French coast of the Dover Strait. For every sortie flown over the area west of Le Havre, two were flown further to the north; for every ton of bombs dropped over Normandy, two tons were dropped north of Le Havre. In Britain's County Kent, the possible launching area for an attack across the Strait of Dover, mock-ups of headquarters buildings and railway installations were built.

8.4 CHINA'S VIETNAM CAMPAIGN, 1979

In his classic treatise *The Art of War,* Sun Tzu writes:

> Making the armies able to take on opponents without being defeated is a matter of orthodox and unorthodox methods.

> . . . Generally in military operations there is always the
> orthodox and the unorthodox, or the straightforward and
> the surprise. . . . In battle, confrontation is done directly,
> victory is gained by surprise. . . . Therefore those skilled
> at the unorthodox are infinite as heaven and earth, inex-
> haustible as the great rivers.[2]

Stratagem No. 8 involves outwardly executing a perfectly normal military operation while secretly carrying out an unusual
one. If Han Xin had not set some troops to visibly repairing the
wooden walkways through the ravines, the secret march of his
main force to Chencang would not have succeeded. According
to some Chinese authorities, militarily unusual moves should
always be coupled with apparently normal operations. The 1989
Beijing stratagem book cited earlier suggests that the terms "visibly" and "secretly" in the formula for No. 8 really stand for
"orthodox" and "unorthodox" or "normal" and "abnormal"
military means. In the ancient Chinese view, an absolutely normal military move should serve as the starting point for every
surprise tactic. Only when the enemy is misled to judge the
actions and intentions of his opponent in terms of normal or
orthodox warfare can the opponent's uncommon action lead to
success. In other words, in order to "march secretly to Chencang" one must first direct the enemy's judgment into the
channels of normalcy by publicly "repairing the walkways."
    The Beijing stratagem book notes that "normal" and "ab-
normal" can mean many things. For example, if a preventive
strike would be the normal thing, the abnormal (or unorthodox)
tactic would be to let the enemy make the first move, and only
then grab the initiative; if standard methods of warfare would
constitute the normal, then special methods such as guerrilla
tactics would be the unusual; if open confrontation would be
the orthodox thing, a surprise attack is the unorthodox; if a
direct frontal attack would be the norm, a flanking maneuver
would be the unexpected. "Normal" and "abnormal" are, then,
linked opposites, and can under certain circumstances flow one
into the other.

The Beijing book cites an example drawn from the 1979 Chinese campaign against Vietnam. Because of the Chinese habit of circumventing an enemy's flanks and attacking from behind enemy lines, the Vietnamese had secretly reinforced their defensive flanks with extra firepower and laid down protective minefields. But their front lines directly facing the Chinese positions were relatively weak. Discovering this, the Chinese suddenly converted their flanking maneuver into a frontal attack, taking the Vietnamese completely by surprise. In this context, the Chinese flanking maneuver was "openly repairing the wooden walkways"—i.e., the conventional Chinese tactic— while the sudden frontal onslaught was the "secret march to Chencang," the unconventional military move.

8.5   Buddha's Tooth

In their chapters on "Secretly March to Chencang," stratagem books published in Hong Kong and Taipei point to amorous applications of this tactic as exemplified in two novels dating from the Ming period: the famous erotic work *The Plum in the Golden Vase* and the previously cited *Water Margin*.

In chapter 4 of *The Plum in the Golden Vase,* a woman named Golden Lotus, wife of Wu Da, meets her lover in the house of old Mother Wang, pretending to her husband that she is making a robe and shoes for the old woman. Here the outwardly normal, credible act is helping an old woman, while hidden behind it is the abnormal thing (in the ancient Chinese view), a wife's rendezvous with her lover.

The help for Mother Wang in *Plum* is analogous to the display of a holy relic in *Water Margin*. But before recounting that episode, a few background remarks are needed.

It is said that, after the death of the Buddha (variously given between 487 and 477 B.C.), his bones were distributed to temples all over the world. During the Tang period, a bone reputed to be from Buddha's body found its way to China. And in June

1987 the Chinese press reported that four bone fragments from his fingers had been discovered in an underground room of the seventeen-hundred-year-old Famen Temple, a hundred kilometers (sixty-two miles) west of Xi'an in Shaanxi Province; the fragments had been preserved in four reliquaries made of iron, gold, silver, crystal, jade, and sandalwood.

In *Water Margin,* the priest Haigong of the Temple of Gratitude becomes aware that Pan Qiaoyun, wife of the governor of Jizhou, is rather interested in him. At one point Pan Qiaoyun and her father come to the temple to say memorial prayers for her late mother. Having completed the ceremony, father and daughter are invited by Haigong into his private chambers, where tea is served. Then the priest ushers his guests into a side room for a delicious meal. Haigong has prepared an especially strong wine for the father, and it is not long before the old man is completely drunk. The priest has him brought to another room and bedded down to sleep it off.

Pan Qiaoyun, the daughter, has also had some wine and is in a playful mood. "Why is it so important to you that I keep drinking?" she asks.

"Because I adore you," the priest whispers, smiling.

"I can't take any more," she replies.

"Please, come look at the tooth of the Buddha which I keep hidden in another room," urges the priest.

"I'd love to see it," says Pan Qiaoyun.

Haigong shows her up to his bedroom, with its invitingly arranged bed.

"What a pretty room," says the woman, "and how clean it is."

"All it lacks is a young woman," replies the monk with a smile.

"Why don't you find yourself one?"

"Where is the generous soul who will provide one for me?"

Says Pan Qiaoyun, "You were going to show me Buddha's tooth?"

"Send your handmaiden away, and I'll bring it out."

"Ying'er," commands the woman, "go down and see if my old father is awake yet."

The maid leaves the chamber, and the priest locks the bedroom door.

8.6   THE MATCH

In *Ernü yingxiong zhuan* (The Tale of the Gallant Maid), written during the early nineteenth century by Manchurian author Wenkang, a young scholar named An Ji undertakes a long journey in order to be at his father's side in time of trouble. Along the way he takes shelter in a monastery where the monks are really bandits in disguise. The novel's heroine, known as Thirteenth Sister, rescues him at the last minute, at the same time freeing the Zhang family from captivity. This family consists of Mr. and Mrs. Zhang and their seventeen-year-old daughter Golden Phoenix (*Jinfeng*). After all the excitement, when the elder Zhangs and the young An Ji are in the monastery kitchen preparing a meal, Thirteenth Sister draws Golden Phoenix aside and asks about her marital status. Learning that the girl is not engaged, Thirteenth Sister offers to serve as matchmaker for her, with a particular view to An Ji. Inwardly, Golden Phoenix is not at all averse to such a match, but she is plagued by certain doubts and reservations.

Golden Phoenix remarks to herself that Thirteenth Sister is previously unknown to her and her parents, a chance travel acquaintance. And yet not only has she rescued them from dire distress, perhaps from death, she is also offering to help her, Golden Phoenix, to a lifetime with a handsome young man. And, in her impulsive and energetic fashion, Thirteenth Sister has insisted that Golden Phoenix commit herself and state that she is willing to make such a match.

All of this, the young girl thinks, is quite extraordinary. What was Thirteenth Sister's purpose in making such a generous but totally unsolicited proposal? Golden Phoenix is a straightforward country girl, but to her mind it seems that there must be some ulterior motive behind the proposition. She thinks, "Thirteenth Sister is a young girl like myself; in fact, she is very like

me in both age and looks. So she would have the same drives
and urges as I do. If that is the case, why does she put her own
interests aside and try to arrange such a fine match for me? Why
does she bring such a fine gift to me, a total stranger? Is that
not something to wonder at and think about? Has she some
ulterior motive for her generous offer? . . . Of course! She wants
the same thing for herself. And since she dare not say so openly,
she is using me to go the long way around. Outwardly, she is
'repairing the wooden walkways,' but secretly she is 'marching
to Chencang.' "

So Golden Phoenix concludes that the matchmaking proposed
by Thirteenth Sister—actually nothing unusual in itself—is
probably a ploy ("openly repairing the walkways") by means
of which Thirteenth Sister hopes to effect her own marriage to
An Ji as his second wife (the "march to Chencang"). Polygamy
was an accepted practice in ancient China. Anyone who receives
unexpected and unsolicited help is likely to wonder why. The
remarkable thing about this case is that Golden Phoenix immediately goes one step farther and finds the answer in a stratagem which she ascribes to Thirteenth Sister: That young
woman, she assumes, is helping her to make a match so that,
at a later point, she and her parents will help Thirteenth Sister
to likewise make a match with the same man. Golden Phoenix
suspects—and it is a suspicion often shared by many others,
even in ordinary, everyday circumstances—that a basically normal and apparently harmless action really masks some stratagem
or ulterior motive.

8.7 CRITIQUE OF ECLECTICISM

During the Cultural Revolution's "campaign to criticize Confucius," the writers' collective known as Luo Siding aimed especially sharp barbs at "eclecticism," a conciliatory philosophy
of "both this and that." Eclecticism has always been a thorn in
the side of orthodox Communist ideology, which accuses it of

seeking peaceful solutions—i.e., seeing the positive aspects on both sides of an issue—when confrontation and struggle should be the order of the day.

When Luo Siding's writings were carefully analyzed, however, it turned out that the accusations of "eclecticism" were invariably aimed against imperial chancellors (or prime ministers) of ancient China. A typical case cited was that of Tian Qianqiu, a chancellor under the Han Dynasty. He was branded as guilty of eclecticism because he had been skillful in smoothing relations among diverse cliques and had avoided taking a clear position on any issue. On closer examination, all the accusations by the Luo Siding collective pointed to only one "imperial chancellor"—namely, to Premier Chou En-lai. As the *People's Daily* later pointed out, explicitly referring to Stratagem No. 8, the essentially unobjectionable criticism of eclecticism turned out to be "visibly repairing the walkways," and the veiled attacks against Chou En-lai constituted the "secret march to Chencang."

From a loftier vantage point, as it were, the Beijing stratagem book in its chapter on No. 8 alludes to the commentary on the hexagram *Yi* (Increase) in the classic Chinese book of oracles, the *I Ching*. The commentary speaks of the "flexibility of the wind," which unexpectedly rushes in to fill a newly created void. And according to a handbook of common Chinese idioms,[3] Stratagem No. 8 creates that void by performing an outward action to divert people's attention, thus gaining for the perpetrator of the stratagem the latitude to pursue a totally different intention.

Observe the Fire on the Opposite Shore

The Chinese characters	隔	岸	观	火
Modern Mandarin pronunciation	*gé*	*àn*	*guān*	*huǒ*
Meaning of each character	opposite	shore	observe (watch)	fire

Applications	With seeming indifference, observe your opponent as he finds himself in a crisis or a difficult situation; refrain from any action—either a rescue operation or a premature attack—until the tide has turned in your favor, and then act to reap the benefits. The stratagem of nonintervention, delay, patient waiting.

The wording of this short formula is derived from a scene in the famous Chinese novel *The Romance of the Three Kingdoms*. The episode depicts Liu Bei, the future founder of one of the three kingdoms, and his adviser Zhuge Liang as they watch the smoldering fires of the Battle of Red Cliff from high up on Fankou Mountain.

In fact, however, no book on the stratagems published in the People's Republic, Hong Kong, or Taiwan provides an example of No. 9 that literally involves a fire on an opposite shore. Oddly enough, the source incident from *The Three Kingdoms* is never cited. The terms of the formula are understood metaphorically. The "fire" represents a crisis situation; the "opposite shore" stands for the opponent affected by the crisis, and the act of "observing" is understood to be done by a seemingly uninvolved third party who hopes to benefit from the crisis.

9.1 THE VICTORIOUS OBSERVER

The source incident drawn from *The Romance of the Three Kingdoms* dates back to the year A.D. 208, when Zhuge Liang succeeded in persuading Sun Quan, ruler of the state of Wu, to join in a coalition against Cao Cao, ruler of northern China, who was approaching with an army of more than 200,000 troops. Cao Cao and his army camped on the northern bank of the Yangtze River, while General Zhou Yu and the Wu forces camped on the southern bank. There, a mountain rises up steeply, and at the spot where it begins sloping up from the riverbank the two Chinese characters signifying "red cliff" were carved into the rock. Thus the clash between the forces of Zhou Yu and Cao Cao became known as the Battle of Red Cliff.

Cao Cao was unacquainted with marine warfare. Through a complex ruse, Zhou Yu had persuaded Cao Cao to tie his boats together side by side so that his troops could walk across the river as if on dry land. It was Zhou Yu's plan to set Cao Cao's fleet afire, with the help of the southeast wind.

Up to this point Zhuge Liang had accompanied Zhou Yu, serving as his adviser. But just before the battle was joined, he returned to his real master, Liu Bei, and the two men climbed up Fankou Mountain to watch the fiery fight on the opposite bank of the Yangtze. Liu Bei thus found himself in the enviable position of being able to observe from a distance the battle between the army of his ally Sun Quan and that of his archenemy Cao Cao. Ultimately, through skillful tactics, Liu Bei was able to exploit Sun Quan's victory in the Battle of Red Cliff to his own advantage.

9.2 FLIGHT INTO DEATH

The following historically based incident is also drawn from *The Romance of the Three Kingdoms*.

Yuan Shang and Yuan Xi were the sole surviving sons of the family of Yuan Shao, who during his lifetime had been a rival of Cao Cao. Pursued by the latter, the two brothers decided to flee to Liaodong with a force of several thousand men, despite the fact that Gongsun Kang, the governor of Liaodong, had been one of their father's enemies. Yuan Shao, their father, had tried repeatedly to conquer Liaodong. But because Liaodong was remote from the scene of the power struggle between Cao Cao and Yuan Shao, Gongsun Kang had not allied himself with either ruler. And so the brothers hoped to find temporary asylum with Gongsun Kang. Their long-term plan was to murder Gongsun Kang when an opportunity presented itself, so that Liaodong could become the base from which they would finally eliminate Cao Cao, who was then in the process of expanding his rule over northern China.

The obvious move at this point was for Cao Cao to pursue the treacherous Yuan brothers to Liaodong. But Cao Cao heeded the advice of his confidant Guo Jia, who proposed that for the time being he should leave Gongsun Kang and the Yuan brothers to their own devices. It would not be long, he predicted, before Gongsun Kang would eliminate them.

Not long afterward, as predicted, Gongsun Kang had the brothers beheaded and their heads brought to Cao Cao. When his generals asked him how the Yuan brothers had been eliminated, Cao Cao offered the following explanation, according to the oldest document on the 36 Stratagems as reproduced in the 1979 Jilin edition:

> On the one hand, Gongsun Kang feared the brothers' obvious desire to annex Liaodong. Their appearance inevitably aroused his suspicions. On the other hand, Gongsun Kang also feared that I [Cao Cao] would attack Liaodong. If I had pursued the brothers, Gongsun Kang would have joined forces with them against me. But I simply let things run their course and refrained from marching on Liaodong. It was my restraint that created the conditions under which Gongsun Kang and the Yuan brothers turned against one another.

Well aware of the deadly antagonism between the brothers and the governor of Liaodong, Cao Cao achieved his ends simply by playing the uninvolved observer.

9.3 THE CONQUEST OF CHANGCHUN, 1948

In June of 1948, during China's civil war (1945–49), the Red Army laid siege to Changchun. The city was defended by about 100,000 troops of Chiang Kai-shek's Guomindang regime, dug in behind strong fortifications. But gradually the food supplies in Changchun began to dwindle, and the Guomindang troops began to fight among themselves for the limited food that could be flown in.

The Red Army kept Changchun surrounded but did not attack the city. Instead it permitted the enemy's "internal contradictions" to ripen and divide the defenders. ("Contradiction" is the term commonly used in the People's Republic for conflicts, differences of opinion, and difficulties of every kind.) A premature attack on Changchun would have caused the Guomindang forces to close ranks once again and overlook their own internal strife.

Just at that time, news arrived of a great Communist victory in Jinzhou. Under the combined political and military pressures exerted by the Red Army, Zeng Zesheng, commander of the Yunnan elements of the Guomindang forces in Changchun, refused to carry out Chiang Kai-shek's order to break through the enemy's siege lines. On October 17, 1948, Zeng Zesheng's troops rebelled, and other units of the Guomindang army in Changchun followed their example.

In this way, remarks the Beijing stratagem book, the Red Army conquered Changchun without spilling a drop of blood or even engaging in combat.

9.4 LOOKING ON WITH FOLDED ARMS

In the Ap[ril] 18, 1981, issue of the *Zhongguo qingnian bao* (Chinese [Yout]h Journal), an article appeared analyzing the So-[viet rea]ction to the Iran-Iraq war. The analysis con-[clude]Kremlin would have to content itself with [...] on the opposite shore." Here the phrase was [use]a stratagem but to describe the allegedly [...] regarding the Iran-Iraq conflict. If Mos-[su]pport Iraq, the Chinese commentator [...]e Iran into the arms of the U.S.A. On [...Krem]lin were to openly support Iran, it [...hostil]ity of most Arab states. So all the [...con]cluded, was to "observe the fire [...w]ithout pulling [anyone's] chest-

er   figh.

f King Hui
Records of

Hui of Qin
sel with his
s opposed.
Chen Zhen.

ngzi's tiger
ling on the
was about
Guan Zhuzi
eding. Wait
en they will
killed and
wait until
tigers with

hid behind
asts began

e formula for No. 9 was made
ost revered twentieth-century
He remarked in a lecture that
rmerly "observed the fire on
arts had served as mere pas-
t not daring to confront vital

ublic[1] the phrase "observing
criticize a superficial or overly
problems. In other contexts it
: to remain uninvolved in any-
self directly and to avoid ex-
itment for the common good.
frequently described with an
Menglong (A.D. 1574–1646):
now from his own doorstep,
; neighbor's roof."

9.5 SIT ON THE MOUNTAIN AND WATCH THE TIGERS FIGHT

This is another formula for Stratagem No. 9:

The Chinese characters	坐	山	观	虎
Modern Mandarin pronunciation	zuò	shān	guān	hǔ
Meaning of each character	sit	mountain	watch	tig

The phrase goes back to an incident in the days o
of Qin (337–311 B.C.) as described in Sima Qian's
the Historian.

The states of Han and Wei were at war. King
wanted to intervene in the struggle, and took coun
ministers. Some were in favor of intervention, othe
The ruler couldn't make up his mind, so he asked (
After lengthy thought, that worthy said:

"Does Your Majesty know the story of Bian Zhua
hunt? One time Bian Zhuangzi saw two tigers fee
body of a freshly killed steer. He drew his sword and
to launch himself at the tigers when his companion (
held his arm and said, 'The tigers have just begun fe
until they become really maddened with gluttony; th
start to fight one another. The smaller tiger will be
the larger tiger probably wounded in the battle. If yo
then, without much effort you'll be able to get two
a single blow.'

"Bian Zhuangzi was struck by this advice. So he
a rock and watched the tigers. After a while the be

to fight. The smaller one was killed, the larger wounded. Bian Zhuangzi then sprang out from behind the rock, drew his sword, and stabbed the wounded animal. In that way he easily obtained two tigers with minimum effort.

"Now," continued Chen Zhen, "Han and Wei are at war. The battle has already lasted a year. There seems no chance of mediation. Ultimately the more powerful Wei will annex the smaller state of Han. But it will have been severely weakened by the war. That will give Your Majesty the opportunity to easily overpower Wei and thus absorb both states into your kingdom."

And that is precisely what happened.

Mao Zedong often used to evaluate foreign and domestic developments in terms of Stratagem No. 9. On June 30, 1939, Mao accused foreign powers of tolerating Japan's aggression against China,

> while themselves sitting on the mountain and watching the tigers fight, waiting for a favorable moment in which to engineer a so-called Pacific Mediation Conference in order to secure for themselves the benefits of the laughing third party.[2]

With reference to the European theater, Mao remarked on September 1, 1939:

> In recent years the international reactionary bourgeoisie—especially in England and France—has consistently pursued a reactionary policy of "nonintervention" toward the aggression of the German, Italian, and Japanese Fascists. Their objective has been to tolerate wars of aggression in order to secure advantages for themselves. . . . The policy of "nonintervention" . . . [is the equivalent] of "sitting on the mountain and watching the tigers fight"—the purest form of imperialist policy designed to secure benefits for themselves at the cost of others.[3]

On September 28, 1939, Mao wrote:

> The governments of England, the U.S., and France had
> absolutely no intention of preventing the outbreak of the
> World War—on the contrary, they accelerated it. . . . [Their
> plan was] to drive Germany into a war against the Soviet
> Union, while they themselves [i.e., England, the U.S., and
> France] would sit on the mountain and watch the tigers
> fight, let the Soviet Union and Germany exhaust themselves
> in mutual combat, and then step into the battleground and
> settle things their own way. This conspiracy was foiled by
> the Soviet-German nonaggression pact. . . . When it came
> to Spain, China, Austria, and Czechoslovakia, these con-
> spirators had not the slightest intention of halting the
> aggression; on the contrary, they gave it free rein, fanned
> the flames of war. . . . This they euphemistically termed
> "nonintervention." In reality it amounted to "sitting on the
> mountain and watching the tigers fight."[4]

On April 24, 1945, Mao accused Chiang Kai-shek's Guomindang regime of being passive in its conduct of the war against
Japan. It had, he said,

> thrown the burden of combat on the liberated territories
> [i.e., those regions ruled by the Communist Party of China]
> . . . making it possible for the Japanese invaders to mount
> large-scale offensives against the liberated areas, while they
> themselves [i.e., the Guomindang] sat on the mountain and
> watched the tigers fight.[5]

In early 1981, Zhang Jian of the Economics Department of
Wuhan University followed in Mao's footsteps in his analysis
of the broad objectives of Soviet foreign policy.[6] According to
Zhang, some Western circles had mistakenly assumed that the
Soviet incursion into Afghanistan was aimed primarily at China.
On the basis of that assumption, these Western parties held the
illusion that the conflict between China and the USSR could
worsen to such an extent that China would ultimately carry
most of the burden of containing Soviet expansion, so that the
West could continue to "sit on the mountain and watch the
tigers fight."

In Zhang Jian's view, however, the Soviet invasion of Afghanistan could be accurately viewed only within the context of the Kremlin's overall strategy, which aimed at achieving worldwide hegemony. The central problem of achieving that dominance, stated Zhang, was control over Western Europe, which required its strategic encirclement. There were, in this view, two Soviet rings of encirclement aimed against Western Europe, one extending from the Arctic Ocean to the Black Sea, the other from the Black Sea to the Pacific. Afghanistan was the point at which these two rings intersected, providing a springboard for actions not only against Western China but also in the direction of the Arabian oilfields and the ports of the Indian Ocean.

Says the 1989 edition of the Beijing stratagem book:

> When dissension appears in enemy ranks, and internal conflicts erupt with increasing openness, then is the time to "sit on the mountain and watch the tigers fight." It would be a mistake to try and benefit immediately from the other side's distress, to "loot a burning house." For hasty intervention often serves only to temporarily unite the fragmented forces of the opposition and increases the danger of a counterattack. It is better to thoughtfully step back and wait until the dissension in the enemy camp has ripened to the point where the enemy forces turn against one another and do themselves in.[7]

But Stratagem No. 9 does not involve only waiting. When the time is ripe, the waiting must be transformed into well-prepared action. To paraphrase a thought ascribed to Laozi, it might be said: "Apparent inaction is the highest form of action."

9.6   FAR FROM THE RED DUST

Beijing linguistics expert Liu Jiexiu has drawn a connection between the words of Stratagem No. 9 and a poem by the Tang Dynasty monk Qiankang. The poem, however, deals not with tactical behavior, or stratagems, but with the seclusion, the remoteness from the world, of Buddhist sages. "Red dust" is a Buddhist expression denoting transitory earthly existence, and "green mountaintops, cool as mute ice" reflects the peace and ascetic seclusion of the hermit.

> *There, on the other riverbank,*
> *in the red dust,*
> *hordes of people, impetuous and irascible*
> *as tongues of flame.*
> *Here, before the gates of the hermitage,*
> *only green mountaintops everywhere,*
> *cool as mute ice.*

A. Hide Your Dagger Behind a Smile

The Chinese characters	笑	里	藏	刀
Modern Mandarin pronunciation	*xiào*	*lǐ*	*cáng*	*dāo*
Meaning of each character	smile	in	hide	dagger

B. Honey in the Mouth, a Sword in the Belt

The Chinese characters	口	蜜	腹	剑
Modern Mandarin pronunciation	*kǒu*	*mì*	*fù*	*jiàn*
Meaning of each character	mouth	honey	belly	sword
Applications	Speak flattery, but plan evil in your heart; mask evil intent with outward friendliness and fine-sounding words. The stratagem of the forked tongue, or the "Judas kiss"; the "two-faced" or "Janus-headed" stratagem.			

10.1 LI YIFU AND LI LINFU

Formula A was coined in the ninth century A.D. by Bai Juyi, one of the most famous poets of the Tang period, to characterize a government official known as Li Yifu. In his poem *"Tian Ke Duo"* (Heaven Can Be Measured), he writes that individuals like Li Yifu "hide a dagger behind their smile and murder people." In a poem cycle about the virtues of drinking wine, the same author ends a poem with another sideswipe at types like Li Yifu:

> *Stop sharpening a dagger behind your smile.*
> *It is better to drink wine and,*
> *deep in your cups,*
> *lie there peacefully.*

Who was this Li Yifu? Historical tradition has it that, in the seventh century A.D., he flattered his way into the favor of Tang Emperor Gaozong and, by toadying and bootlicking, became a high-ranking dignitary at court. According to the *Jiu Tang shu* (Old History of the Tang), written around A.D. 940:

> [Li] Yifu pretended to be soft-spoken and modest; when he spoke with others he always presented a sparkling smile. Inwardly, however, he was deceptive and sly. Anyone who offered him the slightest resistance was earmarked by him for destruction. Consequently his contemporaries said of him that "Li Yifu hides a dagger behind his smile."

The *Xin Tang shu* (New History of the Tang), composed the following century, speaks of Li Yifu in similar terms. And the phrase coined by Bai Juyi also found its way into various novels and plays.

Formula B was handed down by historian Sima Guang. In his *Zizhi tong jian* (Comprehensive Mirror to Aid in Government), he reports as follows about Li Linfu, an eighth-century imperial minister:

> He had a special hatred of the literati. . . . Outwardly he encouraged them, and lured them with sweet words, but secretly he harmed them [whenever possible]. His contemporaries said of him, "He has honey in his mouth, but [carries] a sword in his belly [i.e., in his belt]."

Following the death of Mao Zedong on September 12, 1976, the members of the Gang of Four were repeatedly referred to in the Chinese press as "disciples of Li Linfu." Mao himself, back in 1939, had compared the "imperialists" to Li Linfu and British Prime Minister Neville Chamberlain to Li Yifu. At another point Mao, speaking of China's domestic politics, called for opposition to the attitude embodied by the figures of Li Yifu and Li Linfu, which he described as follows:

> Outwardly yielding, but inwardly resistant, affirming with the lips but denying with the heart, speaking fine-sounding words to people's faces but making mischief behind their backs—this is how hypocrisy expresses itself.

Also worth mentioning in this context are the "sugarcoated bullets" of the bourgeoisie, which Mao regarded as the chief danger to the proletariat after the victory of the Chinese Communists.

The formula "Honey in the mouth, a sword in the belt" also appears in the Chinese edition of Lenin's *Collected Works,* where it is used as the title of a 1907 essay. The commonly used German-language edition of Lenin's writings renders the title as "Honey in the mouth, gall in the heart."

Apropos the Soviet Union: In the 1969 Hong Kong stratagem book,[1] Khrushchev is described as a Li Yifu or Li Linfu type, who appeared to be a most loyal follower of Stalin during that dictator's lifetime but then condemned him at the famous Twentieth Party Congress of 1956.

Stratagem No. 10 seems to be quite popular in China, as indicated by some variations on the two formulas cited so far, such as:

miàn dài zhōnghòu, nèi cáng jiānzhà—"The face displays loyalty and goodness, but the interior harbors cunning and falsehood,"

or

zuǐ shàng fàng mìtáng, xīnlǐ cáng pīshuāng—"There is honey on the lips, but arsenic hidden in the heart."

Needless to say, such hypocrisy is not unknown outside of China. And formulas such as "Hide your dagger behind a smile" need little or no elaboration. But the following cases, taken from various Chinese stratagem books, may cast light on some surprising dimensions of No. 10.

10.2 THE DANGEROUS LIAISON

The first example is drawn from a work ascribed to Han Fei, the most important representative of the so-called School of Legalism.

During the Spring and Autumn period, Duke Wu of Zheng

schemed to annex the state of Hu. But because he had only limited military means, he did not dare a direct attack against Hu. Instead he resorted to Stratagem No. 10. First, he offered his beautiful daughter to the Prince of Hu as a prospective wife. The Prince accepted the offer and thus became Duke Wu's son-in-law. Then, in order to lull Hu's suspicions even more, the ruler of Zheng gathered his ministers around him and said, "I am thinking of attacking another state. I ask you: Which state would be a most suitable target of attack?"

One minister suggested that a strike against Hu would be most rewarding.

In simulated fury, the Duke shouted, "What? You propose war against Hu, which is allied to us by marriage?" And he had the offending minister beheaded.

When the Prince of Hu learned of this incident, his last doubts about Duke Wu's genuine friendship evaporated, and from then on he felt that vigilance against Zheng was unnecessary. Suddenly, however, Duke Wu mounted a surprise attack against Hu and conquered it. For a long time afterward, Zheng remained a powerful state; it was destroyed only in 375 B.C. by Han.

A book on Chinese military phraseology offers the following commentary on the foregoing incident:

> This is a typical example of the military application of Stratagem No. 10. The Duke of Zheng did not hesitate to sacrifice his own flesh and blood and to unjustly execute his own minister, in order to create the illusion of friendliness and thus lull his enemy into a false sense of security. The point, then, is to convince your opponent that you have only the most friendly or peaceable intentions. Your opponent is thus persuaded to relax his vigilance. In secret, however, you plan to strike against him at the first favorable opportunity, and you make the necessary preparations for the strike in such a way that your opponent notices nothing.[2]

10.3   THE KING AS STABLE BOY

In the Spring and Autumn period, China was fragmented into dozens of states, with wars repeatedly breaking out among them and alliances constantly shifting. At one point, Goujian (d. 465 B.C.), King of Yue, was defeated by Fuchai (d. 473 B.C.), ruler of Wu,[3] at the Battle of Fujiao. Goujian's first inclination was to flee abroad with some five thousand soldiers. But his adviser Fan Li counseled him to surrender to Fuchai and, by pursuing a consistent policy of self-abasement, to prepare the ground for future vengeance.

Goujian sent Wen Zhong as an emissary to Fuchai and offered him all the riches of Yue. Goujian also declared himself willing to serve Fuchai forever as a humble servant. Against the advice of one of his own generals, Fuchai accepted the offer. Goujian donned an undyed robe and, with his adviser, his wife, and three hundred men, migrated to Wu. Appearing before his conqueror, he knelt down and, in the humblest terms, expressed his thanks to Fuchai for sparing his life.

Fuchai permitted Goujian to work as a groom in his stables. Whenever Fuchai went riding, Goujian prepared the horses and time after time he expressed his gratitude to the ruler of Wu for not having had him executed. When Fuchai fell ill, Goujian tended him attentively, even examining his feces to determine the cause of the malady.

Since Goujian was so respectful, Fuchai assumed that he had become a loyal subject. After three years he permitted Goujian to return home. There, in order not to forget his dream of vengeance, Goujian slept on a bed of straw and brushwood, and each day, before each meal, he ate a piece of gall. At the same time he quietly set about preparing his hour of revenge.

Finally, the time came. Wu's leading army commander was murdered. The country just then was suffering a terrible drought, so severe that crabs dried up in the streambeds and rice wilted on the stalk. At that inauspicious time, the ruler of Wu went abroad to attend a conference of heads of state. With all these circumstances favoring his enterprise, Goujian launched a major attack against Wu, and in no time his forces had occupied and destroyed it.

10.4 MASQUERADE AS A SWINE TO DEFEAT THE TIGER

Shu Han, author of a stratagem book published in Taipei in 1986,[4] links the story of Goujian with that of Lucius Junius Brutus in Rome of the sixth century B.C.

Legend has it that when Tarquinius Superbus, last king of Rome, defeated Brutus's father and elder brother, Brutus himself was spared because he played the fool. He played the part so well, in fact, that Tarquinius brought him to court as a jester for his own sons' amusement. But after the rape of Lucretia and her suicide, Brutus threw off his disguise. He persuaded Lucretia's husband and father to swear that they would not rest until the tyrant and his shameless sons would be driven from the land. Then he hastened to Rome, bearing Lucretia's body, and with a passionate speech he persuaded the people to topple their king and banish him, also gaining the support of the army. All of this eventually led to the founding of the Roman Republic and the election of Brutus and his loyal comrade Collatinus among its first consuls.

In recounting this tale, author Shu Han gives it the subtitle "Masquerading as a swine to defeat the tiger." This is a well-known Chinese expression. According to the 1969 Hong Kong stratagem book, it is based on the idea that a hunter, by dressing up as a pig and imitating its grunts, can attract the attention of a tiger and kill the surprised beast at close range. In this context the same book cites an aphorism ascribed to Laozi, the legendary founder of Daoism: "[Let] wisdom [seem] like stupidity"—and the eleventh-century poet Su Shi's saying: "The man of great wisdom appears to be a fool." The book then continues:

> "Masquerading as a swine to kill the tiger" is [a tactic] used against a stronger opponent. You hide your sword

from him, pretend to be as stupid as a pig and compliant in all things, keep a friendly smile on your face, and work like a slave. Ultimately, your enemy will be completely deceived. Then, when a favorable opportunity presents itself, quick as lightning the slave turns into an executioner.[5]

10.5 AN OFFER OF CAPITULATION

In the third century B.C., the state of Yan attacked the state of Qi and captured seventeen cities. Only two cities continued to resist, one of them called Jimo. When Jimo's commanding general died in battle, Tian Dan took his place. After trying various devices, Tian Dan ordered elderly and weak men and women to mount the city walls and sent emissaries to the Yan army to negotiate the city's capitulation. The Yan soldiers cheered. Tian Dan took up a collection among the people of his city and raised more than a thousand gold pieces, which he had delivered to the commanding general of the Yan army along with a letter from Jimo's wealthier citizens. The letter said, "Jimo will soon surrender. All we ask is that our relatives, wives, and concubines not be taken prisoner." The Yan general agreed, and the Yan army's vigilance dwindled steadily. This was the moment for Tian Dan to lead a sortie out of Jimo and into the enemy camp, which ended with a devastating defeat for the Yan army.

No wonder that Confucius warned, "Smooth words and an ingratiating expression are seldom paired with humaneness."

In his treatise *The Art of War,* Confucius's contemporary Sun Tzu terms the humble words of the enemy an alarm signal, and warns, "Those who come seeking peace without a treaty are plotting."[6]

In a 1977 edition of Sun Tzu's classic work published in Taipei, this idea is updated with the following formula, described by the Taiwanese regime as having been the guiding principle of the Chinese Communists (in the years 1945–49): "When the enemy attacks, we begin to negotiate. When the enemy negotiates, we attack."

Let the Plum Tree Wither in Place of the Peach

The Chinese characters	李	代	桃	僵
Modern Mandarin pronunciation	*lǐ*	*dài*	*táo*	*jiāng*
Meaning of each character	plum tree	instead	peach tree	wither

Applications	The stratagem of the scapegoat, or the sacrificial lamb:
	a. With the aid of deception, sacrifice yourself to save another.
	b. With the aid of deception, sacrifice another to save yourself.
	c. With the aid of deception, sacrifice someone else to save a third party.
	d. Make a small sacrifice to gain something more valuable.

The formula used to describe this stratagem derives from a famous collection of folk songs and ballads. The collection was assembled by the *Yuefu* (Music Bureau), which was founded by Emperor Wu of the Han (140–87 B.C.) for the purpose of collecting and preserving popular and aristocratic poems and songs. Part of the collection has been preserved in a later compilation, the *Collection of Yuefu Poems,*[1] which contains a chapter featuring Han folk songs that are meant to be performed to the accompaniment of string and wind instruments. One of the songs, "The Cock Crows," contains this passage:

A peach tree grows by a well.
A plum tree grows next to it.
When insects attack the roots of the peach,
The plum tree sacrifices itself and withers instead of the
  peach tree.

If trees sacrifice themselves for one another,
Can brothers forget each other?

11.2 UNDER A FALSE FLAG

To illustrate this stratagem, the 1969 Hong Kong stratagem book[2] cites an incident of Chinese history which occurred more than twenty-five hundred years ago. It is described in the classic Confucian work the *Zuo Commentary,* one of the major collections of writings, biographical incidents, and other material ascribed to chroniclers, scribes, and soothsayers from the tenth to the sixth century B.C.

Duke Xuan of Wei has intimate relations with his father's concubine. She bears him a son named Jizi. Later, Duke Xuan plans to marry off his son Jizi to Xuan Jiang, a woman from Qi. But she is so beautiful that the Duke takes her for his own wife. Xuan Jiang bears two sons, the gentle Shou and the crafty Shuo. At a later point in the story, Xuan Jiang and her son Shuo slander Jizi to the Duke, claiming (among other things) that Jizi cannot forgive his father for taking the beautiful Xuan Jiang away from him and still longs for her. The Duke finally sends Jizi on a mission to Qi, at the same time commissioning a band of robbers to lie in wait for him at a certain place and kill him. Shou, Xuan Jiang's good son, loves his half-brother Jizi. Learning of the plot, he warns Jizi and advises him to flee. But Jizi rejects the advice with a reply reflecting the typical Confucian virtue of absolute filial piety: "If I do not obey my father's commands, how can I be worthy to be called 'son'? If there were a kingdom without fathers, I would be able to flee there."

Prior to Jizi's departure for Qi, Shou gets him drunk, steals the standard designating the crown prince, and himself sets out for the fateful rendezvous. Believing he is Jizi, the robbers kill Shou. Shortly thereafter, Jizi appears and cries, "It was I you were supposed to kill. What had he done wrong? Kill me as well!" And the robbers murder Jizi too.

In this tale, the gentle Shou plays the role of the plum tree. But here the peach tree (Jizi) does not accept the sacrifice.

11.3   OUTWITTING A ROUGHNECK

Another story, this one dating from the eleventh century A.D., also tells of a brother who plays the role of the plum tree. But this incident does not end in calamity.[3]

Di Qing had lost his parents at an early age, and lived with his elder brother Di Su, a poor but upright farmer. One day, as Di Qing was bringing Di Su's lunch to him in the fields, a woman hurrying by called to him that his brother was having a fistfight with Iron Luohan on the riverbank. Iron Luohan was a local good-for-nothing; he had gone out into the fields drunk that day, looking for trouble. Meeting a peasant, he took the man's bread away and ate it. The peasant, trying to resist, was thrown to the ground. At this point Di Su, who had been quietly watching the incident, stepped in and punched Iron Luohan, which led to a brawl between the two strong men. A woman bringing food to her husband in the fields saw the fight, ran for help, and told Di Qing about it.

Arriving on the scene, Di Qing found the fight over and his brother Di Su sitting on a rock, gasping for breath, his forehead wrinkled with worry. Di Qing looked around and saw Iron Luohan, who could not swim, struggling for his life in the river. Di Su had kicked him so hard that he had fallen into the water. Di Qing knew that, if the fellow drowned, his brother would be in serious trouble. Under the laws of the Song Dynasty, in fact, he might be sentenced to death. So Di Qing immediately jumped into the river to rescue Iron Luohan, who was nearing the end of his strength. Sensing a rescuer approaching, the drowning man desperately reached out and clutched the collar of Di Qing's threadbare old shirt. It tore, leaving Iron Luohan with only a scrap of cloth in his grip. Di Qing grabbed him by the hair and pulled him to shore, at the same time whispering in his ear, "I am Di Su, and I've saved your life."

Iron Luohan had swallowed a great deal of water and was half unconscious. He could not tell who had saved him. Hardly had he been brought to land when he fainted and lay there like a corpse.

"I've killed him," said Di Su, horrified. "I'll pay for it with my life. And what will become of you, Little Brother?" The tears ran down his cheeks.

"Calm yourself, Brother," replied Di Qing. "I think he has only fainted. He isn't dead."

"Even so, things look bad for me," answered Di Su. "I've obviously hurt him, and the magistrate will punish me severely for it."

By this time some villagers had hurried to the scene. They consoled Di Su, saying, "Don't worry. You had every right to intervene and try to help someone else. We'll put in a good word for you."

The village headman came hurrying along. He shouted, "Di Su, our Emperor proclaimed the laws. Beating someone is a crime. If you start a fight and kill someone, you must pay for it with your life."

Di Su rose and stood there silently, waiting to be taken into custody.

"Wait!" called his younger brother.

"You dare to oppose me, young fellow?" said the headman with a stony countenance.

"You're confusing things," shouted Di Qing. "It is perfectly clear that Iron Luohan persecuted a weak villager. This infuriated me, and out of fraternal feeling I helped the weaker party. That ruffian Iron Luohan was careless and nearly drowned. But my brother pulled him to shore and saved his life."

The village headman looked at him doubtfully, then looked around at the assembled people as if to ask, "Is this true?"

Immediately some of the people shouted, "It's true. We can testify to it."

Di Qing strengthened his case even more. "You see? He's got a piece of my collar gripped in his hand."

The official bent down to look—and sure enough, Iron Luohan was clutching a ragged collar. He was about to arrest Di Qing, when the youngster said, "Just a moment. It's not certain that Iron Luohan is really dead." Reluctantly, the headman had to agree. "All right," he said, "let's see."

Di Qing immediately jumped on Iron Luohan, sat astride him, and began massaging his stomach. Soon Iron Luohan opened his mouth and vomited dirty water. Then he regained consciousness, and at that moment Di Qing bent over and whispered something to him. Iron Luohan shook himself, stood up, walked shakily over to Di Su, bowed to him with his arms crossed over his chest, and said, "I thank you for saving my life." Then he trotted off.

Di Su was astonished. A storm cloud that had suddenly gathered above him had passed with equal swiftness. The spectators, realizing that there was nothing more to gape at, took themselves off. On their way home, Di Su asked Di Qing, "Younger Brother, I do not understand why Iron Luohan thanked me after our life-and-death struggle. What happened?"

Di Qing replied, "When Iron Luohan took the peasant's bread from him, then fought with him and with you, he was very drunk. He didn't remember much of all that. When I pulled him out of the river, I deceived him by saying, 'I am Di Su, and I'm saving your life.' Later, when he came to, I whispered to him that he should thank you. And that's exactly what he did."

Di Su profoundly admired his younger brother's clever use of such a stratagem, which had saved him from a nasty fate. According to the tale as told in *Children's Epoch* magazine, Di Qing was only fifteen years old at the time. He later became a famous general of the Northern Song Dynasty.

11.4 SWAPPING CLOTHES WITH THE KING

Vietnam's war of resistance against Ming China lasted from A.D. 1418 to 1427. In the year 1419 the Vietnamese army, headed by the peasant leader Lê-Loi, was surrounded at Chi-Linh. A vassal by the name of Le-Lai then said to Lê-Loi, "Give me your robe. I will dress myself in it and leave the camp."

When the Chinese saw him they thought he was Lê-Loi, so they captured and killed him. In the meantime, the real Lê-Loi escaped and later went down in history as King Lê-Thai-To, founder of Vietnam's Lê Dynasty (which lasted from A.D. 1428 to 1793). Today this application of Stratagem No. 11 is still recalled by the Vietnamese expression "Le-Lai rescues the King." There is reportedly also a street named Rue Le-Lai in Ho Chi Minh City (formerly Saigon), commemorating the one who sacrificed himself for his leader.[4]

11.5 THE ARREST OF CHIANG KAI-SHEK

After the Chinese Red Army's "Long March" in 1934–35 and its arrival in northern Shaanxi, Chiang Kai-shek gave precedence to fighting the "Communist menace" over resisting the Japanese invaders of his country. In Xi'an, capital of Shaanxi Province, he set up an anti-Communist command that was supposed to deal with the bases that were being directed from Communist headquarters in Yan'an. The dominant personality of the anti-Communist command was Zhang Xueliang.

The general situation at that time was characterized by two major elements: on the one hand, a growing wave of Chinese patriotism in the face of the Japanese threat, with mounting calls for an end to the civil war between the Guomindang and the Communists; on the other hand, the desire of the Comintern (the Kremlin-directed Communist International) to forge a united front of Chinese Communists and non-Communists.

Even the Guomindang troops in Xi'an were vulnerable to the influence of the Communists' slogan: "Chinese should not kill Chinese, but unite all their strength for the struggle against the Japanese."

Zhang Xueliang shared that viewpoint. In June 1936 he made contact with Chou En-lai and concluded an agreement on the practical cessation of hostilities. In August 1936 an unofficial representative of the Chinese Communist Party was sent to serve on Zhang Xueliang's staff.

Word of all this reached Nanking, then the Chinese capital, prompting Chiang Kai-shek to travel to Xi'an at the end of October, just when the Japanese were attacking Suiyuan. This attack triggered numerous anti-Japanese strikes in China, notably in Shanghai and Qingdao. Even the military commandants of Guangxi and Guangdong called on Chiang Kai-shek to halt China's civil strife and organize the resistance against the Japanese. But Chiang rejected these demands, along with that of Zhang Xueliang to form a united front with the Communists against the Japanese. Chiang also refused to transfer at least a part of the Xi'an garrison to Suiyuan.

On December 4, Chiang Kai-shek called for a general offensive against the Communists to be launched on December 12. But he failed to obtain the cooperation of either Zhang Xueliang or Yang Hucheng, who at that time was serving as the "pacification commissar" for Shaanxi. When Chiang relieved Zhang Xueliang of his post on December 10, the opposition decided to intervene. On December 12, 1936, an elite group of Zhang Xueliang's bodyguards took Chiang prisoner. In subsequent negotiations, Chiang was presented with a list of eight demands and confronted with the necessity of a united front against Japan.

The arrest of Chiang Kai-shek created a great stir throughout China and the rest of the world. The leadership of the Chinese Communist Party immediately sent a delegation to Xi'an, which included Chou En-lai. After long and complicated negotiations, Chiang accepted the demands which had been presented to him, and on December 25 he flew back to Nanking accompanied by

Zhang Xueliang. Zhang was brought to trial, summarily removed from office, and sentenced to ten years in prison. His punishment continued even after the Nationalist (Guomindang) regime fled to Taiwan in 1949, and as of 1990 Zhang was still living there, now a more or less free man.

The Hong Kong stratagem book[5] emphasizes that Zhang Xueliang took full responsibility before the military tribunal for the arrest of Chiang Kai-shek, thus saving his colleagues, and particularly Yang Hucheng, from prosecution. With that noble deed, continues the author of the Hong Kong book, Zhang Xueliang demonstrated the spirit of the plum tree that sacrifices itself for the peach tree.

11.6 THE EMBROIDERED SLIPPER

The phrase representing Stratagem No. 11 was also used by seventeenth-century author Pu Songling in the most famous of his works, *Liaozhai zhiyi* (Strange Stories from the Leisure Studio), a collection of more than 490 tales. This story is entitled "Yanzhi."

In Dongchang there lived a man named Bian, who was a quack veterinarian. His daughter Yanzhi was beautiful and talented. He would have loved to see her married to a scholar. But his poverty and low social status stood in the way. Yanzhi was fifteen years old and still not betrothed.

In a house across the way lived Mrs. Wang, wife of Gong and a friend of Yanzhi. Mrs. Wang was a flighty woman and loved practical jokes. One time after a visit, Yanzhi accompanied her back to her door and saw an elegant young man pass by, all dressed in white. Yanzhi seemed to catch fire. Her eyes continued to follow the young man, even as he receded into the distance. Mrs. Wang noticed what had happened and laughingly suggested to Yanzhi that this was the perfect mate for her. Yanzhi blushed but said nothing. Mrs. Wang told her that she had once lived in the same street as the young man's parents. His name was E Qiuzhun, and he was uniquely gentle and obedient. His father had died and, more recently, his mother as well, which was why he was dressed in mourning. Mrs. Wang then proposed going to E Qiuzhun and prompting him to request Yanzhi's hand in marriage. The girl said nothing. Mrs. Wang laughed and went her way.

For several days nothing happened. Doubts arose in Yanzhi's mind. Had Mrs. Wang not done as she intended? Or was she, Yanzhi, simply of too low a class? She began to worry, stopped eating, fell sick, and took to her bed. One day Mrs. Wang came to visit and asked Yanzhi what was ailing her. The girl claimed to have no idea. She had felt poorly after their last parting, she said, and now she was exhausted and had no idea what was to become of her.

Mrs. Wang reported that her husband had been away on business, so that she had had no chance yet of speaking with E Qiuzhun. Could that be why Yanzhi was ill? When the girl heard this she blushed furiously. Mrs. Wang said jokingly, "If that's how things are with you, and that's what your sickness is all about, you can stop worrying. I shall have Mr. E come to you this very night, and the two of you will be happily united. How could he refuse you?"

Yanzhi replied, "As things stand, there is no room for shame. If he doesn't feel that I am socially too far beneath him, and he sends an intermediary to ask for my hand, I shall feel well again in an instant. But I'm not at all prepared to meet him face-to-face myself."

Mrs. Wang nodded her approval and departed.

Since her youth Mrs. Wang had kept up an intimate relationship with her neighbor Sujie. Since her marriage, he had visited Mrs. Wang whenever her husband was away on a trip. On this day Sujie came to see her and she told him about Yanzhi just to amuse him. Sujie had long thought Yanzhi to be very beautiful, and now he conceived a scheme to have her. Fearing Mrs. Wang's jealousy, he feigned a lack of interest but listened carefully and took note of the exact location of Yanzhi's bedroom. The following night he climbed the wall of her house and knocked on her window.

"Who's there?" she asked.

"E Qiuzhun."

Yanzhi replied, "I think about you day and night, about being with you forever, growing old together—but not about sharing just one night's pleasure. If you really love me, find an intermediary quickly and arrange our marriage. But I won't receive you privately like this."

Sujie saw no alternative but to pretend agreement. He passionately begged her, however, to at least let him press her hand once as a pledge of their troth. Yanzhi could not bring herself to refuse, rose weakly from her bed, and opened the window. Sujie pushed his way roughly into the room, grabbed her, and pressed her to make love. Yanzhi, being too weak to resist, fell to the floor gasping. Sujie tried to lift her, and she threatened to scream.

Afraid he might be discovered, Sujie did not dare to push his luck. He asked only that she set a time for their next meeting. Yanzhi replied that their next meeting would be their wedding day. The false suitor grabbed her foot, pulled off an embroidered slipper, and disappeared out the window.

Sujie went straight to Mrs. Wang's. Lying in bed there, he kept thinking about the slipper and secretly felt for it in his sleeve pocket. But the slipper wasn't there. He searched for it everywhere, failed to find it, and finally could not avoid telling Mrs. Wang the whole story and asking her help. But even working together they could not find the slipper.

There lived in that same narrow street a good-for-nothing by the name of Mao Da, who had pursued Mrs. Wang in vain, spied on her, and knew about her relationship with Sujie. He hoped to obtain proof of her infidelity and blackmail her with it. On that evening he went to her house and sneaked into her garden. Suddenly he stepped on something soft. Picking it up, he found it was a woman's slipper. Listening at the window, Mao Da heard Sujie's detailed description of his visit to Yanzhi. Delighted, he left the garden.

A few evenings later Mao Da climbed over the garden wall of Yanzhi's house. Not knowing the way, he landed outside her father's room. Yanzhi's father, looking out his window, saw a man and immediately suspected someone of being after his daughter. Furious, he grabbed a knife and stormed out of the house. Mao Da took fright and ran away. He tried to climb back over the wall, but the man was right behind him. Mao Da turned around and forced the knife out of the older man's hand. Yanzhi's mother now began to scream too. Desperate, Mao Da killed Yanzhi's father and fled.

Yanzhi now came hurrying into the garden with a lantern. She saw her dead father and her slipper next to him on the ground. Asked about it, a weeping Yanzhi told her mother the story of the slipper, though she could not bring herself to involve Mrs. Wang in the matter and mentioned only E Qiuzhun.

The next day, charges were made against E Qiuzhun at the district magistrate's office, and he was arrested. At this time he was only nineteen years old and still little more than a child. Brought before the magistrate, he did not know what to say. He denied nothing, just stood there and trembled. The magistrate became increasingly convinced that E was the culprit. He had the youngster interrogated under torture, for in imperial China only someone who confessed could be convicted. The young scholar couldn't stand the pain, admitted everything, and was sentenced to death.

A report of the entire matter was sent to the superior authorities in Jinan. After one look at E Qiuzhun, the prefect in Jinan began to doubt his guilt. He had an agent in disguise placed in E's prison cell, so that the young man would speak freely. What he learned in this way strengthened the prefect's belief in E's innocence. By confronting Yanzhi with E Qiuzhun and interrogating Mrs. Wang, the prefect finally was led to Mrs. Wang's lover Sujie. He, however, while admitting his adventure in Yanzhi's room, denied killing her father. Under torture, however, he too confessed and was sentenced to die. Desperate for help, Sujie wrote a letter to the highly regarded Commissioner Shi Yushan, who came to the conclusion that something was wrong with the case and had all the files brought to him for review.

Further questioning of Mrs. Wang revealed the names of several men who had been after her, including the scapegrace Mao Da, whom Shi Yushan immediately suspected. But since Mao Da refused to confess, Shi Yushan said, "Now the spirits of the temple must unmask the culprit."

All of Mrs. Wang's male friends, stripped to the waist, were forced to enter a darkened Buddhist temple and stand in front of a wall. There, Shi Yushan told them, "The spirit of the temple will place a sign on the back of the guilty man." After a while the wily commissioner called the men out and looked at their backs. He pointed to Mao Da: "You are the murderer." And indeed, there was a mark on the man's back. The wall had been covered with ashes in advance, and Mao Da, knowing himself guilty, had pressed his back against the wall to prevent the spirit from marking him. Finally, Shi Yushan wrung a confession from Mao Da.

In reading his sentence, Shi Yushan declared that Sujie had "let the plum tree wither instead of the peach tree," because in his nighttime encounter with Yanzhi he had pretended to be E Qiuzhun. And Mao Da, having been caught in the act, had "put Zhang's hat on Li's head"—that is, he had diverted responsibility for his own act to Sujie—by leaving the embroidered slipper at the scene of the crime.

11.7   THE HIDDEN OFFSPRING

The examples cited so far have involved two-sided relationships, in which the "plum tree" voluntarily sacrificed itself for the "peach tree" or else was made to do so by the latter. At another level of interpretation of Stratagem No. 11, a third party is involved who assigns the role of "plum tree" to someone else.

In the year 607 B.C., Duke Ling of Jin was assassinated by a member of the powerful Zhao clan. A few years later a former favorite of Duke Ling, a man by the name of Tu'an Gu, was appointed to high office by Ling's successor, Duke Jing. Tu'an

Gu yearned for revenge against the murderers of his old patron and plotted to exterminate the Zhao clan.

A general who did not approve of the plan revealed it to the head of the Zhao family. That worthy, seeing no other way out and willing to accept the necessity of his own death, had his pregnant wife, a princess from the house of Duke Jing, brought to the Duke's palace to live. Shortly thereafter, Tu'an Gu's troops stormed the residence of the Zhao family and killed all its members. The only survivor was the wife of the clan's chief, who was now living safely in the palace.

Some time later she gave birth to a son. Tu'an Gu immediately sent his men to the palace with orders to bring the child to him. But the mother managed to hide the infant, and Tu'an Gu, believing it had already been smuggled out of the palace, had his men search for it everywhere.

Meantime two loyal vassals of the Zhao family, Gongsun Chujiu and Cheng Ying, sought a way to save the clan's only male offspring. Finally they hit on the following plan: Cheng Ying searched for a male child of the same age. When he had found it, Gongsun Chujiu hid with it in a mountain hut. Cheng Ying then revealed the hiding place to Tu'an Gu, whose men searched for the substitute child and killed both it and its guardian Gongsun Chujiu. While this was going on, the real Zhao child was smuggled out of the palace and brought to a safe place, where it grew up unrecognized.

When the boy was fifteen years old, Duke Jing rehabilitated the Zhao clan. Young Zhao revealed himself to Duke Jing, and the ruler permitted him to wreak vengeance on Tu'an Gu, who was killed together with his entire family.[6]

In this tale the innocent little boy who lost his life in place of the noble Zhao child, who could then grow up in safety, was selected to play the role of the "plum tree" by the vassals Gongsun Chujiu and Cheng Ying. Gongsun Chujiu also appears in the role of a voluntary "plum tree," while the surviving "peach tree" is, of course, the last scion of the Zhao clan. Gongsun

Chujiu's behavior inevitably calls to mind a saying ascribed to Confucius and quite typical of the Confucian virtue of unconditional loyalty:

> If you are another's subject, and can be of service to him by being beheaded, you should do so.

11.8 THE VACILLATING RULER

In the conflicts among the various states which occupied the territory of pre-imperial China (i.e., prior to 221 B.C.), one of the principal goals was to avoid falling victim to the attempts by rulers of the stronger states to gain predominance. In such cases the game often involved surviving as the "peach tree" instead of ending in the role of the "plum tree."

During the Warring States period, the Han state, whose ruler King Xuanhui was a temporizer, was caught between the two mighty states of Qin and Chu. The King of Qin regarded the Chu as his sole rival for hegemony in the land. He would have liked to attack Chu, but the Han state was in his way. So, in 317 B.C., he sent Zhang Yi, a specialist in forming alliances, to persuade Han to join him in a common war against Chu. But the ruler of Han opted for a policy of neutrality toward both his powerful neighbors. This infuriated the ruler of Qin, who decided to subjugate Han.

The Qin army marched into Han, encountering no serious resistance. Desperate, the King of Han summoned Minister Gongzhong. But that notable avoided taking a direct stance on the matter, instead citing the popular song, "The plum tree withers in place of the peach tree." The Han ruler, however, did not understand what his minister was getting at. So Gongzhong pointed to two trees in the royal garden and said, "Let us assume that the smaller is a peach tree and the larger a plum. The peach tree is suddenly attacked by insects. The only way to save it is to cause the insects to attack the plum tree instead."

Now the Han ruler understood what Gongzhong had in mind. The calamity which threatened Han was to be diverted to Chu, which would serve as Han's sacrificial lamb. Whereupon the King of Han sent his minister to Qin, with a promise that it would be rewarded with an important Han city if Qin would enter into an alliance for a war against Chu.

These developments were reported to the King of Chu, who asked the counsel of his adviser Chen Zhen. The latter laughed and said, "Han is planning to use the stratagem 'Let the plum tree wither in place of the peach tree' against us. Let us fight Han with its own stratagem!"

The King of Chu approved his adviser's plan. He prepared his army militarily for an attack and at the same time spread the rumor through other states in the region that he was heeding Han's call for help and would soon send troops into that state. The King of Chu also sent an emissary to Han bearing many costly gifts for its ruler and proposing an alliance against Qin. The Han chancellor rejected the proposal, saying that it would simply mean Han would suffer to protect Chu. Whereupon the Chu emissary declared that his country had already mobilized its entire army and swore that, together with Han, Chu would fight Qin until final victory was won. Han's vacillating monarch took these clear words of the Chu emissary at face value and annulled the old plan of joining forces with Qin to attack Chu.

The King of Qin did not at first credit the news of the Han-Chu alliance. So he sent spies disguised as merchants to both states. His spies confirmed the news.

Angered at the Han ruler's vacillation, the King of Qin marched his troops into Han even before those of Chu had gotten there. The Han army put up brave resistance, but as the situation grew more critical the Han King sent messengers to Chu requesting troop support. In accordance with Chen Zhen's plan, the ruler of Chu had sent troops marching toward Han, but only for the sake of appearances, in order to prompt Qin to conquer Han as a preemptive move. The King of Chu assured the Han emissaries that support troops were already on their way. In reality, of course, he had no intention of helping Han.

The Han troops waited for the Chu army, which did not arrive. The morale of the Han troops declined and fear spread through the ranks. Many soldiers deserted. At that point, Qin mounted a general attack against Han and conquered its main army. Han became Qin's vassal state.

Following the Qin victory over Han, the ruler of Chu feared an attack by the Qin army. But his adviser Chen Zhen told him that he was worrying unnecessarily. The plum tree had already fallen, so that the survival of the peach tree was assured for the time being.

The Qin ruler's advisers pushed for a campaign against Chu. But the King himself opposed the idea. The war against Han had caused serious losses. The Chu troops were well prepared and awaited their exhausted enemy at their ease. So the King of Qin returned with his army to his own country. Chen Zhen's stratagem had succeeded totally. Han had been sacrificed and the security of Chu thus assured.[7]

11.9 GENERAL TIAN JI'S HORSE RACE

In the Warring States period, General Tian Ji often held horse races with the Prince of Qi—and the stakes were high. The races consisted of three heats, each with a different horse from each contestant's stables. Tian Ji lost regularly.

One day he was in the company of Sun Bin, a descendant of Sun Tzu and himself a military writer and strategist. Sun Bin saw that Tian Ji's horses were inferior to those of the royal house. Yet Tian Ji's steeds, like the royal ones, could be divided into three classes: good, mediocre, and poor.

The next time a race with three heats was scheduled, Sun Bin advised Tian Ji to run the first heat with his poorest horse against the royal house's best, then in the second heat to use his best against the prince's mediocre animal, and finally to run his mediocre horse against the poorest of the royal house.

Tian Ji followed this advice. The result was that he had to

sacrifice one heat, the first, in which his poorest horse lost to the best of the royal house, but won the other two heats and thus emerged the victor of the race as a whole.

In this instance, letting the plum tree wither in place of the peach tree meant making a partial sacrifice as the price for an overall victory. If Tian Ji had pursued the usual course and tried to win all three heats with his inferior horses, he would inevitably have lost them all.

11.10   GENERAL TIAN JI'S BATTLE PLAN

The same Sun Bin made military use of Stratagem No. 11 after saving the state of Zhao by surrounding the capital of Wei (see Section 2.1, "With the Army into the Void"). By surrounding the city, Sun Bin forced the Wei army to give up its siege of Zhao and return to its home territory. On its hurried march homeward, the Wei army was divided into three columns: left, middle, and right. The left-hand column was the strongest, the middle column next, and the right-hand column the weakest.

General Tian Ji of the Qi army, accompanied by his adviser Sun Bin, wanted to apply the method he had learned in the horse racing episode (see Section 11.9, "General Tian Ji's Horse Race"), dividing his own army into three columns, strong, medium-strong, and weak, and attacking the enemy's strongest division with his own weakest, the enemy's medium-strong column with his own strongest, and the enemy's weakest division with his own medium-strength column.

But Sun Bin pointed out that this time the objective was not to win two out of three but to destroy as many enemy troops of Wei's generally superior forces as possible. He proposed that the weakest Qi troops attack the strongest Wei column and the medium Qi troops be used to attack Wei's medium-strong column. This yielded a segment of the battlefront where the enemy was superior and another where the two sides were well matched. But Sun Bin ordered those two Qi divisions merely to involve the two Wei columns in battle and to hold their own for a while. At the same time he used his own strongest troops in a lightning attack against the weakest enemy column, which was easily defeated. Next he hurried his elite troops to the central segment of the front, where they helped the medium-strong troops defeat the enemy's medium-strong column. Finally both victorious Qi divisions joined forces with the weakest Qi unit to decimate the strongest enemy column. The result was absolute superiority which secured the victory of the Qi army in the Battle of Guiling.

11.11   THE TANG EMPEROR'S TACTIC

According to an overview of Chinese history by Fan Wenlan,[8] a tactic similar to Tian Ji's was used by Tang Emperor Taizong. During the civil war that preceded the founding of the Tang Dynasty in the seventh century A.D., Taizong had amassed a wealth of experience which enabled him to judge at a glance which were the weak and strong positions of an enemy combat formation. He often used his own weaker units against the enemy's stronger and his own stronger units against the enemy's weaker. Pressed by the stronger enemy force, his own weaker unit would fall back a certain distance, while his own stronger unit would penetrate the weaker enemy's front line. Then Taizong's stronger unit would turn and attack the stronger enemy unit from the rear. Caught in a pincers movement between Taizong's strongest and weakest units, the enemy troops would usually be totally wiped out.

Here the "plum tree" that is initially sacrificed is the weaker division of Taizong's army. The "peach tree" that is saved is embodied by the ultimately victorious army.

11.12   THE RED ARMY VICTORY AT THE DNIEPER

In the autumn of 1943, during the Battle of the Dnieper, two commando units of the Soviet 381st Rifle Battalion crossed the river north of Kiev. After the raiding party had occupied a base on the far riverbank, they were discovered by the Germans, who saw through the Soviet plan and mobilized a large number of tanks for a counterattack. The Soviet command swiftly shifted gears to accommodate the new situation. Orders were given to the commando units that had crossed the river to hold on to their newly acquired base at all costs and to launch an offensive against the Germans from there, so that the enemy would think that the main Soviet force was concentrated on that bridgehead and would send the German troops against it.

Meantime, the main body of the 381st Rifles, which originally was supposed to have crossed the Dnieper north of Kiev after the advance units had paved the way, was regrouped, absorbed into the 38th Attack Unit, and sent to a new bridgehead south of Kiev. By the time the two commando units had been almost wiped out, the main Soviet force had already easily crossed the Dnieper at the other point and established more than twenty operational bases on the far bank.

This example, cited in the 1989 edition of the Beijing stratagem book, illustrates how a sudden emergency can necessitate recourse to Stratagem No. 11. The two Soviet commando units were the "plum tree" that was sacrificed to save the "peach tree," in this case the successfully operating Soviet main force.

11.13   THE SECRET WEAPON OF THE WEAKER PARTY

In their interpretations of Stratagem No. 11 as illustrated by the last few examples, Chinese stratagem books employ the following considerations:

a. The clash of forces in war is based on objective, generally measurable factors, which form the basis for each force's superiority or inferiority. But subjective factors play a significant role in how this superiority or inferiority is played out tactically on the battlefield.

b. Battle command based on objective factors (e.g., weapons stocks, technology, reconnaissance, etc.) should be supplemented by subjective factors (estimates of the situation, vigilance, speed of reactions, etc.). The proper application of one's own subjective factors may make it possible to transform objective inferiority into tactical superiority.

c. Accurate estimation of one's own strengths and weaknesses and those of the enemy is decisive for victory. Stratagem No. 11 can serve as a powerful secret weapon with which the weaker party may defeat the stronger. It is to be used whenever a situation arises in which some loss is unavoidable. At that point you sacrifice a part for the sake of the whole.

Highly relevant here are three of the ten secret rules of Chinese chess (called *Go* in Japanese)[9] formulated by Wang Jixin in the eighth century A.D.:

Yield some stones, if it helps you to gain the upper hand.
Accept a small loss of territory, if it makes possible a greater gain of territory.
Faced with certain dangers, you must give up some stones.

Stratagem No. 11, then, helps one to accept some partial losses in order to avoid a total loss and possibly to gain ultimate victory. The essence of the process is to choose the greater of two benefits and the lesser of two disadvantages.

11.14 CAPITALIST CONTRACTS WITH A PROLETARIAN GOVERNMENT

These thoughts about calculated military sacrifices naturally can be extended to civilian life as well. The theme of accepting a sacrifice was sounded, for example, in the following passage from a July 1979 commentary published in Canton's *Southern Daily* dealing with China's economic opening to the outside world:

> In order to transform China into a strong, modern socialist state in the not-too-distant future, we must pay a price, pay our "dues" [i.e., the "plum tree"]. From an overall, long-range standpoint, however, it is worthwhile to permit foreign investors to earn certain profits.

It is not difficult to find passages in the works of Lenin which touch on the idea of calculated losses. In August 1978, just before the official start of China's policy of opening (December 1978), the Beijing newspaper *Guangming Daily* cited the following passages from Lenin's writings:

> If we want trade with other countries—and we do want it, we recognize its necessity—what we are most interested in is to acquire from the capitalist countries as soon as possible those means of production (locomotives, machinery, electrical equipment) without which we cannot restore our own industries. . . . Let us bribe the capitalists with high profits. . . . To hell with those excessive profits [the "plum tree"]. We [the "peach tree"] will thus acquire what is important, with the help of which we will grow strong, finally get ourselves on our feet, and economically defeat Capitalism.[10]
> This is even more true in granting concessions. Without

in the least eliminating [its policy of] nationalization, the Workers' State leases certain mines, forests, oil fields, and other resources [the "plum trees"] to foreign capitalists, in order to obtain from them additional machinery and equipment which enable us [the "peach tree"] to accelerate the buildup of Soviet heavy industry.[11]

The concession-holder is a capitalist. He manages the enterprise in capitalist fashion, for the sake of profit; he signs contracts with the Workers' State in order to achieve profits that go beyond the ordinary, or to acquire raw materials which he could otherwise not obtain at all or only with great difficulty [the "plum tree"]. The Soviet State [the "peach tree"] thereby gains an advantage by developing its productive forces and increasing its quantitative output, whether immediately or in a very brief time.[12]

Some well-meaning Western observers have at times regarded the expansion of Chinese trade relations with the West as at least a partial "sellout." Their fear has been that China might lose its hard-won independence. But it may be fruitful to apply the perspective of Stratagem No. 11 to this matter.

The sacrifice, the "plum tree" being given to the insects to eat, could be interpreted in this context as a certain carefully calculated loss of Chinese economic independence, involving certain concessions and obligations undertaken to foreign trade partners. The great goal to be thereby won by China—the "peach tree" rescued in the formula for Stratagem No. 11— would be a degree of modernization not to be achieved without Western help. In the final analysis (as Lenin noted in the quotes cited above), the sacrifice turns out to be only an apparent loss, since it is more than adequately compensated by the ultimate gain.

This "sacrificial lamb" stratagem calls to mind the Confucian saying "A lack of tolerance in small things endangers great plans." In this case, however, in view of China's sheer size, the "small things" for which tolerance is needed may not be so small—at least from the standpoint of some of China's Western business partners.

Seize the Opportunity to Lead the Sheep Away

The Chinese characters	順	手	牽	羊
Modern Mandarin pronunciation	*shùn*	*shŏu*	*qiān*	*yáng*
Meaning of each character	easy (effortless)	hand	lead away	sheep

Applications   Alertly seize the opportunity that presents itself when a sheep happens to cross your path, and lead the animal away.

The stratagem of chance: Constant vigilance and psychological readiness to exploit opportunities to one's own advantage, whenever and wherever they arise.

The stratagem of serendipity.

The sheep, the eighth animal in the Chinese zodiac, was considered a symbol of filial piety in ancient China, because it kneels as it nurses from its mother. But it can also stand for *yang*, masculine power. Modern scholars maintain that the present-day Chinese character denoting "beauty" is derived from the characters for "large" and "sheep." A large sheep was regarded as tasty (i.e., "beautiful") food, much favored by the Chinese.

The formula used to describe Stratagem No. 12 appears in a number of literary sources, beginning with the thirteenth-century drama *Armed only with a whip, Wei Chigong takes the lance from Yuanji,* by Guan Hanqing. There, however, it is less a stratagem than a flowery description of how the protagonist disarms his enemy.

Another usage appears in chapter 99 of the popular vernacular novel *Water Margin,* where the phrase serves as a comment on how a priest, happening along at the right moment, uses his staff to trip up an escaping villain so that he can be caught.

In the sense most germane to our discussion, the phrase is used by Wu Cheng'en in his novel *Journey to the West,* in describing an incident involving the attempted theft of Buddhist monk Tripitaka's radiant robe (see Section 5.1, "The Radiant Robe"). Tripitaka's companion, the Monkey King, watches as some monks ignite firewood they have heaped around Tripitaka's room, and ponders:

> They want to kill us and steal the [radiant] robe. . . . I could attack them with my magic wand, but that would be too easy. One blow and they'd all be dead. But then my Master would surely accuse me of violence. So let's leave that. Instead I'll use the tactic "Seize the opportunity to lead the sheep away" and turn their own murder plans against them, so that they, instead of we, lose their lives.

Here the "sheep" is the murderous scheme hatched by the host monks in an attempt on the lives of Tripitaka and the Monkey King. The latter "borrows" it, in the sense of Stratagem No. 3 ("Kill with a borrowed knife"), in order to turn the tables. "Leading the sheep away" in this instance involves the comprehension and reworking of the enemy's insidious plan.

The essence of No. 12, then, is the alert recognition and exploitation of favorable opportunities and, in particular, of an enemy's suddenly revealed weaknesses. To quote a relevant Chinese proverb: "The crumbling of a great wall may start at an insignificant corner, and a branch may begin to rot at the forking of a twig."

12.1 XIANG YU VS. TIAN RONG

The 1989 edition of the Beijing stratagem book cites the following historical example.

As was recounted in Section 8.1, "The Burned-Out Wooden Path," in 206 B.C. Xiang Yu declared himself "Hegemon of Western Chu" and installed eighteen vassal lords in as many fiefdoms. But Tian Rong, who had expected to receive a fiefdom, was passed over. That same year he rebelled, killing or driving out several of the vassal lords and occupying three segments of the former state of Qi, which Xiang Yu had awarded to his own men. Xiang Yu then launched an attack in an effort to neutralize Tian Rong. At that point Liu Bang, who was supposed to have withdrawn to Hanzhong in the west, took advantage of Xiang Yu's momentary inability to attend to the western part of his realm and secretly marched his troops to Chencang, where they easily conquered three sections of the former state of Qin. (This episode is recounted in greater detail in Section 8.1.)

In this example the "sheep" is the temporary weakness of Xiang Yu, who is preoccupied with the campaign against Tian Rong. By "leading the sheep away" in the sense intended here, Liu Bang laid the groundwork for establishment of the long-lived Han Dynasty.

12.2   Zhao Calls for Help

In 354 B.C., King Hui of Wei hatched a plan to annex the state of Zhao to the north. A strong Wei army, commanded by General Pang Juan, marched into Zhao and easily reached its capital, Handan, which was surrounded in the year 353 B.C. At that point the King of Zhao sent a plea for help to the ruler of Chu, a powerful state situated south of Wei. But the Chu ruler hesitated to grant the requested aid. At a meeting of his advisers, Minister Zhao Xixu opposed helping Zhao, suggesting that they instead strengthen Wei, which would force Zhao to put up tough resistance until, ultimately, both states would be seriously weakened by the war and Chu could play the role of the "laughing third."

Jing She disagreed and instead advocated his own plan for weakening both Zhao and Wei. The King of Chu approved the plan, commissioned Jing She a general, and gave him command of a medium-size army, which quickly crossed the border between Chu and Zhao on the pretext of bringing help to Zhao. The Zhao commanders spread the word about Chu's aid among their own defending troops. But despite the brave resistance of

'seizing the opportunity to lead the sheep away.' Maybe Yiz-uomao is trying to use that stratagem against us. If we try to get up that canyon, we'll probably be wiped out."

The reconnaissance squad in this example is not being lured up Tiger Mountain but itself wants to get up there. The enemy spy is simply making alert use of this sudden chance to mislead his enemy and send them into a trap. But his attempt is foiled by the suspicions of Shao Jianbo, who suspects that the allegedly safe way up Tiger Mountain indicated by the spy is an application of Stratagem No. 12.

12.5 AN EMPEROR FLEES

Imprisoned by rebels in the imperial capital of Chang'an, Emperor Xian escapes at the first opportunity and heads for Luoyang. But a group of rebel horsemen pursue him and are getting very close. His old imperial adviser Dong Cheng says, "Let us scatter all our jewelry and treasures along the road."

And so it happens. All their precious goods are unloaded, including even the jade-studded crown and the Empress's necklaces. Seeing these treasures lying on the ground, the rebel soldiers stop their horses, leap from the saddle, and, ignoring their commander's angry orders to keep riding, feverishly begin gathering up the precious objects. What they stand to gain here is more than most of them would otherwise ever see in their lifetime. So they forget about pursuing the Emperor. They gladly take possession of the "sheep" encountered by the wayside—i.e., the tangible treasure in front of them—and thus lose sight of their original purpose.

This case brings to mind a deceptive maneuver often used in Chinese warfare. In order to seduce the enemy, you accumulate valuables (gold, silk, foodstuffs, etc.); if the enemy goes after the booty, his troops fall into disarray, and at that point your own forces, lying in ambush, can deal them a devastating blow.[1]

One must judge by the overall situation whether a newly

visible advantage (a "sheep") is really worthwhile and should be "led away." A mistake one must avoid is losing the important goal for the sake of something of lesser value. As one of the ten secret rules of the game of Go[2] puts it, "Yield smaller things to win the big one."

12.6 THE SEVEN VOYAGES OF ZHENG HE

According to a 1973 stratagem book published in Taipei,[3] an excellent example of the application of No. 12 is linked to the unknown fate of the Ming Dynasty's Jianwen Emperor (r. 1399–1403). After ascending the throne, the Emperor wanted to smash the power of feudal lords in his empire, to which end he dethroned several feudal princes and demoted them to the status of common subjects. Finally, the only one left was the ruler of the fiefdom of Yan, who organized a rebellion which led to a three-year civil war. The conflict ended when the Prince of Yan conquered the imperial capital, Nanking, and put the imperial palace to the torch. But what happened to the Jianwen Emperor remained a mystery. His disappearance was surrounded by legends, including one that said that he had escaped abroad disguised as a monk. His enemy, the Prince of Yan, became his successor and ruled as the Yongle Emperor from 1403 to 1424.

Noteworthy during Yongle's reign were the naval expeditions which he entrusted to the command of Zheng He, a Muslim eunuch from Yunnan. Between 1405 and 1433, Zheng He went to sea seven times. The first expedition (1405–7) involved more than three hundred ships and twenty-seven thousand seamen, and took Zheng He to the southern coast of Vietnam, to Java, Sumatra, Malacca, Ceylon (Sri Lanka), and Calicut (on the west coast of southern India). In the process, Zheng He intervened in the affairs of some other states, including a conflict over royal succession in a Javanese kingdom. During subsequent expeditions Zheng He made the kingdoms of Calicut, Cochin, and Ceylon vassals of the Ming empire, and Chinese troops intervened in the internal affairs of a sultanate in Sumatra. The longest expedition, in the years 1417–19, brought Zheng He to the Arabian Peninsula and the East African coast.

According to later depictions of Chinese history, the Emperor's purpose in mounting these expeditions was to gain prestige on the seas of East Asia. But the author of the Taipei stratagem book claims that such prestige was only "the sheep that fell by chance into China's hands," while the real goal of the expeditions—the destruction of the Jianwen Emperor, presumed to be living abroad—was never achieved. The political gains, says the Taipei author, were exploited later through the use of Stratagem No. 12, in order to mask the failure of the expeditions' real purpose. He supports this assertion by pointing out that never before had a Chinese Emperor felt the need to demonstrate his authority outside the boundaries of his realm. Moreover, if prestige had really been the main objective, the Emperor would certainly not have entrusted the foreign missions to a eunuch, since eunuchs were not considered the highest representatives of Chinese culture.

The biography of Zheng He included in the *Ming shi* (History of the Ming Dynasty), published in China in 1739, seems to support that assertion. It includes this statement:

> Emperor Chengzu (the Yongle Emperor) suspected that Emperor Hui (the Jianwen Emperor) had fled abroad; he wanted him pursued. He also wanted the splendor of his army to penetrate remote regions and to display China's wealth and power.

12.7 WAITING FOR THE PEACH

Zhao Zhongsen, a factory worker from Kaifeng, was quoted in the February 5, 1977, issue of the *People's Daily* with a variation on the original formulation of Stratagem No. 12:

> To work is to struggle. Again and again one encounters opposition and resistance. Responding to these is a serious

problem. There are people who depend entirely on "wait-and-see." They wait and wait for the problem to resolve itself. If waiting proves unsuccessful, they disclaim all responsibility by pointing out that they have done nothing. But if the problem clears up while they wait, they then "pluck the peach as they go" [i.e., they exploit the opportunity to take credit for themselves].

12.8 JUGGLING WITH THE FACTS

In an issue of the Beijing newspaper *Guangming Daily* published in December 1978, one Shi Qiao attacked the operations of the so-called Gang of Four and its supporters:

> They select individual facts from overall reality, isolate them from the rest, and then proceed to draw absurd conclusions from them. For example, one or two mistakes by an official are selected from a total of 100 acts, and by keeping silent about the 90-plus percent of positive achievements, the [isolated mistakes] are put forward as proof of his incompetence.

According to Shi Qiao, over the years this "counterrevolutionary trick" has led some Chinese comrades into the bad habit of juggling with facts. They emphasize how important it is to keep contact with reality but then confine themselves to "seizing the opportunity to steal the sheep that cross their path"—i.e., selecting a few fragmentary data and bits of documentation out of a whole range of material. "In this way they try to prove that they are in the right."

12.9 PROMOTING THE SHEEP

An editorial comment in the Heilongjiang periodical *Party Life* about strategies and tactics used in gaining or awarding promotions was deemed important enough to be picked up by the official *People's Daily* on April 3, 1984:

> In considering the promotion of young Party officials, one repeatedly encounters generally favored "sheep." These are people with a malleable character; they say "Yes" and "Amen" to everything, are mediocre in their morals and expertise, and never cause the leadership any difficulties. . . . Promotions fall readily into their laps. [Such people] are "raised up with a light hand."
>
> This is inappropriate . . . not because these individuals might cause disorder or unrest, but out of concern that they will contribute nothing, have insufficient qualifications . . . will undertake nothing and achieve nothing, indeed, that they will pull down the general level of achievement. It is obvious that someone who always says "Yes" and "Amen" and looks to the leadership before making a move, when he himself is elevated to a high post, will continue to look to the higher leadership [for guidance] and will continue to do only second- or third-class work. It is easy to "seize the opportunity to promote [such] a sheep," but that will not help to bring about a new beginning [for China].

12.10 SPOONS FLY WITHOUT WINGS

In the Chinese press, Stratagem No. 12 is often cited in connection with casual or petty theft, which aptly illustrates an interpretation of No. 12 made during the Qing period by Gu Zhangsi:

> "Seizing the opportunity to steal the sheep" means lying in wait for an opportunity to commit a theft.

In March 1983 the *People's Daily* complained that certain people "seize the chance to steal the sheep," the sheep here standing for publicly owned objects, or the intellectual property of others.

In June 1984 the Shanghai newspaper *Jiefang ribao* (Liberation Daily) used the phrase "Grabbing the chance to take a plate away" as a headline over the story of a teacher who, during lunch at a school picnic, said to his neighbor, "You can't buy this kind of plate at the market. I'm going to take it home."

"Stop people from 'stealing the sheep'!" was used by a regional Chinese newspaper as the title of an article in which an officer of a tobacco and alcohol company in a Shanghai district observed, "Lately many restaurants have noticed that quite a few of their spoons seem to have flown away without wings."

12.11   TAKING HOME THE ROPE

A necessary condition for the execution of Stratagem No. 12, says the Taiwanese stratagem book,[4] is that the "sheep" be led away unobserved and unhampered. If one is disturbed in the act, however, the ability to present a clever and plausible excuse is a further requisite for success of the stratagem. In this context, the 1969 Hong Kong stratagem book[5] offers the following anecdote:

> A cattle thief was brought before the judge and accused of theft. But the thief defended himself by saying, "Since when am I a cattle thief? I saw a piece of rope lying on the road. I picked it up and brought it home with me. The cow that was attached to the rope came along on its own."

The Taiwanese stratagem book describes the essence of No. 12 this way:

> The use of Stratagem No. 12 involves not concentrating one's attention on a single concern, but keeping one's field of vision wide open so that all objective opportunities for gain may be (*a*) recognized and (*b*) exploited.
>
> Even the smallest advantage, hardly worth mentioning, is not to be lightly dismissed. For small drops fill an ocean.

The value of the stratagem "Seize the opportunity to steal the sheep" lies not in snatching an individual sheep, but in the invisible gain generated by a permanent and fundamental alertness to every possibility—and that gain is of far greater value.

Beat the Grass to Startle the Snake

The Chinese characters	打	草	惊	蛇
Modern Mandarin pronunciation	*dǎ*	*cǎo*	*jīng*	*shé*
Meaning of each character	beat	grass	startle (frighten)	snake
Applications	Beat the bushes: The stratagem of indirect warning or deterrence. Intimidation: The "warning shot" stratagem. Provocation: The "agitation" stratagem.			

13.1 A SHOCKED CONSCIENCE

One of the oldest sources for the formulation of this stratagem is the work *Nan Tang jin shi* (Timely Facts from the Southern Tang Dynasty), written by Zheng Wenbao in A.D. 977. He reports that, during the Southern Tang Dynasty, a certain Wang Lu, a greedy and corrupt official, was prefect of Dangtu District. One day the people of his district submitted an official complaint against his secretary, accusing the man of being open to bribery, among other things. When Wang Lu read the accusations, which applied equally to him, he was deeply shaken. While in that mood he wrote, "You [i.e., the people of his district] have only beaten the grass, but I am already a frightened snake."

Tradition does not confirm whether the intimidation of Wang Lu was a deliberate aim of the complaint. In any case, his statement is the source for the standard formulation of Stratagem No. 13, which even found a place in Chinese Buddhist writings. In the *Chuan deng lu* (Notes on Handing on the Lamp), a collection of Buddhist teachings from the Song period, a Buddhist master says, "I beat the grass, and the snake takes fright." The allusion here is to the use of a stick or staff to administer "clouts of illumination" to novices, a Buddhist pedagogical practice reportedly introduced by the monk Deshan during the Tang period. The novice's body receiving the blows is the "beaten grass," while the novice's soul, thus rudely jolted out of its worldly dreams—or, to use Chinese imagery, dreams steeped in the "red dust" of this world—is the "snake."

13.2 EXECUTE ONE TO WARN A HUNDRED

Yin Wenggui, governor of Donghai during the reign of Emperor Yuan of the Han (74–49 B.C.), is still remembered in the People's Republic for his exemplary use of this stratagem in combatting crime. Tradition has it that Yin Wenggui was a conscientious official who kept strictly to the law. He always investigated personally all criminal cases within his territory and ordered that executions of those who had committed serious crimes be carried out during his own tours of inspection or during the assemblies of officials held every spring and autumn. Behind this was the intention of "warning a hundred by executing one." According to Yin Wenggui's biography in the *Han shu* (History of the Han Dynasty), officials and commoners alike were duly impressed by this procedure; overcome by fear, they changed their ways and began to lead better lives.

Yin Wenggui personally executed the prominent criminal Xu Zhongsun, whom Yin's predecessors had not dared to punish. This execution shook the entire province. In the words of the biography, "The whole area [under his governorship] was overcome with fear and trembling, and no one dared break the law anymore. The result was that peace and order returned to Donghai during Yin Wenggui's time in office."[1]

The "beating of the grass" in this instance is the exemplary punishment of an individual, by means of which other criminal elements ("frightened snakes") are deterred from further illegal acts.

13.3   KILL A CHICKEN TO FRIGHTEN THE MONKEY

Author Li Boyuan (1867–1906) uses a variant of Stratagem No. 13 in chapter 53 of his political novel *Guanchang xianxing ji* (Exposing the World of Officialdom). Wenming, the Manchurian governor-general of Jiangnan, is about to eat his lunch when a foreign visitor is announced, the consul of some other country. Why has he come? Some time ago Governor-General Wenming executed a soldier in his bodyguard. That in itself, says the visitor, is no great matter; His Excellency doubtless had his reasons. "But the sentence was carried out in the wrong place —that is, not on the parade ground but immediately next to my consulate!" expostulates the aggrieved foreign official. And he demands an explanation.

The governor-general is old but fortunately also very experienced and quick in his responses. "The Honorable Consul has not asked me," he replies after a brief pause for thought, "just who it was that I had executed. That soldier was a bad lot; he belonged to the Boxers and had taken part in all the harassment aimed at your worthy country and other countries in our nation's capital during the Boxer Rebellion."

"If he was a Boxer, he certainly deserved execution," says the consul. "But why did it have to take place right next to our consulate?"

Once again the governor-general pauses, and then responds, "There was ample reason. The execution was meant to serve as a warning to other Boxers. The Honorable Consul may not be aware that these rebels wanted to topple the Qing Dynasty and wipe out all foreigners. That is why I used this stratagem. I had the scoundrel executed next to your consulate so that his fellow conspirators could see what awaited them. There is an old saying: 'Kill a chicken to frighten the monkey.' I had only one soldier executed, but having seen it, the other Boxers will now no longer dare to molest your consulate or your countrymen."

The foreign consul erupts in loud laughter, praises the governor-general's foresight, and departs. After which the governor-general returns to his chair, weak with relief at having gotten himself out of a most unpleasant situation. For in reality the execution had been held next to the foreign consulate purely by oversight, with no particular motive behind it. His quick thinking and application of Stratagem No. 13, however, turned a potential embarrassment into something that redounded to his credit—an illustration of how the rhetorical use of stratagems (provided they are correctly applied, of course) can rescue someone from a tight spot.

As the governor-general presented it, the soldier executed next to the consulate was the "beaten grass," and his fellow Boxers the "startled snakes."

13.4 SURVEYING THE LAND AND WINNING A CONCUBINE

In many cases the application of No. 13 is not limited to intimidating the "snake" in order to neutralize it, so to speak. At another level of interpretation, according to other examples cited in the relevant Chinese literature, "beating the grass" can be used to agitate the snake and provoke it to certain actions.

In the brief tale "Surveying the Land and Winning a Concubine," recounted in the Prologue to this volume, the boy's brazen references to his eventual inheritance ("beating the grass") not only infuriate his aunt ("the snake") but, since she is determined not to let the boy inherit, provoke her into urging her husband to take a concubine, thus yielding what she had previously been denying him.

13.5   MARRIAGE AS A WAY OUT

The King of Zhongshan had two concubines, court ladies named Yin and Jiang. Both hoped to become queen, and they secretly fought each other bitterly. The rivalry between the ladies seemed to offer Counsellor Sima Xi an opportunity to gain wealth and influence. So he sent an emissary to Lady Yin, to deliver the following message anonymously:

> It is no easy thing to become queen. If you achieve it, you become the first lady in the land, with power and authority. But if you fail, not only your life but those of your family will be in danger. So either give up that goal or else take up the challenge. If the latter, do so only if victory is assured. Sima Xi is the only person who can guarantee your success.

Lady Yin thereupon paid a secret visit to Sima Xi, who enchanted her by laying out a clever plan. When he had finished, she thanked Heaven and Earth and said, "If you succeed, I will reward you richly," leaving him with an advance gift of money.

In keeping with his plan, Sima Xi sent a memorandum to the King with a plan for strengthening their own kingdom and weakening those of their neighbors. The monarch was highly intrigued and sent for Sima Xi to give him more precise details. The counsellor proposed that he be sent on a state visit to the kingdom of Zhao, where he would secretly study the military installations, topography, and political situation. Only after his return would he be in a position to work out a precise plan. His ruler gave him gold and gifts and sent him off to Zhao.

After the official talks with the ruler of Zhao, Sima Xi remarked during the confidential part of their discussion that he had heard great praises for the beauty of Zhao's women. "To be honest," he continued, "I've traveled all over the world, have seen beautiful women everywhere, but never have I found one to compare with Lady Yin in my own country. To me she seems like a fairy who has floated down to earth. No one can describe her beauty in words or depict it with brush and ink."

The King of Zhao's heart beat faster at these words, and he quickly asked, "Could she be acquired on my behalf?"

Growing thoughtful, Sima Xi replied, "I was just remarking on it. If Your Highness wishes the lady for himself, alas, I can be of no help. Although she is but a lady of the court, our King loves her passionately. But I beg Your Highness, do not speak of this to anyone or it may cost me my head."

The King of Zhao smiled craftily and let it be understood that he wanted that woman at all costs.

Sima Xi returned to Zhongshan and reported to his king. In doing so, he complained about the immorality and corruption of the King of Zhao, who thought only of women. "Incidentally," he added, "I have it from an impeccable source that the King of Zhao is secretly planning to get his hands on Lady Yin."

The ruler of Zhongshan roared his displeasure, but Sima Xi admonished him to keep calm and said, "At present, Zhao is stronger than we are. We could not conquer it. If the King of Zhao demands Lady Yin, we must hand her over. If we do not, Zhao would regard it as a hostile gesture and would attack and destroy us. Of course, if we do turn her over, we will become a laughingstock and people will say that we are so weak we are even forced to hand Your Highness's concubine to another ruler."

"What shall we do?" asked the King.

Calmly Sima Xi replied, "There is only one way out, and that is to formally make Lady Yin your queen. That will dampen Zhao's desire. No ruler has ever desired as his wife the queen of another land."

"Excellent!" said the King. And so Lady Yin easily became queen of the realm.

Here, Sima Xi's sexual titillation of the Zhao ruler may be regarded as "beating the grass," and the King of Zhongshan is the startled "snake." In this instance No. 13 serves as a stratagem of provocation by which the King of Zhongshan is provoked into marrying his concubine Lady Yin.

13.6   The Dangers of Yaoshan

In 627 B.C., Duke Mu of Qin decided to invade the remote state of Zheng. Minister Jian Shu warned against a campaign with tired troops in a distant territory, but the ruler ignored him. Jian Shu sadly accompanied the departing army a little way along the road and warned General Meng Mingshi about Yao-shan (Mount Yao), which would have to be dealt with on the homeward march and where there was danger of an ambush. But the general, self-confident and high-spirited, paid no attention to the adviser's warning.

Having failed in his campaign, General Meng Mingshi returned over Mount Yao without sending any advance scouts ahead of the main army. All he did was divide his troops into four columns, which marched one behind the other. The forward column was ambushed by a small squad of enemy soldiers, who quickly retreated, however. Without further scouting the territory, Meng Mingshi marched his troops into a narrow valley, until they were completely surrounded by enemy units waiting to attack. The Qin army was wiped out completely.

This incident was first recounted in Sima Qian's *Records of the Historian* and retold in the 1989 Beijing stratagem book. It illustrates the possibly catastrophic consequences of ignoring the stratagem "Beat the grass to frighten the snake." In this case, that tactic would have meant sending an advance party ahead to lure the waiting enemy out of ambush, instead of marching an entire army into unknown territory without first scouting the situation.

13.7 THE CAUTIOUS SIMA YI

After the fall of the Han Dynasty in A.D. 220, three kingdoms were formed in China: Wei in the north, Wu in the southeast, and Shu in the southwest. As we have already seen, Shu was founded by Liu Bei, a descendant of the imperial Han clan. In an effort to restore the rule of the Han Dynasty over the entire empire, Shu undertook several campaigns against Wei between A.D. 225 and 234.

In the year 231, Shu's Prime Minister Zhuge Liang launched the fifth campaign against Wei. Once again his opponent was General Sima Yi. For a long time the two armies faced each other on Mount Qishan without engaging in combat, since Sima Yi preferred avoiding a direct confrontation. Suddenly the news reached Zhuge Liang that Wei had come to an agreement with the kingdom of Wu and was taking advantage of Zhuge Liang's absence to attack the western part of Shu. In order to avoid becoming entangled in a two-front war, Zhuge Liang sounded the retreat. Sima Yi learned of this from spies, though he had heard nothing as yet about the alliance between Wu and Wei. Suspecting that Zhuge Liang was employing the stratagem known as *yin she chu dong,* or "lure the snake from its hole," he refrained at first from pursuing the Shu troops and rejected the advice of Zhang He, one of his unit commanders, that they give chase immediately. Only when new intelligence reached him about the Shu army's withdrawal did Sima Yi leave his mountain stronghold. However, fearing that Zhuge Liang might have laid a trap for him, he decided to employ the stratagem of "Beat the grass to frighten the snake."

This time when Zhang He pressed to launch the pursuit, Sima Yi agreed. But, with Stratagem No. 13 in mind, he allowed him to take only a few thousand cavalry troops with him, keeping the main force to march behind them. Having waited impatiently for a direct clash with the Shu army, Zhang He rode furiously ahead with his men. But, as Sima Yi had suspected, Zhuge Liang had laid a trap in the valley into which hotheaded

Zhang He now galloped. The latter did not suspect that he had been chosen by Sima Yi as the "stick" with which to startle the "snake" out of hiding. When Zhang He had penetrated deep into the valley, a group of Shu soldiers suddenly sprang out of the woods and their leader, Wei Yan, challenged Zhang He to combat. After only a few passes, however, Wei Yan turned tail and appeared to flee. Without hesitation, Zhang He and his troops pursued the apparently retreating Shu. As darkness fell, the Wei vanguard rode through a ravine. Suddenly tree limbs came crashing down from all sides and Shu soldiers waiting in ambush showered the Wei troops with arrows, wiping out all of them.

When the news reached Sima Yi, he congratulated himself for having used Stratagem No. 13 and thus having kept his main fighting force intact.[2]

In dealing with No. 13, books on the 36 Stratagems sometimes cite a statement from the chapter on "Maneuvering Armies" in Sun Tzu's classic *The Art of War*:

> When an army is traveling, if there is hilly territory with many streams and ponds or depressions overgrown with reeds, or wild forests with a luxuriant growth of plants and trees, it is imperative to search them carefully and thoroughly. For these afford stations for bushwackers.[3]

13.8 THE BATTLE ON KOREA'S CHONGDONG PLATEAU

In the Beijing stratagem book reissued in 1989,[4] reference is made to the Chinese army's attack on the northwestern highlands of Chongdong during the Korean War. The enemy was dug into positions in two tunnels and a large number of bunkers and dugouts. The Chinese attackers had two regiments, supported by some artillery and a few tanks. On the evening of

November 4, 1951, two Chinese squads made a sudden advance and fired at the enemy from both flanks. A bitter twenty-minute exchange of fire forced the enemy to leave their fortifications and enter the fray. Once the enemy's troop strength and firepower had become visible, the two advance squads pulled back quickly and the Chinese opened up with rocket launchers, field artillery, howitzers, and tanks, inflicting heavy losses on the enemy.

Here, the initial attack by the two advance squads is the equivalent of "beating the grass" to lure the enemy, like the snake, out of its hiding place.

13.9   FIRING AT DUMMIES

According to the Beijing stratagem book, when the British and French launched their landing operations at Port Said, on the Suez Canal, in November 1956, they first sent wood-and-rubber dummies down by parachute. The Egyptians, believing they were real paratroopers, opened fire with their land-based artillery. Then Egyptian soldiers were sent out to pin down and kill the paratroopers. In this way the Egyptians revealed what they had in the way of artillery and troops. With this information in hand, the French and British sent in their aircraft and dealt the Egyptians heavy losses.[5]

13.10   THE DREAM OF THE HUNDRED FLOWERS

In its chapter on No. 13, the Hong Kong stratagem book cites the following example:

In 1957 the Communist Party of China wanted to uncover all elements hostile to it inside Party ranks, the bureaucracy, and cultural circles. To that end, the campaign known as "Let a hundred flowers bloom" was launched, ostensibly to create an atmosphere in which diverse opinions could be freely expressed. There was an enormous reaction throughout the country. From peasant villages to major cities, from public school teachers to university professors, countless Chinese gave vent to their disaffection. The movement did not last long, however. It was quickly broken off and followed by renewed repression aimed at liquidating the "right." Many of those who had openly expressed themselves during the days of the "hundred flowers" movement now suffered the consequences.

Years later, the use of that ruse to "startle the snakes" out of their hiding places was still a source of bitterness to many Chinese. In November 1979 the Beijing newspaper *Guangming Daily* wrote:[6]

> There are [still] people who regard the Party norm "Let a hundred flowers bloom, let a hundred schools contend" as a stratagem, employed to "lure the snake out of its hole."

In 1986, the thirtieth anniversary of the "hundred flowers" movement was celebrated throughout the People's Republic. Even today, the "hundred flowers" party norm is still upheld, in the sense of a certain degree of pluralism in literature and the arts and sciences—limited, of course, by a strict insistence that the Party's absolute authority not be endangered. At the same time, this party norm also continues to be applied as a stratagem, insofar as it repeatedly encourages some "snakes" to leave their "holes," whereupon they are promptly caught by the Party.

13.11 THE RETURN OF THE MONKEY KING

"Get out of my sight!" said the monk Tripitaka to his companion, the Monkey King Sun Wukong. With those words, Tripitaka dismounted from his horse and told his other companion, Sha the Sand Monk, to bring him paper and a brush. Then he drew a little water from a nearby stream, wet his ink stone and rubbed it against a rock to get some ink, and wrote out a certificate of dismissal on the spot.

"Mangy ape! Take this paper. I don't want you as a disciple anymore. If I ever set eyes on you again, I'll cast you down into the deepest cavern of Hell!"

The Monkey King hastily took the document and said, "Master, there's no need to swear an oath. I'm going!" He bowed reverentially before Tripitaka, and then gave a bit of advice to the Sand Monk.

"If during the journey a monster comes and overpowers the Master, you need only tell the monster that I, the Monkey King, was the Master's first disciple. Since my abilities are known to all fiends and monsters, none will dare to do the Master any harm."

The Monkey King had every reason to be self-confident. Born in ancient times of a Heaven-fertilized stone egg, he had become ruler of the Monkey Kingdom to the east, in the middle of the Great Sea, on an island named Flower-Fruit Mountain. A Patriarch taught him the secret of immortality and inducted him into all the magic arts. The Monkey King was able to change his form at will, to multiply himself, and even to make himself invisible. He was master of all the elements and could fly on the clouds across thousands of miles in a twinkling. His diamond pupils saw through everything and everyone. As a weapon he carried a huge iron cudgel with golden hooks on all sides, and he used it without hesitation whenever he spotted a monster, no matter in how pleasant a form it appeared. The cudgel would grow to monstrous proportions whenever he commanded it to do so, or it would shrink to the size of a needle, which he could then stick behind his ear for safekeeping. Once, however, he had sent all the Heavens into an uproar with his unruly behavior, and none of its inhabitants could stop him. So the Heavenly King had had no choice but to acknowledge his power and give him the rank of "Great Sage, Equal to Heaven."

But the Monkey King continued to misbehave. He ate fruit from the Immortal Peach Garden which he had been entrusted to supervise, drank of the Heavenly Nectar without permission, and gobbled down all the Pills of Life concocted by Lao-tse. It was only the Buddha himself who managed to imprison the Monkey King under the Mountain of the Five Elements. He remained there for five centuries, until he finally repented of his former behavior and was freed in order to help the monk Tripitaka to obtain the sacred scriptures from the West.

Now Tripitaka wanted nothing more to do with him. "I am a good monk," he said. "Never again will the name of a villain such as you cross my lips. Now get out of here!"

Seeing that his Master would not relent, the Monkey King took his departure, somersaulted onto a cloud which instantly transported him thousands of miles away, and headed for his old kingdom on the Flower-Fruit Mountain.

What had brought things to this pass?

On his journey westward to India to seek the sacred scriptures of Buddhism, Tripitaka, who was traveling with his two stalwarts Sha the Sand Monk and Zhu Bajie the pig, as well as the Monkey King, had reached the mighty White Tiger Mountain, where the demon Lady White Bone lived. She had already heard of the monk Tripitaka and knew that anyone who ate the flesh of that pious man would gain immortality. To get near him, the demon disguised herself as a charming girl and offered the hungry monk food. With his diamond pupils, the Monkey King immediately recognized the demon for what she was and, raising his great cudgel, dealt the "girl" a mighty blow. But the demon knew some magic, too, and just before the blow landed she slipped away into the air, leaving behind her the horribly mauled corpse of what apparently had been a beautiful maiden.

Horrified by the Monkey King's brutality, Tripitaka was prepared to dismiss him from his service but was softened by his pleading and forgave him. The demon, however, did not give up. She came back down from the cloud on which she had been recovering, took on the form of an old woman, and walked down the mountain toward the pilgrims, crying bitterly. Seeing this figure, Zhu Bajie cried to Tripitaka, "That is doubtless the mother of the girl killed by the wicked monkey."

Once again the Monkey King saw through the demon's disguise and swung his cudgel. And once again the demon left a false corpse behind, in the form of the old woman. Tripitaka was so dismayed that he fell off his horse. Once more he was on the verge of dismissing the Monkey King but was persuaded to forgive him again.

The third time was too much. The demon came down the mountain in the form of an old man with white hair, reciting Buddhist sutras. His daughter had disappeared, he said, and now his wife as well, and there had been nothing left for him but to take to the road himself, to see what had happened to them.

The Monkey King, seeing through the ruse, ordered the local spirits and the mountain god to position themselves in the air around the spot, so that the demon could not get away. And this time his blow not only smashed the demon's external form, it truly destroyed the she-monster forever. All that remained was her original substance: a heap of white bones. Seeing them, Tripitaka was prone to believe the Monkey King's insistence that he had indeed killed a demon. But his pig-shaped disciple Bajie shouted, "It's murder! He was afraid of your punishment, Master, and so he turned the old man's body into a heap of bones to deceive you."

Tripitaka believed Zhu Bajie, and so he banished the Monkey King—which is where we began this tale.

Now the monk, his two remaining disciples, and his white horse cross White Tiger Mountain and come to the Black Pine Forest. There Tripitaka is overcome by hunger. Dismounting from his horse, he sends Bajie on a search for vegetarian nourishment. Zhu Bajie hikes for ten miles or more without encountering a living soul and eventually sinks down into the grass and falls asleep. Since his emissary fails to return, Tripitaka sends Sand Monk to look for him.

Left alone in the forest, Tripitaka cannot sit still for long and sets out to look around him. Soon he comes to a golden pagoda, not knowing that it is inhabited by the Yellow Robe Fiend. The fiend takes him prisoner, but thanks to the intercession of the

Third Princess of the Precious Image Kingdom, he is released. This princess had been captured by the Yellow Robe Fiend thirteen years earlier and forced to become his wife. Now she secretly gives Tripitaka a letter to take to her parents—which is why she so warmly urges the fiend to let the monk go.

Arriving in the Precious Image Kingdom, Tripitaka gives the letter to the King, who, having read it, asks the monk to go back and subjugate the fiend. But Tripitaka is incapable of such a thing. His two disciples Sand Monk and Zhu Bajie, who have some magical abilities, offer to go instead. But they have overestimated their abilities. Sand Monk is taken prisoner, and Bajie runs off in the middle of the fight with the fiend and hides in the grass.

The Yellow Robe Fiend now transforms himself into a handsome youth and thus gains entry to the court of the Precious Image Kingdom, with the pretext of asking acceptance as the King's son-in-law. Before the King's eyes, he changes Tripitaka into a tiger, claiming that he is in fact a tiger who has only assumed the form of a monk. Tripitaka is caught and caged.

Left alone, Tripitaka's white horse—really a small dragon king who had been changed into Tripitaka's horse as a punishment for his crimes—hears news of his Master's fate and regains his original form in order to save him. Seeing the fiend alone in the throne chamber, he turns himself into a lithe young court lady who serves the fiend a great deal of wine and then tries to kill it while performing a sword dance. A battle ensues, in which the fiend injures the dragon-horse-lady with a candlestick. Weakened, the dragon manages to escape into the water of the palace moat and that same night meets with Zhu Bajie, who has returned. After some effort, the dragon persuades Zhu Bajie to set out for the Flower-Fruit Mountain, where he is to get the Monkey King to return, defeat the fiend, and rescue Tripitaka.

Zhu Bajie, going on this mission reluctantly, tries to lure the Monkey King back with a lie. He has been sent by Tripitaka, he claims, who misses the Monkey King and wants him to return. (It is Zhu Bajie's idea that, if the Monkey King goes back and sees his former Master in desperate straits, he will surely help.) But the Monkey King shows Bajie his realm, seems very content, and is not inclined to return. So Zhu Bajic leaves the Monkey Kingdom in failure. Hardly has he gone a few miles, however, when he turns around and shouts curses back at his former companion. Spies report this to the Monkey King, who angrily has Bajie arrested and brought before him. Now Zhu Bajie has no choice but to reveal his real purpose in coming.

"The white dragon-horse said that you are good, honorable, and noble. A noble soul does not cling to old hurts, he said, and you'd surely be willing to rescue our Master. I plead with you, Elder Brother. Remember the saying 'He who is your teacher for one day is your father for a lifetime.' For the sake of Heaven, come back with me and save Tripitaka!"

"Fool," cries the Monkey King. "Didn't I tell you when I left that, if ever some demon should pursue our Master, you were to say that I, Sun Wukong, am his chief disciple? Why didn't you heed my advice?"

Zhu Bajie says to himself, "Asking a general to act is not as good as provoking a general to act. So . . . I'll provoke him." And aloud he says, "Elder Brother, it would have been better if I had never mentioned you. As soon as I did, the demon became livid with rage."

"What did you tell him?"

"I said, 'Fiend, don't be so impudent. Leave our Master in peace. Do you know who my Elder Brother is? Sun Wukong, the Monkey King, whose magic powers can overcome any monster. If he should turn up here, you wouldn't find an inch of ground in which to rest your corpse.'

"But hearing this, the fiend grew even more furious and started to curse. 'Sun Wukong, is it? You don't think I'm afraid of him, do you? Let him come. I'll skin him alive, strip his muscles, gnaw his bones, and devour his heart. He may be a skinny monkey, but I'll cut him up into little pieces and fry him in oil.'"

Hearing this, the Monkey King springs up wildly, scratches his cheeks, pulls his earlobes, and howls, "Who was it who had the nerve to speak thus of me?"

"Calm yourself, Elder Brother," says Zhu Bajie. "It was the Yellow Robe Fiend who spoke of you with such disrespect. I am merely repeating his words."

"Rise, dear Brother," says Monkey. "I don't really want to leave here, but since the fiend has had the temerity to abuse me this way, I cannot let him go unpunished. I'm coming with you. Five hundred years ago I turned Heaven upside down, and all the celestial spirits bowed before me, respectfully calling me 'Great Sage.' Now an uncouth demon dares to slander me behind my back! Well, he'll pay dearly for it. I'll catch him and cut him up into mincemeat. And after taking my revenge, I'll return home again."

"Fine, Brother," says Zhu Bajie hurriedly. "You come with me now and take care of the fiend. After that, whether you return or not is entirely up to you."

Thus it was that Zhu Bajie, in *Journey to the West,* applied the stratagem of provocation, formulated in the words "Asking a general to act is not as good as provoking a general to act," and succeeded in persuading the Monkey King to return to earth and rescue Tripitaka.

Ji jiang ji, also known as *Ji jiang fa,* the stratagem of "provoking the general," is virtually identical with No. 13. Some form of provocation is used to emotionally motivate another person to perform an act which, under normal circumstances —if merely asked or cajoled—he would not perform. An appeal is made to his vanity or pride, so that he loses his head, or else (as a Beijing University professor suggested) he is persuaded to a belief in his own omnipotence or the inevitability of his plans. Alternatively, feelings are aroused in him of anger, shame, honor, jealousy, envy, etc. In any case, the matter is handled in such a way that the person does not notice how he is being manipulated by his opponent, and under the latter's guidance he does what the provocateur wants him to do—as in the next case.

13.12   THE PAVILION OF THE BRONZE SPARROW

As the army of Cao Cao, ruler of northern China, advanced, many voices were raised in the eastern kingdom of Wu calling for capitulation. General Zhou Yu, who served as the leading foreign policy adviser to the ruler of Wu, inclined toward accepting Cao Cao's rule. Wu's ruler was undecided and waited for Zhou Yu's decision in the matter. War or peace depended on that one man.

Suddenly, Zhou Yu received a visit from Zhuge Liang, commander of Liu Bei's army. Shortly before, Liu Bei had paid three visits to Zhuge Liang's mountain hut [see Section 16.13, "Three Visits to the Thatched Hut"] to recruit his help in strengthening Shu in southwestern China. Having thrown in his lot with Liu Bei, Zhuge Liang realized that if the kingdom of Wu were to fall into Cao Cao's hands, Cao Cao would then become so powerful that his realm would sooner or later envelop all of China. Such a fatal development had to be prevented if Liu Bei were to have any chance of achieving his ambitious objectives.

At first Lu Su, a military adviser to the court of Wu who was accompanying Zhuge Liang, pressed Zhou Yu to agree to a war against Cao Cao. But Zhou Yu replied that he had no wish to oppose Cao Cao, who was, after all, acting in the name of the Han Emperor. He was also very strong. An attack against him was simply too risky. "In my opinion," said Zhou Yu, "war would mean certain defeat, while conciliation will bring peace."

"You are mistaken," stammered Lu Su. "Our land has been ruled by the same dynasty for three generations. It cannot be suddenly ceded to another. Why do you adopt the stance of a weakling?"

"If the people of this land were to be devastated by war as a result of my decision, I would earn their hatred. So I am determined to advise our ruler to yield to Cao Cao."

"But you are underestimating the power of our ruler, and the favorable topography of our land. If Cao Cao attacks us, it is highly questionable whether he will attain his objective."

The two men continued to dispute one another for a time, while Zhuge Liang sat there smiling. Finally Zhou Yu asked him the reason for his smile, whereupon Zhuge Liang replied, "I am smiling at your interlocutor, Lu Su. He does not realize what hour has struck."

"Sir, what do you mean by that?" inquired Lu Su.

"I mean," said Zhuge Liang, "that Zhou Yu is quite right in advocating capitulation."

"Clearly, Zhuge Liang understands the signs of the times," interjected Zhou Yu. "He agrees with me."

Said Lu Su, "Is that really your opinion, Zhuge Liang?"

Zhuge Liang responded, "Capitulation means safety for the women and children; it will bring wealth and high position . . ."

Lu Su broke in angrily, "Do you really wish my Master to kneel before that rebel Cao Cao?"

Zhuge Liang replied, "I have a stratagem. If we apply it, you need give no sheep and no kegs of wine as gifts to Cao Cao nor cede him any land or seals of high office. It will not even be necessary to cross the river to meet him. All you would have to do is send a boat with two people in it to Cao Cao. As soon as he has these two individuals in his grasp, his army will lay down its weapons, roll up its flags, and withdraw."

"With which two persons could one achieve such a huge effect?" inquired Zhou Yu.

"Two people who are as expendable in this populous land as two leaves from a great tree or two grains of corn from a granary. Yet, if Cao Cao could get his hands on them, he would gladly depart."

"Well, about which two people do you speak?" Zhou Yu insisted impatiently.

Finally, Zhuge Liang explained. "When I was living in the Longzhong Mountains,[7] I heard that Cao Cao had had a pavilion built along the Zhang River and called it the Pavilion of the Bronze Sparrow. It is a most magnificent place. Cao Cao then searched out the most beautiful women in the land and bade them take up residence there. He is, as you must know, a great womanizer. For a long time now, he has known about two beauties who live in this area. They both come from the Qiao family. So beautiful are they, that at the sight of them fish sink thoughtfully beneath the waves, birds tumble from the skies, the moon hides its face, and blossoms blush with shame. Cao Cao has sworn that he lusts after only two things in this world: the imperial throne, and the two beauties named Qiao, with whom he hopes to amuse himself in his old age at the Pavilion of the Bronze Sparrow. According to his oath, having attained those two goals he will go to his grave one day without regrets. The real motive for his advance upon this land is possession of those two women!"

Turning now to Zhou Yu, Zhuge Liang continued, "One could approach the father of those two beautiful sisters, buy them from him for a thousand gold pieces, and send them across the river to Cao Cao. Once he has achieved the real objective of this war, he will withdraw satisfied. Why not employ this little stratagem?"

"What proof do you have that Cao Cao feels such fiery lust for the Qiao sisters?"

Zhuge Liang replied, "At his behest, his son Cao Zhi composed the 'Ode to the Pavilion of the Bronze Sparrow.' The entire poem deals only with Cao Cao's burning desire for the imperial throne and for the two Qiao women. I believe I could recite the poem by heart, if you wish it, since I admire it for its beauty."

"Go ahead, try it," said Zhou Yu.

So Zhuge Liang recited the "Ode to the Pavilion of the Bronze Sparrow"—a lengthy poem in which Cao Cao sings of his anticipated lusty life after gaining the imperial throne, sporting with the two beauties in the wondrous pavilion. Or so, at least, it seemed to Zhou Yu, as he heard lines such as these:

> *Two towers rise to the left and right,*
> *one called Jade Dragon and the other Gold Phoenix,*
> *united with the two Qiaos, in the east*
> *and in the south, in the thicket of desire.*

Zhou Yu listened to the entire poem and then suddenly sprang up in fury. Shaking his fist toward the north, the direction from which Cao Cao's army approached, he thundered, "You old rebel, you humiliate me too deeply now!"

Zhuge Liang also jumped up, and inquired, "Why are you so excited about two common women?"

"You clearly do not know, sir," said Zhou Yu, "that the elder of the two sisters is the widow of Sun Ce, father of our present ruler, and that the younger is my wife."

Zhuge Liang pretended vast astonishment and said, "No indeed, I did not know. What a fatal error I have made. What a fatal error!"

Now Zhou Yu intoned, "Either I or the old rebel will have to die. We cannot both continue to live. That I swear!"

This episode is drawn from *The Romance of the Three Kingdoms*. Cao Cao had indeed built a Pavilion of the Bronze Sparrow. But in the poem which Zhuge Liang recites, the passage dealing with the "two Qiaos" and their being united in the "thicket of desire" actually referred to two suspension bridges connecting the towers to one another. For one of the meanings of the word *qiao* in Chinese is "bridge." Zhuge Liang exploited the similarity of sound between the word and the family name Qiao to make Zhou Yu believe that the poem (which, incidentally, appears in no source other than the novel itself) referred to the two sisters. By so doing he kindled the general's anger and so arrived at his goal indirectly: winning Zhou Yu's support for a campaign against Cao Cao. (See Section 9.1, "The Victorious Observer," for the outcome of that campaign.)

13.13 HOW A HISTORY LESSON WON
THE CHAMPIONSHIP

In his handbook on sports tactics (published in Beijing, 1985), world table tennis champion Zhuang Zedong relates the following:

> It was evident before the twenty-sixth Ping-Pong World Championships [in Beijing, 1961] that the finals would be between China and Japan. The Japanese were favored by the public and the experts, and China was not given much of a chance. Several members of our team were very fearful, and a dark shadow lay over my heart as well. Before the final matches I was sitting on a stool, torturing myself with the question of how to beat the Japanese. Suddenly I heard a soft voice address me. I looked up and saw an old sports official. I quickly rose and offered him my seat. But, unexpectedly, he did not sit down. There was an intense, gloomy look on his face, the muscles of which kept working. I wondered why this old master, who usually expressed nothing but good cheer and sunshine, had such a dark visage that day. As I stood there, he stretched his arms out, rolled up his sleeves, and began to speak. He talked about the scandalous humiliations our nation had suffered in the past from imperialist aggressors. At that time, he said, the great powers saw us as "the Sick Man of Asia." Time and again we were the victims of ruthless attacks. "But today," he added, "as competitors on behalf of the Chinese people, it is incumbent upon us to win honor for our nation and increase its prestige in the world."
>
> When he had finished speaking, he threw me a brief glance and then silently left. Suddenly, my fearful feelings had vanished totally. An unparalleled élan surged through me and I was determined to give my all for victory. This energy did not fail me even when I was unexpectedly called on to play two final matches against the Japanese. In retrospect I see that the fighting spirit which the old sports leader evoked in me was a decisive factor in our triumph over Japan.

In this instance the "provoked general" is the Ping-Pong player Zhuang Zedong. The old sports official pulled him out of the emotional depths by inciting his patriotic emotions. In the course of that year's world championship matches, a Chinese team won the crown for the first time, and in the men's singles Zhuang Zedong defended the title that had been won by a Chinese player in 1959 in Dortmund, Germany.

13.14   THE TRICKY HARE

Hare went to God
and asked him for a new trick.
God spoke:
"Good. I have heard your request.
But first you must prove yourself.
You will bring me a live python.
You will bring me the fresh milk
of a buffalo cow.
You will bring me a gourd full of flies.
You will bring me a gourd full of mosquitoes.
When you have done all that,
you will bring me a live hyena.
Then I will add a new trick
to those you already know."
Hare went forth.
He took a gourd, went with it to the buffalo cow,
and said,
"This fills it, this fills it not,
this fills it, this fills it not."
"What are you saying?" asked the buffalo cow.
Hare answered, "If I were to milk
one of your udders, it would not suffice
to fill my gourd."
Said the cow, "Just wait, you'll see
how wrong you are."

And Hare began to milk.
When the gourd was full, he closed it.
Then he went to the flies and said,
"This fills it, this fills it not.
This fills it, this fills it not."
The flies replied,
"Good Brother Hare, what are you talking about?"
"This gourd says that if all of you fly into it,
you would not fill it up."
They buzzed, metemetemete, *and flew into the gourd.*
Hare closed it up, menemeneku,
and went on his way.
He came to the mosquitoes and said,
"This fills it, this fills it not,
this fills it, this fills it not."
The mosquitoes asked: "Hey, Big Brother Hare,
what're you up to?"
"This gourd says that if all of you fly into it,
you would not fill it up."
"Well, let's see," they said,
and they flew into the gourd and filled it.
Hare closed it up, menemeneku,
and went on his way.
He cut himself a big stick.
The python asked, "Hey, what's happening?
What's up with you, Little Brother Hare?"
"This stick wants to prove that it's
bigger than you," said Hare.
"Fine, let's measure," said the python.
And when it had stretched itself out
alongside the stick,
Hare tied them together, krrr,
put the stick and the snake over his shoulder,
and carried them away.
Then he went to the hyena.
The hyena asked, "Hey, where you goin'
with all that stuff?"

Said Hare, "We're going together!
If you can carry me,
I'll climb on your back with all my things
and we'll go.
They've killed a great steer,
we'll go there and eat some meat together."
The hyena said, "What?"
"It's true," said Hare.
"Okay, I'll follow you."
"No, I'll climb on your back."
"Right. Get on!"
Hop. *Hare jumped onto the hyena's back,*
grabbed its short mane,
and quickly put a bridle around its snout.
Then Hare began to sing.
They marched and marched
until they came to the Great God.
Hare offered God everything he had collected.
The Great God said, "Leave everything here.
Go and bow down."
Hare ran a distance off and bent his back.
The Great God took a heavy object and—wu!—
threw it at Hare.
Hare jumped up and stood stock-still.
"Ha!" said the Great God,
"if I would teach you another trick,
you'd trick me right off my throne."[8]

In this tale Hare seeks greater wisdom, an increase in his knowledge of stratagems, in order to lord it over the other creatures.
Interestingly enough, it is God he approaches to teach him new
tricks. God sets him some "impossible tasks." Hare uses various
stratagems to accomplish them. In each case he opens with No.
13, the stratagem of provocation, by uttering arcane phrases
which arouse his victim's curiosity. Then he uses No. 13 again
to provoke the other's self-esteem. The victim, of course, tries
to prove that he can do what Hare has claimed he cannot—

and promptly falls into Hare's trap. In the case of the hyena, Hare uses Stratagem No. 7, "Create something from nothing," and then uses the image of the slaughtered steer as the "brick" (see Stratagem No. 17) with the aid of which he gains the "jade"—that is, the prize, the hyena itself.

Finally, the Great God sets Hare one last task: to run off, bowing as he goes. Then God throws something heavy at Hare, who, hearing the sound of its passage through the air, jumps up and then stands absolutely still—thus violating the divine commandment but probably saving his own life in the process. In doing so, Hare has passed the final test: He has remained alert even in the presence of God. But here the African deity refuses to teach him any more tricks, because with greater wisdom Hare would become godlike and thus dangerous to God (just as Adam and Eve, having eaten of the Tree of Knowledge of Good and Evil, had become, as God says in Genesis, "like one of us"). One of the aspects of this African tale is to present the Great God as the highest source and wielder of stratagems.[9]

13.15   RHETORICAL PROVOCATION

The stratagem book published in Taipei in 1986[10] recommends No. 13 as a rhetorical tactic. It suggests that, in certain critical conversations, one should not talk incessantly oneself but rather provoke one's opponent with a few brief remarks so that he begins to speak. The opponent's stream of verbiage should thereafter be interrupted only with a few provocative words, in order to deduce from his pattern of reactions what he really thinks about the matter under dispute. On no account, continues the author of the Taipei book, should one suddenly embark on a lengthy sermon oneself, because that would give the opponent a chance to return to quiet contemplation and reserve. In this usage, "beating the grass" would be using a few provocative remarks, while the "startled snake" is the opponent who is provoked into excessive speech.

The philosopher Schopenhauer offers another variant of No. 13 when used rhetorically:

> Contradiction and contention irritate a man into exaggerating his statement. By contradicting your opponent you may drive him into extending beyond its proper limits a statement which, at all events within those limits and in itself, is true; and when you refute this exaggerated form of it, you look as though you had also refuted his original statement.[11]

Here, the "provocation" stratagem aims at so agitating an opponent that he is provoked into making extreme statements, which can then be easily disproved or shown to be lacking in credibility. Schopenhauer continues his "Twenty-third Stratagem" with the following advice:

> Contrarily, you must take care not to allow yourself to be misled by contradictions into exaggerating or extending a statement of your own. It will often happen that your opponent will himself directly try to extend your statement further than you meant it; here you must at once stop him, and bring him back to the limit which you set up. "That's what I said, and no more."[12]

13.16   THE DISCOURTEOUS HOST

The following incident, dating from the year 625 B.C., shows that an opponent's tongue need not always be loosened by purely rhetorical means. It is drawn from the Confucian classic the *Zuo Commentary*.

Against the advice of his minister, the King of Chu named Prince Shangchen to be his successor. Later the monarch came to regret his decision, preferring that his son Zhi succeed him. So he decided to kill Shangchen. The Prince heard about the plan but was unsure whether the rumor was true. He asked his teacher Pan Chong how he could find out the truth. Pan Chong told him, "Give a dinner for the King's sister, and treat her rudely."

The Prince followed this advice. His rudeness provoked the lady to anger, and she shouted, "Base scoundrel! No wonder His Majesty intends to kill you and make Zhi his heir instead."

Shangchen told his teacher that the rumor was indeed true. He then carried out a coup, during which the King of Chu was killed. Shangchen succeeded him as King Mu and reigned from 625 to 614 B.C.

In this instance Shangchen's calculated discourtesy is the equivalent of "beating the grass," while the infuriated and therefore loquacious royal sister is the "frightened snake."

Of course, like every stratagem, No. 13 can be turned into foolishness through clumsy or thoughtless application. The result may be described by the phrase "waking a sleeping dog" or "stirring up a hornets' nest." A premature warning, moreover, could cause an opponent to be on his guard or to launch a quick, preemptive strike.

Borrow a Corpse
for the Soul's Return

The Chinese characters	借	尸	还	魂
Modern Mandarin pronunciation	*jiè*	*shī*	*huán*	*hún*
Meaning of each character	borrow	corpse	return	soul

Applications	
	a. Revive something from the past by infusing it with new purpose. The "renewal" stratagem.
	b. Explicitly or implicitly, give new polish to old ideas, traditions, customs, works of literature, etc., and thus harness them for contemporary ideological or political purposes. The "warming-over" stratagem.
	c. Apply a patina of venerable age to something that is actually new. The "patina" stratagem.
	d. Use new institutions as instruments for carrying out old behavior patterns; use new personnel to carry out old policies. Don new shoes, but tread an old path. Pour old wine into new bottles. The "renovated façade" stratagem.
	e. Acquire the goods (or position or reputation) of another by absorbing his strength or power, in order to build up your own. The "parasite" stratagem.
	f. Exploit every possible means to overcome a difficult situation. The "comeback" or "phoenix" stratagem.

14.1 Li of the Iron Crutch

One of the oldest sources for the phrase expressing Stratagem No. 14 is the drama *Lü Dongbin Instructs Li Yue of the Iron Crutch*, written by Yue Bochuan during the Yuan period (A.D. 1271–1368).[1] The phrase for No. 14 crops up about half a dozen times in the course of the play, though it is used in a completely Buddhist-Daoist context and thus somewhat literally, rather than metaphorically as a stratagem.

In the first act the play's protagonist, a Zhengzhou district official named Yue Shou, reports that the Emperor has sent Han Weigong, a provincial circuit judge, on a secret mission to the district, with orders to behead incompetent and corrupt officials. As a result, says Yue, many of the officials have fled. But he himself has not fled because he does not regard himself as crooked. In fact, he goes to welcome Han Weigong on his arrival but fails to meet him.

On the way back home he encounters a Daoist priest at his gate, who calls to him, "Yue Shou, you headless demon, you shall die." Angered, Yue Shou orders his subordinate to hang the priest from the gatepost. The priest is in reality a Daoist immortal, Lü Dongbin, who has recognized in Yue Shou a likely candidate for entry into the Realm of the Immortals. But in order to gain entrance, Yue Shou must first be purified. This initial scene was the first step in the purification process.

A little later an old farmer comes along and unties the priest from the gate. This causes an altercation between Yue Shou and the old farmer. Yue calls him an unreasonable peasant and boasts of his own powers. Finally, the old man reveals himself as none other than the imperial emissary Han Weigong and orders Yue Shou to wash his neck clean and present himself at the district offices early the following morning, when he will test the edge of his sword on him.

This threat of death so frightens Yue Shou that he dies and goes to the Underworld. Yama, the Prince of Hell, is about to spear him with a pitchfork and dip him in a vat of boiling oil, when the Immortal Lü Dongbin appears and begs Yama to rescind the punishment, give Yue to him as a disciple, and permit him to return to the Upper World. Yama checks his books and replies, "I regret to inform you that his wife has already burned the body, so his soul cannot return."

"Please help us, Yama," says Lü Dongbin.

Yama goes through his books again and reports, "Illustrious Immortal, in Fengning, in Zhengzhou District, just inside the eastern gate, a young butcher named Li has just died. His body is still warm. What if we were to borrow Li's corpse so that Yue Shou's soul could return to earth?"

"Very good," says Lü Dongbin. And, addressing Yue Shou, "But who would have thought that your wife would already have burned your body?"

Yue Shou's soul enters the corpse of the young butcher Li. Since Li had one lame foot, Yue Shou now needs a crutch. Immediately upon awakening, he sets out to see his family. Now, he abruptly realizes how crookedly he had behaved in his former incarnation as a district official:

I lied with brush and ink,
made the crooked look straight,
deceived Heaven and Earth in my heart.

. . .

How often did I accept bribery,
declare right to be wrong.

. . .

When an accused man stood before me,
guilty, but with ready cash,
I managed to acquit him swiftly.
But if he was innocent and poor,
he soon felt the bailiff's grip.
I numbed my conscience, forgot my duty,
seeking only to extort money.
Why is one of my legs now too short?
Because in my former life
I walked a crooked path.

After a brief meeting with his wife and interrogation by the imperial emissary Han Weigong, Yue Shou follows Lü Dongbin and withdraws from the world. Eventually he is transformed into one of the Eight Immortals.

In Fuzhou, in Fujian Province, a statue of the lame Li with his crutch adorns the shore of West Lake.

The phrase for Stratagem No. 14 also appears in the play *Emerald Peach Blossom*, by an unknown author of the Yuan period. Here the deceased Xu Bitao borrows the corpse of her dead sister in order to return to life and marry. The rebirth motif is also a key part of the drama *Peony Pavilion* (also known as *The Tale of the Soul's Return*), by Tang Xianzu (1550–1617). This play is still popular in China today.

In all these cases the Chinese text uses the word *hun* for "soul." In classical Chinese there was also another word for soul: *po*. The *po*-soul gave a person life; after death it hovered for a while about the individual's grave. The *hun*-soul gave a person his personality; it too lived on long after the body's death, watching over the deceased's surviving loved ones. When sorcerers had dealings with the dead, they worked through the *hun*-soul.[2] As a stratagem, of course, the expression "Borrow a corpse for the soul's return" is understood figuratively.

14.2 THE SHEPHERD XIN BECOMES KING OF CHU

During the Spring and Autumn period, there were scores of separate states on Chinese soil. Of those, only about twenty were left at the beginning of the Warring States period. Seven of them, including Chu and Qin, were the most powerful. They battled one another for domination over all China. Qin ultimately defeated and annexed the others, including Chu (in 223 B.C.), which had the largest territory of all.

When the first Qin Emperor died in 210 B.C., he was succeeded by his twenty-one-year-old son, Hu Hai, who led a dissolute life at the expense of his neglected people. During the first year of his reign, there were uprisings led by Chen Sheng and Wu Guang in the territory of the former state of Chu. Chen Sheng was killed in the year 208 B.C., but his rebellion gave the signal for uprisings throughout the land, most of them occurring within what had been Chu territory. This was no mere coincidence. The people of Chu nurtured a special hatred for Qin because, back in 299 B.C., King Huai of Chu had been lured to Qin and assassinated, a national affront which the people of Chu never forgot.

Among the rebel leaders were Xiang Liang and his nephew Xiang Yu. Xiang Liang was the son of a famous Chu general. When another rebel chieftain declared a descendant of an old noble clan to be the King of Chu, Xiang Liang was advised by the hermit Fan Zeng to find a genuine scion of the royal house and declare him king. If he could do that, he would win the sympathy of the Chu people and thereby also gain the support of the other Chu rebels against Qin domination.

Xiang Liang followed that advice and searched everywhere, until he finally found a grandson of King Huai named Xin, who was working as a shepherd. Xin was willing to have himself declared King of Chu, and took the name of Huai, the Chu monarch who had been so shamefully imprisoned and killed by Qin. The crowning of the new King of Chu gave greater impetus to the popular Chu rebellion, which smoothed the path for Xiang Liang and his nephew Xiang Yu to gain a dominant position in the empire.[3]

In this example of No. 14, the young shepherd Xin, grandson of the murdered King Huai, serves as the "corpse" or "body" which is borrowed by Xiang Liang and Xiang Yu to breathe new life into the defunct royal house of Chu. By also injecting new vitality into the name of King Huai, who had been assassinated almost a century earlier, they at the same time rekindled the hatred of the Chu people against Qin and gave their rebellion the appearance of a legitimate struggle on behalf of a venerable old dynasty.

According to the authors of a stratagem book published in 1983 in Guizhou, in the People's Republic, the peasant rebel chieftains Chen Sheng and Wu Guang also used Stratagem No. 14, to the extent that they fought in the name of the old state of Chu and inscribed the words *Da Chu* (Great Chu) on their flags.

The 1989 edition of the Beijing stratagem book points out that descendants of a bygone dynasty (the "corpse") are often "borrowed" and placed in the service of a political program (the "soul" manipulating the corpse) which may be quite irrelevant or even inimical to the old dynasty. The hope is that, by so doing, the loyalty of the people to the old dynasty can be channeled to the new political system. A twentieth-century example, made familiar by the film *The Last Emperor,* was that of Pu Yi (1906–67), the last Manchu Emperor of China, who was deposed in 1911. In 1932 he was crowned head of the puppet regime of Manchukuo (Manchuria) by the occupying Japanese, who tried to pass it off as a continuation of the Manchu Dynasty.

14.3   WANG MANG FIDDLES WITH HISTORY

The machinations of Emperor Wang Mang (r. A.D. 8–23) also call to mind Stratagem No. 14. In order to secure power for himself and his followers, he harnessed the so-called Old Script School to his own purposes.

Under the Qin Dynasty, there had been a vast book-burning of Confucian writings in the year 213 B.C. After the downfall of the Qin Dynasty, there was a great desire to restore the old classics. During the reign of Emperor Wu of the Han, texts written in an archaic script were allegedly found, under unusual circumstances, in the wall of what had once been Confucius's house. The scholars who concerned themselves with these writings came to be known as the adherents of the Old Script School.

The texts in question were suspected by many scholars of not being genuine. But Emperor Wang Mang and his supporters lent strong support to the Old Script School. The old writings were reissued and, according to sinologist Wolfram Eberhard,[4] in the process certain passages suiting Wang Mang's purposes were inserted into the texts. The Emperor also had other works reissued and falsified.

In all his actions, Wang Mang now assumed the pose of one who meticulously adhered to what had been written down in the books of earlier rulers and ministers. He insisted that his new laws were simply amplifications of decrees from the "Golden Age." In doing so, he constantly cited the old texts, either totally distorting the meaning of relevant passages or else smuggling appropriate remarks into the new editions. According to Eberhard, there can be no doubt that Wang Mang and his clique deliberately falsified and deceived at first, but that eventually the Emperor began to believe in his own falsehoods.

This is an instance of combining Stratagem No. 14, "Borrow a Corpse," and No. 7, "Create Something from Nothing."

14.4 VIETNAM INVOKES HISTORY

According to a commentary published in the *People's Daily* in July 1978, the Vietnamese exploited real events from premodern history for contemporary political purposes. Without specifically referring to Stratagem No. 14, the author of the Chinese commentary made the following observations:

> For a long time Vietnamese newspapers, magazines, and radio broadcasts have been running features on the history of aggression by Chinese feudal rulers against Vietnam. [In those presentations] civilian and military officials of the Vietnamese royal dynasties are presented more fully and magnificently than are modern proletarian heroes. . . . The Vietnamese rulers organize many activities each year commemorating historical events or personalities related to [Vietnamese] resistance against Chinese aggression. Relevant historical dramas, stories, news reports, and propaganda photos are disseminated; schoolchildren are assigned to collect material about the struggles of old Vietnam against Chinese feudal rulers. Every means is used to illustrate the aggression from the north. . . . This is the trick of speaking about old matters while really referring to new ones.

In other words, the constant representations of past Chinese incursions against Vietnam and of heroic Vietnamese resistance were being used, according to the Chinese commentator, as a means of provoking the Vietnamese people's hatred of the present-day People's Republic. The long-dead Chinese aggressors and their Vietnamese opponents served as the "corpse," so to speak, into which new life was being breathed to deliberately stimulate anti-Chinese resentment.

14.5 NEW PEOPLE'S PRINCIPLES

The stratagem book published in 1973 in Taiwan[5] accuses Mao Zedong of using No. 14 by invoking a popular old doctrine to pursue a new and totally different goal. Well before he gained power, says the author of the Taiwanese book, Mao used the stratagem in the full knowledge that the Chinese people were generally opposed to Marxism and, though disappointed in its performance, approved of the Guomindang regime's basic doctrine, the Three Principles of the People—nationalism, democracy, and a secure livelihood.

The Three Principles had been formulated by Dr. Sun Yat-sen, founder of the Guomindang. In order to deceive the people and weaken their power of resistance, says the author of the Taiwanese stratagem book, in January 1940 Mao wrote an essay on the so-called "Three New People's Principles," in which he used Sun Yat-sen's ideas as postulates for the period of transition to socialism. Mao pretended that all he wanted to do was topple the unpopular Guomindang regime and that he was not at all opposed to Sun Yat-sen's Three Principles. By doing this, he convinced many academics and university graduates and won them to his cause. But once he came to power, says the Taiwanese writer, there was no more talk of New People's Principles reminiscent of those enunciated by Sun Yat-sen. In effect, then, he borrowed the old Three Principles as a "corpse" into which he breathed new life with a Communist "soul."

The interesting thing about this example is the manner in which Mao's writing is analyzed by a Taiwanese author from the perspective of a particular stratagem. But a careful reading of Mao's essay shows that his New People's Principles read very differently from those of Sun Yat-sen. Mao's New Principles are solidarity with the Soviet Union, solidarity with the Communist Party of China, and support for the peasants and workers. Moreover, in the version of the essay published in 1949, after the establishment of the People's Republic, Mao clearly distanced himself from Sun Yat-sen's Three Principles. So, on the basis of the currently available version of the essay, it cannot fairly be maintained that he set out to deceive the Chinese people.

14.6   THE VICTORIOUS CORPSE

In the year A.D. 234, Zhuge Liang, minister and chief strategist of Shu, mounted his fifth field campaign against the kingdom of Wei in northern China. His opponent was once again Sima Yi, commander of the Wei army. Because of the distances involved and the resulting supply problems, Zhuge Liang was anxious to engage in a decisive battle as quickly as possible. But, under Sima Yi's command, the Wei army prepared for a long war of attrition and dug itself in along the banks of the Huai River.

Time and again Sima Yi was urged by his lieutenants to engage in open combat. But he clung to his porcupine tactics. After a while, Zhuge Liang sent an emissary to Sima Yi bearing a chest. Suspecting that Zhuge Liang's messenger brought a declaration of war, all the eager Wei officers crowded into Sima Yi's tent and watched tensely as their leader opened Zhuge Liang's letter. In that document, the Shu minister insulted Sima Yi mercilessly, saying that he was anything but a general, that he clung to life and feared death and therefore resembled a woman more than a man. Inwardly Sima Yi boiled with rage, but he did not show it. Smiling, he opened the chest. It contained nothing but women's clothing.

Seeing how Zhuge Liang had derided and insulted their commander, Sima Yi's officers demanded the immediate execution of the emissary and a battle to the death with Zhuge Liang. But, according to a comic-strip version published in Lijiang, Sima Yi answered them with a quote from Confucius: "A lack of tolerance in small things endangers great plans." Instead of executing Zhuge Liang's messenger, he invited him to dinner. During the meal, Sima Yi avoided military subjects and drew from the emissary information about Zhuge Liang's general circumstances and the state of his health.

After dismissing the emissary, Sima Yi said to his officers, "Zhuge Liang is trying to use the stratagem of provocation. We must not let ourselves be tricked. He is overburdened with military and political work, is not eating, and sleeps badly. I believe that he will not live much longer. Now, you are to prepare yourselves well for his death. As soon as news of his demise reaches us, we will launch the battle."

So the Wei army remained in its fortifications, which made Zhuge Liang furious. The war had already dragged on for more than a hundred days. Every day Zhuge Liang took counsel with his generals on what to do next, and every night he thought sleeplessly about how he could defeat Sima Yi. Zhuge Liang thus exhausted himself; he began to spit blood, grew steadily weaker, and finally died.

The generals of the Shu army were overcome with grief and wanted to hold the burial ceremony immediately. But the commanders Yang Yi and Jiang Wei, who were privy to Zhuge Liang's will, determined to follow its instructions and persuaded the other generals to postpone the burial. Zhuge Liang's body was laid in a coffin and the order was given for the army to retreat.

The next morning Sima Yi received the news that Zhuge Liang had died and the Shu army was preparing to withdraw. Now Sima Yi and his army finally left their entrenched positions and began pursuing the enemy. Along the way, Sima Yi climbed a hill from which he could observe the Shu army at a distance. He saw that the enemy forces were maintaining exactly the same battle formation and running the same flags as they had under Zhuge Liang's command. Sima Yi now began to question whether his opponent were really dead, suspecting that the news had been given out simply to lure him onto the battlefield. But, at the urging of the other generals, he felt constrained to continue the pursuit.

Suddenly the Shu army halted its retreat and, at a signal, turned in perfect battle formation to face the pursuing Wei forces. This was precisely in keeping with Zhuge Liang's tactics. Sima Yi again was beset by doubts, and just then Zhuge Liang's standard-bearer appeared between two trees, with the flags of Shu, surrounded by several generals and among them a wagon in which the allegedly dead Zhuge Liang sat upright. When Sima Yi saw all this, he immediately gave the signal for a general retreat. At the same time the Shu army continued its withdrawal until it had reached a position of safety. And now the funeral of Zhuge Liang was held with all proper ceremony. Only then did Sima Yi discover that his old enemy was truly dead and the figure riding the wagon had been just an effigy. Sima Yi immediately resumed the pursuit, but by this time the opposing forces were well away.

The Wei officers were furious at the lost opportunity of destroying the Shu army. But Sima Yi said with a sigh, "Yang Yi led the Shu forces exactly as Zhuge Liang used to do. It was as if the soul of the dead Zhuge Liang had come back to life in Yang Yi. And I was taken in by the stratagem of 'Borrow a corpse for the soul's return.' "[6]

14.7   The Origin of Christmas

In the Weekend Supplement to the Christmas Day 1983 edition of the German-language Swiss daily newspaper *Neue Zürcher Zeitung*, author Anne-Susanne Rischke described an important episode in the history of religion that, from the standpoint of the stratagems, could well be regarded as an application of No. 14:

Celebrating the turn of the year is an ancient custom. The Romans celebrated the Saturnalia, the festival of Saturn, god of the harvest, between December 17 and 23. It was the most cheerful festival of the year. All work and commerce stopped, and the streets were filled with crowds and a carnival atmosphere. Slaves were temporarily freed, and the houses were decorated with laurel branches. People visited one another, bringing gifts of wax candles and little clay figurines.

Long before the birth of Christ, the Jews celebrated an eight-day Festival of Lights [at the same season], and it is believed that the Germanic peoples held a great festival not only at midsummer but also at the winter solstice, when they celebrated the rebirth of the sun and honored the great fertility gods Wotan and Freyja, Donar (Thor) and Freyr. Even after the Emperor Constantine (A.D. 306–337) declared Christianity to be Rome's official imperial religion, the evocation of light and fertility as an important component of pre-Christian midwinter celebrations could not be entirely suppressed.

In the year 274 the Roman Emperor Aurelian (A.D. 214–275) had established an official cult of the sun-god Mithras, declaring his birthday, December 25, a national holiday. The cult of Mithras, the Aryan god of light, had spread from Persia through Asia Minor to Greece, Rome, and as far as the Germanic lands and Britain. Numerous ruins of his shrines still testify to the high regard in which this god was held, especially by the Roman legions, as a bringer of fertility, peace, and victory.

So it was a clever move when, in the year A.D. 354, the Christian church under Pope Liberius (352–66) co-opted the birthday of Mithras and declared December 25 to be the birthday of Jesus Christ.

Thanks to that clever move, says this author, a "body" already in decline but still with considerable impact and influence—i.e., the Mithras cult—was imbued with a new "soul," the Christian one, so that something ancient lived on endowed with new meaning.

14.8 THE EMPRESS OF CHINA

In February 1977, a writer in the newspaper *Guangming Daily* suggested that, since direct public relations efforts on behalf of the Gang of Four, and particularly Mao's widow Jiang Qing, had been rejected by the masses, indirect methods had been used to get the message across, including Stratagem No. 14. For example, the Gang of Four's propagandists had praised the historical figure of Lü Hou, wife of Liu Bang, the founder and first emperor of the Han Dynasty. She helped her husband in his conquests and after his death loyally carried out his wishes. To the author of the *Guangming* article, this was a clear demonstration that Jiang Qing was determined to take up the scepter after Mao's death.

Another example: A 1974 essay by a Beijing writers' collective known as Liang Xiao idealized the Tang Empress Wu Zetian, saying that she had dominated China's political stage in the midst of a struggle between two political lines. But according to an April 1977 commentary in *Guangming Daily*, what the 1974 essay had glorified as her "blows against conservative forces" and "struggle against reaction" was in reality the use of brutal methods to gain and retain imperial power, involving secret agents, assault, murder, etc. What was really a struggle for power and wealth was distorted by the Liang Xiao writers' collective to appear as "a struggle of political lines" between the reformer Wu Zetian and reactionary Confucians. The underlying purpose of presenting Wu Zetian as "a woman with new ideas," however, was to glorify Jiang Qing. In other words, maintained critics of Jiang Qing, the "corpse" of Wu Zetian, dead for more than a thousand years, was to have breathed into it the "soul" and political aspirations of Mao's widow, who wanted to become the Wu Zetian of the twentieth century.

14.9   CHANGE THE INFUSION BUT NOT THE HERBS

Stratagem No. 14 can also be interpreted another way: Something outwardly new is presented (as a "new body"), but the soul breathed into it is actually old. This may be thought of as "pouring old wine into new bottles," "putting on new shoes but walking an old path," "putting new labels on old goods" —or "changing the infusion but not the herbs."

This latter phrase was used by the Beijing periodical *Shijie zhishi* (World Knowledge) as the headline over a June 1986 commentary on the replacement of Babrak Karmal by Najibullah as chief of Afghanistan's ruling Democratic People's Party.

The Chinese commentator Mei Wen came to the conclusion that the "change of horses," as he termed it, meant only that the Kremlin's old Afghanistan policy was to be continued under a new name, while nothing fundamental would change. On the one hand, the Soviets wanted to intensify their military activities in order to crush the resistance of the Afghan people and expand their own political dominance, in order to create favorable conditions for an eventual bloodless troop withdrawal. At the same time, they were trying to disarm world opinion by demonstrating a flexibility aimed at a political solution (e.g., via Afghanistan negotiations in Geneva), postpone the time of their troop withdrawal, and get the other side to offer negotiating terms which would be favorable to Moscow.

This interpretation of Stratagem No. 14 can also be extended to cover the veiled restoration of an old order, with new institutions serving as instruments of an old mode of behavior.

14.10   AN INVITATION TO SHU

In a military context, Chinese stratagem literature moves the expressive image of No. 14 onto an abstract level, in which the starting point is a poor or hopeless situation, and the "soul's return" is a comeback or the "rise of the phoenix."

The 1989 edition of the Beijing stratagem book cites the following example, based on the *Zizhi tong jian* (Comprehensive Mirror for Aid in Government), by Sima Guang:

Following the Battle of Red Cliff (see Section 9.1, "The Victorious Observer"), both Sun Quan and Liu Bei turned their desire for conquest to the territory of Shu. As a result of his military weakness, Liu Bei found himself in an unfavorable position.

In the winter of the year A.D. 214, Cao Cao attacked Hanzhong. This posed a threat to the internally divided group around Liu Zhang, which had occupied Yizhou in Shu. Liu Zhang feared an attack by Cao Cao after he had conquered Hanzhong. So he asked Liu Bei for help and gave him permission to march into Shu. Liu Bei took advantage of the opportunity and headed for Shu with his forces. Two years later he had gotten rid of Liu Zhang and annexed Yizhou, thus laying the groundwork for establishment of the later kingdom of Shu (one of the three great realms of the third century A.D.) and securing his own political ascent. Liu Bei did not have the military strength to conquer the region of Shu. Yet the strategic plans of his adviser Zhuge Liang designated that territory as an essential power base if he hoped to extend his political influence. In that situation, Liu Zhang's invitation to come to Shu was the "corpse," so to speak—i.e., in less abstract terms, the favorable opportunity—with which Liu Bei could win the territory necessary for his political rise (the "return of the soul").

This example shows the Chinese word *ji*, which I have translated as "stratagem," used more in the sense of a "calculated move" rather than an actual combat tactic. The Chinese word has many layers of meaning, which cannot always be completely covered by our rather more narrow concept of "stratagem."

14.11 CONCLUSION

According to the 1986 Taipei stratagem book,[7] No. 14 can also be applied in business, for example by seeking new shareholders or creditors when an enterprise finds itself in crisis. They are the "corpse" or "body" which is borrowed to make it possible to put the business back on a firm footing—the "return of the soul."

In closing, a comment from the Beijing stratagem book:[8]

> No one is always victorious. Setbacks are normal. The important thing is to keep a clear head in a period of failure, to analyze the situation calmly, and borrow all available "corpses," that is, discover all useful ways to regain the initiative and turn defeat into victory.

Lure the Tiger Down from the Mountain

The Chinese characters	调	虎	离	山
Modern Mandarin pronunciation	*diào*	*hǔ*	*lí*	*shān*
Meaning of each character	move	tiger	leave	mountain

Applications	Get the tiger to leave the mountain; lure it from its mountain stronghold down onto the plain. Separate the enemy from his base.

a. Lure the enemy down onto the plain in order to neutralize him.

b. Lure the tiger away from the mountain in order to capture the mountaintop (and perhaps to kill the tiger as well).

c. Weaken the enemy by separating him from his main supporters.

d. Separate the tiger from those it protects, in order to more easily neutralize them once they are defenseless. The stratagem of isolation.

The following passage appears in the book *Guanzi* (Master Guan), ascribed to the early political philosopher Guan Zhong:

> When the tiger and the leopard leave their lair and approach humankind, they fall prey to humans. As long as the tiger and the leopard rely on their lair, they can retain their positions of power.

Han Fei is said to have written:

> It is the claws and fangs which enable the tiger to tame the dog. If you remove the tiger's claws and fangs and give them to the dog instead, the dog will tame the tiger.

In the sentence that formulates Stratagem No. 15, "tiger" is a metaphor for the enemy, while "mountain" stands for the enemy's stronghold, the familiar ground on which he finds it most convenient and comfortable to fight. The objective of No. 15 is to separate the enemy from that familiar ground. This is especially important when the tiger is powerful. By permitting a powerful tiger to fight on its home territory, one is, in the words of another Chinese expression, *Wei hu fu yi*—"lending wings to the tiger"—that is, making a powerful enemy even stronger.

There are, naturally, many "tigers" who are not only powerful and courageous but clever as well and not so easily lured off course or away from their "mountain." Odysseus was one such. Sailing past the island of the Sirens, he plugged his crew's ears and had them bind him to the mast, which permitted him to sail undeviatingly onward.

No. 15 has many possible variants, of which the main ones are listed under the Applications above.

15.1　JOURNEY TO THE SON OF HEAVEN

Duke Wu of Zheng had two sons. The elder, Wusheng, had come into the world by a breach birth (i.e., feet first), and because of his difficult birth he was spurned by his mother. She loved their second son, Duan, more than anything in life, and wanted him to succeed to the throne. But the Duke refused to violate the traditional order of succession. Besides, he pointed out, his elder son had done nothing wrong. So Duan was given only a small legacy, while Wusheng became the heir apparent and assumed the throne after his father's death. He ruled as Duke Zhuang of Zheng.

Highly dissatisfied with her favorite son's insignificant position, the Duke's mother asked that a large city, Zhi, be assigned as his brother's fiefdom. Duke Zhuang refused, since Zhi was far too important a center, whereupon his mother requested the city of Jing for her younger son.

Zhai Zhong, one of the Duke's advisers, objected. According to traditional rules, the largest vassal cities were not to be any more than one-third the size of the capital. This was by no means the case with Jing. And just as two suns did not shine in the sky, added Zhai, so there could not be two rulers in their state. The city of Jing was centrally located, large and populous, almost as important as the capital politically and militarily. Moreover, Duan was the favorite of the old duke's widow. "If he is given the city, whether we like it or not there will suddenly be a second ruler on the scene."

But Duke Zhuang replied that his mother had ordered it and it must be done. So he gave Duan the city of Jing as a fiefdom. Before setting out, Duan met with his mother, who advised him to use his new power base to prepare himself to seize the throne when an opportunity should present itself.

Some time afterward Duan ordered the commanders of the northern and western border territories to obey his commands, especially in military matters—though as a vassal ruler he was not really entitled to such obedience. Duan also occupied some neighboring territories, and grew more powerful each day.

This became known at Duke Zhuang's court, but the Duke did nothing about it. A dignitary by the name of Gongzi Lü advised the ruler to have his younger brother eliminated as soon as possible, but the Duke replied, "Duan is my mother's favorite. He is my younger brother. How could I let myself be angered by a few territorial adjustments and act against my mother's wishes?"

Gongzi Lü remarked, "To hesitate at decisive moments is a sure road to disaster. And once disaster has arrived, it is too late for regrets."

Duke Zhuang sighed. "Oh, I have thought about this problem only too often. Duan is certainly aiming to usurp the throne. But so far he has not openly rebelled. If I move against him now, my mother will use it against me and I will be universally blamed for a lack of brotherly love and insufficient respect for my mother. The only thing I can do is pretend that I've noticed nothing, leave my brother alone, and wait until he actually commits a rebellious act. Then I will have tangible proof of his criminal intent."

Gongzi Lü objected. "On the one hand, you are right to hesitate. But on the other hand, your brother grows mightier each day. Ultimately he will be stronger than you. How would it be if we give him an opportunity to reveal his intentions as soon as possible, so that we can be rid of this threat without further delay?"

Gongzi Lü proposed the following: The Duke had not traveled outside his own realm for a long time, for fear of his brother's machinations. Now he would journey to the imperial court for an audience. The Duke's absence would lure his brother to march on the capital and try to capture it. But Gongzi Lü would lead troops a little way outside of Jing, where they would lie in wait, and as soon as Duan left the city they would march in and take it. That would rob the Duke's brother of his base, and then it would be an easy matter to neutralize him.

The Duke approved the plan and made Zhai Zhong his deputy during his absence. The Duke's mother, seeing that the moment had come to realize her plans, sent an emissary to her favorite son with a secret message about taking the capital. But Gongzi Lü captured the emissary, killed him, sent the letter to Duke Zhuang, and sent another messenger to Duan, pretending he was from the old Duchess and bearing the same message. Duan sent the emissary back to his mother carrying a reply in which he revealed the date of his planned military action. Gongzi Lü intercepted this letter as well and sent the messenger on to the Duchess with a forged note containing the same information.

Now Duke Zhuang had the proof he wanted. He took his leave of his mother and, accompanied by a guard of honor, set off with great pomp and circumstance for the imperial court. At the same time, Gongzi Lü and his troops established themselves near the city of Jing and waited for the "tiger" to leave his "mountain." Duan mobilized all the soldiers in Jing and marched them toward the capital, insisting that they had to safeguard the city during his brother's absence. Gongzi Lü sent some saboteurs into Jing; they set fires and instigated riots— and the city was easily captured.

En route to the capital, Duan learned that his own city had fallen and immediately ordered his troops to march back. Outside the city walls, he and his army set up camp, preparing to retake Jing. But his army's morale was deteriorating. Some of Gongzi Lü's people infiltrated the camp and spread the news it laid the foundation for the later kingdom of Wu, one of the three major realms in the first half of the third century A.D.[2]

15.4 THE LETTER IN THE CARP

On the northern shore of a reed-rimmed lake stood the village of Sanheshe, to the east was the village of Huozhuang, to the south the village of Gaobaozhuang, and to the west the village of Lüshi. During China's war against its Japanese invaders (1937–45), there was a man named Ba Sanfu who had a farm in Gaobaozhuang. The Communists in the area regarded Ba as a local despot. As the village headman, he had curried favor with the invading Japanese.

The parents of fourteen-year-old Hong Yazi, a fisher girl, had failed to pay their taxes. So Ba Sanfu incited the Japanese to kill the family. The girl managed to escape and went to her grandfather's house in Sanheshe. Her grandfather was a contact man for the Chinese Communist Party, so Hong Yazi became a courier for the local "armed work unit" (the term used to designate anti-Japanese resistance groups operating under the leadership of the Communist Party).

Hong Yazi would go out fishing in her little boat, and during her excursions she would secretly gather and transmit information. On the basis of her reports, the Communists one night carried out an attack against a Japanese outpost on the western shore of the lake, killing the commandant there. As a result, a unit commanded by an officer named Kameno was assigned to reinforce the Japanese position in the village of Gaobaozhuang on the southern lakeshore and to establish a communications link with the Japanese troops in Huozhuang on the eastern shore. Working from those two points, the Japanese hoped to catch the Communists in a pincers movement.

The fisher girl learned of all this and reported it to the leader of her work unit, who now gave her a special assignment. Hong Yazi went out onto the lake in her boat and began fishing near

that Duan was really out to dethrone his brother, the Duke. Overnight, half of Duan's army deserted him.

Duan wanted to flee to Yanyi with his remaining loyal soldiers, but the Duke's troops had already occupied it. Finally, with nowhere else to go, Duan retreated to the small town he had been given in the first place but with which he had not been content. However, the Duke's troops soon advanced on the town, which was too small to withstand the attack. So Duan saw no alternative but to take his own life.[1]

15.2 OUT ON A LIMB

In an extended sense, the first variant of Stratagem No. 15 as illustrated above can also be applied in debate or rhetoric. The trick is to lure your opponent out of his reserve and, through standard debating techniques, lead him into unfamiliar territory, where he can be tripped up more readily.

No. 15 may also be applicable when signing contracts with foreign businesses, in formulating the clause dealing with the venue of arbitration in case of dispute. This clause may be so designed that, in the event of a disagreement, the foreign partner would have to leave his usual legal environment and operate on unfamiliar, and therefore unfavorable, judicial terrain.

15.3 SUN CE CALLS FOR HELP

During the last decades of the Han Dynasty, large portions of China came under the domination of various warlords. South of the Yangtze River there were two main centers of power: one in the southeast, on the territory of today's Jiangsu Province, under the command of Sun Ce, governor of Guiji, and another northwest of there, on the territory of today's Anhui Province, ruled by Liu Xun, governor of Lujiang. These two potentates vied with each other for domination of all South China.

By the year A.D. 199, Liu Xun had extended his power far enough to become an immediate threat to Sun Ce. What was to be done? Many of Sun Ce's advisers urged a direct military confrontation as soon as possible, in which Liu Xun would be destroyed. But others felt that this would be a dangerous course. Zhou Yu in particular advocated a more indirect method. It was his belief that the tiger must be lured down from the mountain before one entered its den.

Sun Ce decided to follow Zhou Yu's advice. He knew Liu Xun's character: greedy, ambitious, and a bit stupid. On that basis, Sun Ce sent a special emissary bearing a letter and gifts for Liu Xun. On his way to Lujiang, where Liu Xun resided, the emissary saw several army encampments; preparations for war were clearly under way. Going to his audience with Liu Xun, he had to pass a line of warriors armed to the teeth. Arriving before the warlord, the emissary handed him Sun Ce's letter. It read:

> We look up to Your Excellency with great respect and desire good relations with you. However, as a result of constant warfare we have not had the leisure to pay you a visit. Now Shangliao is sending troops and persistently harassing the weaker territories south of the Great River. We ourselves are too weak to mount a long-range campaign. Hence we send you this message, along with precious gifts, and request that Your Excellency mount a punitive expedition to conquer Shangliao. It is our opinion that, if you carry out such a campaign, you will be giving immeasurable aid and support to the weak states south of the Great River.

Now the emissary presented the warlord with Sun Ce's gifts. Liu Xun was convinced of Sun Ce's sincerity. He had heard about the wealth of Shangliao, possession of which would mean great power and prosperity. And now Sun Ce was asking for his support, had even sent a large number of precious gifts! Beside himself with delight, Liu Xun threw a splendid banquet

for Sun Ce's emissary, during which the latter raised his goblet many times to toast victory in Liu Xun's forthcoming war against Shangliao. Liu Xun's generals likewise drank to the coming victory. Only one civilian official, by the name of Liu Ye, showed concern. After the banquet, Liu Xun asked him why he was disturbed. The official replied, "Shangliao is small, it is true, but the city is surrounded by strong walls. It is difficult to take. I fear that Sun Ce is employing the stratagem of 'Lure the tiger down from the mountain' against us. I fear certain defeat."

Autocratic and pigheaded, Liu Xun grew furious and shouted, "Silence! If Sun Ce really wanted to match himself against me, he would not have sent an emissary." And Liu Xun's generals agreed completely. So the campaign against Shangliao was organized. The threatened city heard about the impending attack and made all necessary preparations for defense. Though Liu Xun's troops were weary after their long and difficult march, he ordered them to surround the city and attack it from all sides. Well rested and with their morale intact, the defenders fought valiantly against their tired attackers, sending countless arrows, rocks, and tree trunks down upon the troops trying to scale the city walls. Liu Xun's offensive failed, leaving his troops demoralized.

At the same time, Sun Ce had learned that Liu Xun was attacking Shangliao with his main forces, leaving only a small detachment behind to guard Lujiang. Said he to his advisers, "The tiger has now been lured from its mountain. We can first capture its lair and then easily deliver the final blow."

So Sun Ce's army stormed Lujiang, which surrendered without a fight. Sun Ce then turned his attention to Liu Xun's main force, whose morale had already dwindled to nothing at the news of Lujiang's fall. The battle ended in catastrophe for Liu Xun, who after his total defeat lamented to the Heavens, "Why didn't I listen to Liu Ye's advice? I was tricked by Sun Ce's stratagem of 'Lure the tiger down from the mountain' and misfortune is the result!"

Liu Xun subsequently took service with Cao Cao. As for Sun Ce, this proved to be the easiest of his military campaigns, and

Gaobaozhuang. Suddenly she heard a loud voice from the shore: "Come here, or I'll shoot." This was what she had been waiting for. She rowed ashore and was interrogated by Japanese soldiers. She said simply, "I'm just fishing here."

At that moment Ba Sanfu came along. He lived in that village and had been ordered to prepare a welcoming meal for the Japanese commandant Kameno. But he had no fresh fish. As she had been instructed, Hong Yazi hid her hatred of Ba Sanfu. The headman ordered her to show him her fish baskets. But he found the fish too small. Hong Yazi said there were no big fish in the immediate area but indicated that large ones were to be found around Sanheshe to the north.

"Really big ones?" asked Ba Sanfu.

"You may believe it or not, as you wish," replied the girl. "Yesterday I saw an old fisherman catch a carp as big as a man. And there were others like it in the water. But he wouldn't let me fish there, because I was a stranger."

"Go and get me some big fish," commanded Ba.

"Those fish aren't for sale," said the girl. "If you want to buy some, go get them yourself!"

A little suspiciously, Ba Sanfu asked, "Are there any men of the Eighth Army around there?" (The Eighth Army was a military arm of the Chinese Communist Party in the anti-Japanese war.) Hong Yazi reassured him that there were not. So Ba Sanfu sent his cook Lan Hongyan to go with the girl and get the fish.

Hong Yazi rowed out into the lake, singing a fishing song in her melodious voice. Suddenly a shot sounded from the reeds on the shore. The cook Lan Hongyan cowered in the bottom of the boat. Hong Yazi pretended to be afraid as well, and dropped an oar. The next moment an armed figure popped up among the reeds and said gruffly to the girl, "What are you doing here?"

"I'm going to buy some fish," said Hong Yazi, not revealing that she knew the man, who was the commander of her work unit. She pointed to Lan Hongyan. "He's Ba Sanfu's cook. Ba sent him out to buy fish." The other suddenly doffed his hat and said courteously, "Mr. Ba is our friend. Please continue on your way and fulfill your task." The cook recovered from his fright and bowed low to the man in the reeds. Hong Yazi rowed on.

After a while they came to the northern shore of the lake. There, the girl's grandfather was seated beneath a ginkgo tree fixing his nets. Hong Yazi said, "That's the old fisherman I saw yesterday. Go and get your fish."

Lan Hongyan rudely commanded the old man to give him some fish. At first the fisherman said he had none. But Lan Hongyan said, "Mr. Ba sent me. He wishes to serve a meal to Commandant Kameno. Would you rather have the Communists of the Eighth Army take your fish, instead of feeding the Imperial Japanese Army?"

"Oh, why didn't you say so in the first place?" said the old man, suddenly the soul of courtesy. "So you come from Mr. Ba? Why, of course I have a fish for you." And he brought out of his house a huge carp of at least thirty pounds. Lan Hongyan took the fish without paying for it and ordered Hong Yazi to row him back. Arriving at Gaobaozhuang, he commanded the girl to tie her boat to a tree and help him.

In the kitchen the cook cut the carp open, and in its stomach he found a piece of oiled paper with writing on it. "Come quick!" he shouted, "there's a letter hidden in the carp." People came rushing in, Ba Sanfu among them. He took the piece of paper and saw on it the words "Strictly Confidential" and "Personal to Mr. Ba." He was frightened.

Hong Yazi took this opportunity to go into the dining room and get hot water to brew tea. She told everyone she met about the letter in the fish. The Japanese officer Kameno, who was drinking tea at the time, heard the news and hurried into the kitchen. Since the attack on the Japanese camp in Lüshi he had been hearing rumors linking Ba Sanfu to the Communist Eighth Army, so he was already suspicious of the man. Now, striding into the kitchen, he demanded to see the letter.

After reading the document Kameno went silently out of the room. Ba didn't know what to do. Kameno called the cook and interrogated him. The cook told the truth as he knew it: Ba Sanfu had sent him to Sanheshe; along the way he had met a soldier of the Eighth Army who said that Ba was a friend. Kameno then questioned Hong Yazi, whose statement coincided perfectly with the cook's. Now Kameno returned to the kitchen and confronted Ba Sanfu. The more Ba cringed and fawned, the more suspicious Kameno became. When Ba tried to pour him a glass of wine, Kameno threw the drink in the man's face and drew his sword.

Ba stammered, "It's all a mistake!"

Kameno ordered him to read the "fish letter." It said:

> Tonight we attack Huozhuang. We hope you can make the pig Kameno drunk and prevent him from helping Huozhuang. You will be rewarded later for this and for your help at Lüshi.
>
> Armed Work Unit: Jiang Qi

Kameno beheaded Ba Sanfu on the spot. Leaving the house, the Japanese officer heard shots from the vicinity of Huozhuang. Commandeering two motorboats, he and some troops immediately set out to reinforce the garrison at the other village. As soon as they had departed, a group of armed Communists turned up at Ba Sanfu's farm, tied up the two surprised Japanese guards, and set the place on fire.

In the meantime, Kameno approached Huozhuang without finding any sign of the Communists. Angry, he turned his head and saw in the distance his base at Gaobaozhuang going up in flames. Only now did he realize that he had wrongly killed Ba Sanfu and fallen victim to the stratagem of "Lure the tiger down from the mountain." He immediately ordered a return to Gaobaozhuang. But by this time the armed work unit had laid a trap and dealt the Japanese a devastating defeat.[3]

15.5 AGRARIAN REFORM IN SUIFENDADIANZI

The novel *Forest in the Snow*, by Qu Bo (see Section 12.4, "An Easy Climb Up Tiger Mountain") deals with China's 1945–49 civil war. Chapter 29 is titled "Luring the Tiger from Its Mountain." It tells this story:

Shao Jianbo, commander of a reconnaissance unit of the Communist People's Liberation Army, has a problem. He is trying to figure out how to dislodge Ma Xishan, the leader of three hundred men fighting on the Guomindang side, who is holed up with his troops in a cave on a peak in the Guokui Mountains. The summit is very difficult to reach; the only access is by a narrow path through dense woods. The nearest village is Suifendadianzi, many miles away.

Some of Shao Jianbo's comrades propose a direct attack; others suggest using deception to cause Ma to flee and thus expose himself to attack. Shao Jianbo opts for Stratagem No. 15. He sends his men to give agricultural aid to the village of Suifendadianzi, near the foot of the mountain. His assumption is that, since the Guomindang troops have links to the village elders, these revolutionary measures will cause the enemy unit to leave its stronghold in order to attack the Communists in the valley below.

As the first step in the plan, grain, tools, and horses are confiscated from the village's three richest landowners and distributed to the poor. As anticipated, one of the landowners runs off to the Guokui Mountains and describes the situation to Ma Xishan. The Guomindang officer thinks that, with his three hundred mounted troops, it should be an easy matter to handle the fifty or so Communist guerrillas whose only transportation is their own skis. That night Ma Xishan gives the order for his men to leave the mountaintop, in order to surprise the Communists down in the village the next morning.

On that same night, however, Shao Jianbo's troops also get moving. Leaving the village, they take a detour and ski their way up to the summit. Early the next morning, Shao observes the enemy searching for him down in the village far below. "Comrades!" he calls out to his men. "The tiger has been lured from his mountain. Now our work really begins. We must enter the tiger's lair and destroy it, so that those bandits have nowhere to hide. Then, with the aid of the snow, we can attack them whenever and wherever we wish."

15.6 JOSHUA'S AMBUSH

Some authorities[4] regard the Bible's Book of Joshua as a virtual handbook of military strategy. For example, in chapters 7–8 the story is told of how the Israelites conquered the city of Ai in Canaan. First Joshua and his troops attempted a frontal assault, in which they were defeated and fled (mainly, according to the biblical tale, as punishment for prior transgressions, which had to be expiated before other matters could proceed). On the second try, Joshua divided his army into two segments. One part was sent westward to wait in ambush, while Joshua himself led the remainder of the troops in another frontal attack against the city. The King of Ai, having been victorious the first time around, mustered his troops and marched out of the city to do battle. Joshua and his men pretended to flee and the army of Ai pursued them ("Not a man was left in Ai; they had all gone out in pursuit of the Israelites and . . . had left the city undefended"—Joshua 8:17). The other part of the Israelite army now quickly advanced on the city, occupied it, and then hastened back to help their comrades. Joshua's troops in the field now turned on their pursuers and attacked them, while the Israelites returning from the city fell on the enemy from behind. Caught in a pincers, the Ai army was destroyed to the last man.[5]

According to some reports, England's famous Battle of Hastings (A.D. 1066) was decided in much the same way. The Norman army under William the Conqueror had tried in vain to defeat the Anglo-Saxon forces, which had fortified themselves on a rise behind strong earthworks. So William resorted to a version of Stratagem No. 15: His troops made another unsuccessful assault, then turned tail to flee. This time the Anglo-Saxon troops went after them, confident that they could destroy the Normans. But suddenly they found themselves surrounded.

The "flight" of the Norman forces had only been a ruse to lure the Anglo-Saxons out of their invulnerable defensive position.[6]

15.7   FAN ZENG'S FURY

As noted at the beginning of this chapter, one variant of No. 15 is to weaken the "tiger" by separating it from its main supporters.

In the year 204 B.C. Liu Bang, founder of the Han Dynasty, was threatened by a powerful enemy, Xiang Yu. Liu Bang's adviser Chen Ping proposed a stratagem to sow discord among Xiang Yu's troops, based on his knowledge that Xiang Yu was a mistrustful leader.

Chen Ping had rumors circulated in the enemy camp that Xiang Yu's advisers and chief supporters were dissatisfied, because they had not been amply rewarded for their efforts on his behalf, and they were therefore interested in allying themselves with Liu Bang to destroy Xiang Yu. The rumors reached Xiang Yu, who immediately grew suspicious. In an effort to investigate the matter, he sent an emissary to Liu Bang's camp. Liu Bang had a festive banquet prepared, and when Xiang Yu's messenger arrived Liu Bang pretended to be surprised. "Why, I expected Fan Zeng's emissary. But you're a messenger from King Xiang!" And Liu Bang sent his caterers and staff away and had Xiang Yu's emissary served only a scanty meal. Returning to his home base, the messenger recounted all this to his master. Xiang Yu was filled with suspicion of Fan Zeng, his chief adviser. Was the man turning against him and allying himself with Liu Bang?

Some time later, Fan Zeng advised his master Xiang Yu to mount an attack against the city of Xingyang. But Xiang Yu did not follow his advice. When Fan Zeng realized that his lord no longer trusted him, he was furious and said to Xiang Yu in effect, "Continue the campaign without me. I quit. I'm going back home." Filled with rage, he left Xiang Yu and died a short time later.

In this instance, the "tiger" is Xiang Yu and the "mountain" is his adviser Fan Zeng, from whom Xiang Yu is tricked into parting.

15.8 THE CARAVAN OVER THE LION CAMEL MOUNTAINS

In previous chapters, we have recounted some of the adventures of the monk Tripitaka and his entourage, consisting of Sun Wukong the Monkey King, Sha the Sand Monk, and Zhu Bajie the pig (see Section 5.1, "The Radiant Robe," and Section 13.11, "The Return of the Monkey King"). Told in the sixteenth-century novel *Journey to the West,* these adventures take place as the little group goes on a mission to India, to bring sacred Buddhist scriptures back to China.

One day, Tripitaka and his companions come to a huge mountain which bears the fantastic name Eight-Hundred-Mile Lion Camel Mountain. An old man warns them not to proceed, since forty-eight thousand fiendish demons led by three archdemons live on the mountain and devour any passing mortals. The Monkey King reconnoiters and successfully battles two of the archdemons, who finally agree to accompany Tripitaka and his followers safely over the mountain. As they are discussing this in their cave, the third archdemon says, "Yes, by all means let us escort them. They will surely fall prey to my stratagem of 'luring the tiger down from the mountain.' "

"What do you mean by that?" asks the oldest archdemon.

The third archdemon, named Great Bird of the Three-Thousand-Mile Cloud Path, explains his plan, to which the other two archdemons gleefully agree. The third archdemon came originally from the Lion Camel City some four hundred miles away. Five hundred years earlier he conquered the city, which is now inhabited exclusively by monsters and demons. He has heard that a pious monk had been assigned by the Tang court to travel westward and collect certain sacred writings. The Tang monk is reputed to be a good person who has lived a pure life for ten generations. Whoever would eat of his flesh, it was said, would prolong his own life and never grow old. Realizing that he was not strong enough by himself to overpower the monk and his traveling companion Sun Wukong, wielder of magic powers, this archdemon has come to the Lion Camel Mountain to join forces with the other two archdemons.

In accord with the third archdemon's plan, the monk Tripitaka is borne over the mountain in a sedan chair by eight demons, with the unsuspecting Monkey King going on ahead, the Sand Monk bringing up the rear, and Zhu Bajie carrying the luggage. After a march of four hundred miles, a city suddenly appears that radiates a sense of evil. Now the Monkey King grows suspicious, and turning around he sees that the third archdemon is about to hurl a huge halberd at him. Immediately he assumes a defensive posture, and a violent battle ensues. At the same time the other two archdemons attack Sand Monk and Zhu Bajie. And while this is going on, the eight litter bearers quickly carry Tripitaka into the city, where he is taken prisoner.

Here the "tiger" is Tripitaka, who is deliberately isolated from his "mountain"—i.e., his three protecting companions.

15.9 CONCLUSION

A professor of contemporary Chinese history once told me that Stratagem No. 15 was used often by the Chinese Red Army in its mobile two-front war against the Japanese and the Guomindang. The object was to maneuver the enemy forces into a situation or a location in which they could carry out no useful function and constitute no genuine danger. By tricking the enemy into moving his main force to some strategically useless or tactically disadvantageous place, the Communists, though almost always inferior from a purely military standpoint, were able to win battles or to defeat enemy units which had been cut off from their main force, and thus weaken the enemy as a whole.

A Hong Kong book on the stratagems points out that

No. 15 finds special application in political conflicts, where the objective is an increase in power and each participant may be both "tiger" and "hunter."

A Beijing stratagem book closes its observations on No. 15 by citing Friedrich Engels's essay "The Siege of Silistria":

> One may be forced to retreat, one may suffer a setback, but as long as one is in a position to exert pressure on the enemy [i.e., to force the "tiger" from its "mountain"] instead of being subjected to the enemy's pressure, one remains superior to him to a certain extent.

Finally, in the famous Chinese book of oracles *I Ching* (Book of Changes), there is a sentence dealing with the hexagram *Chien* (Obstruction), which reads:

> Going [to the enemy] leads to obstructions,
> Coming [i.e., letting the enemy come to you] meets with praise.

To Catch Something, First Let It Go

The Chinese characters	欲	擒	姑	纵
Modern Mandarin pronunciation	*yù*	*qín*	*gū*	*zòng*
Meaning of each character	want	catch	temporarily	let go
Applications	The "cat-and-mouse" stratagem; the "laissez-faire" stratagem; the "winning the heart" stratagem.			

In the *Zuo Commentary,* one of the thirteen Confucian classics, it is said, "If you release an enemy for one day, it will bring evil to many generations."

Yet there are situations in which Stratagem No. 16 seems absolutely called for. The classic example of No. 16 cited in all the Chinese sources will be given in Section 16.2, "The Seven Releases of King Menghuo." It is taken from the novel *The Romance of the Three Kingdoms,* which we have drawn upon several times in previous chapters. In the novel it is preceded by the following episode, in which No. 16 also plays a central role.

16.1 VICTORY THROUGH FRIENDLINESS

Liu Bei, ruler of Shu in what is now Sichuan Province, died in the year A.D. 223. Cao Cao, ruler over the northern kingdom of Wei, felt that the critical phase of transition in Sichuan provided a favorable opportunity for an attack against Shu, victory under Gao Ding's command, I shall permit you to return to him. But do not fight against me again. Next time, I will show no mercy."

The soldiers thanked Zhuge Liang, returned to their base, and spread the word of what they had heard about Yong Kai. To find out more, Gao Ding sent a spy into Zhuge Liang's camp. But the spy was caught. When the man was brought before him, Zhuge Liang pretended to believe that the spy was an emissary from Yong Kai. "Your commander has offered me the heads of Gao Ding and Zhu Bao," he roared. "Why has he not kept his promise? You're not very clever. What are you sniffing around here for?"

The spy could give no clear reply. Zhuge Liang served him food and finally gave him a letter, saying, "Bring this dispatch to Yong Kai and tell him to finish the business quickly."

Returning to Gao Ding, the spy handed him the note. When he had read it, Gao Ding was furious. "I've always been loyal to Yong Kai. Now he proposes to kill me!" He then decided to tell the whole thing to his military adviser E Huan, who was already very well disposed toward Zhuge Liang. Said E Huan, "Zhuge Liang is a most benevolent master. It would ill become us to stand against him. It is Yong Kai who misled us into this rebellion. The best thing would be to kill Yong Kai and go over to Zhuge Liang's side."

And so it was. Gao Ding killed both Yong Kai and Zhu Bao and pledged allegiance to Zhuge Liang, who appointed him prefect of Yizhou.

In this case, Zhuge Liang used more than one stratagem. He not only applied No. 16, he also employed No. 33, "The Stratagem of Sowing Discord,"[1] and No. 3, "Kill with a Borrowed Knife." In Chinese, such a combination is often referred to as *lianhuanji* (a chain of stratagems).

16.2 THE SEVEN RELEASES OF KING MENGHUO

On his subsequent march southward, Zhuge Liang was told that an emissary from the Shu ruler had arrived. It was Ma Su, who had been ordered by Liu Bei's son, the Emperor, to bring gifts of wine and silks for the troops. Zhuge Liang said to him, "Our ruler has commanded me to pacify the tribal territories. The fame of your sage advice has reached my ears, and I hope to benefit from your words."

Ma Su replied, "These alien people to the south refuse to recognize our rule, because they believe that they are protected by the mountains and the remoteness of their lands. You may conquer them today, but tomorrow they will fall away again. Wherever you come with your army, of course, peace will immediately descend. But as soon as you pull your armies out of the south for an attack against Cao Cao to the north, those alien tribes will seize the opportunity and invade Shu once more. An important maxim in employing military means is 'Better to win hearts than cities; better to battle with hearts than with weapons.' I hope you will succeed in winning the hearts of these people."

"You read my very thoughts," said Zhuge Liang.

Word reached Menghuo, King of the southern tribes, that Zhuge Liang was personally taking the field against him and had already used stratagems to eliminate his three allies Yong Kai, Zhu Bao, and Gao Ding. So he gathered the leaders of the Three Gorges before him and proclaimed, "Zhuge Liang is leading a huge army and will attack our land. We must stand together and resist him!"

The leaders of the Three Gorges assembled three separate columns of about fifty thousand men each and marched against Zhuge Liang. But they could not match his skill in the art of war. One of the three leaders fell during a surprise nighttime attack, and the other two, Dongtuna and Ahuinan, were captured. When they were brought before Zhuge Liang, he immediately untied their fetters, had refreshments served, and released them with an admonition to refrain from hostile acts in future. With tears in their eyes, the two leaders thanked him and hastily departed.

When they had gone, Zhuge Liang said to himself, "Tomorrow Menghuo himself will certainly mount an attack against us. That will give us an opportunity to capture him." Whereupon he issued instructions to two officers, who then left the camp with five thousand troops each, followed by two more commanders and their units.

Zhuge Liang had now made all the necessary preparations for the clash with Menghuo, who did indeed attack the following day. After a brief skirmish, the Chinese troops turned tail and fled. Menghuo pursued them for about twenty miles. Suddenly he found himself surrounded by Chinese soldiers appearing from ambush to the left and the right; his rear was cut off as well. With a few of his officers, Menghuo managed to flee to the Jindai Mountains, pursued by the enemy. Suddenly he was faced with Chinese troops there too. Thus Menghuo and his entourage were captured.

Back at his base, Zhuge Liang awaited them with meat and wine. The commander's great tent was surrounded by seven squads of armed guards; the entire camp, with Zhuge Liang at its head, made an imposing impression. When all the prisoners except Menghuo had been brought before him, the minister had their chains removed and addressed them.

"You are all upright men. It is Menghuo's fault that you find yourselves in such unpleasantness. I believe you all have parents, brothers and sisters, wives and children waiting for you at home. The news of your defeat will have affected them terribly; they are doubtless shedding bitter tears at your fate. I am going to release you, so that you can return home to your loved ones and comfort them."

Whereupon he had food and wine served to them and released them. The men were deeply touched and thanked Zhuge Liang with tears in their eyes. Then Zhuge Liang sent for King Menghuo and asked him, "The late sovereign of Shu never treated you badly. Why have you rebelled?"

Replied Menghuo, "You invaded our land without the slightest provocation. How can you accuse me of rebellion?"

"You are my prisoner," rejoined Zhuge Liang. "Do you admit your inferior position?"

"As a result of my own carelessness, you captured me in wild mountainous terrain. Why should I feel myself inferior?"

"If I release you," asked Zhuge Liang, "what will you do?"

"I will pull my army together again and lead it against you in a decisive battle. But if you capture me a second time, I shall bow to your superiority."

Zhuge Liang ordered that Menghuo's fetters be loosened and that he be given food and clothing and accompanied back to his camp. As a final gesture, he made him a gift of a horse and saddle.

The Shu officers were upset at the release of the foreign chief. They went to Zhuge Liang's great tent and said, "Menghuo is the most powerful leader of the southern border peoples. He was in our power today. The South could have been pacified. Why did you let him go?"

Zhuge Liang replied, "I can capture that man as easily as I can draw something from my pocket. I am trying to win his heart. When I do, peace will come of itself here in the South."

The Chinese officers absorbed these words without much enthusiasm.

In the meantime Menghuo had reached the Lu River, where he met some of his scattered troops. They had been trying to learn what had happened to their leader, and now they were joyful at his return. They asked him how he had been able to make his escape. Menghuo lied. "They held me prisoner in a tent. I killed more than ten guards and fled under cover of darkness. Then I met a mounted spy and killed him as well. That's how I got this horse."

No one doubted him. Delighted, they helped him cross the river and set up camp. Menghuo immediately began reassembling his troops and mustering a new army. Once again he called upon Dongtuna and Ahuinan, the two glen chieftains who had been captured and then released by Zhuge Liang. Though reluctant, they could not avoid responding to the call. Menghuo declared, "Zhuge Liang is a master in the use of stratagems. We cannot defeat him in direct combat. But his people have had a long march, and the hot season approaches. Those are factors in our favor. We also enjoy the protection of the Lu River. So we will dig in here. The heat will debilitate Zhuge Liang's army so badly that he will be forced to withdraw. Then we can strike and take him prisoner."

Faced with Menghuo's defensive tactics, Zhuge Liang ordered an officer named Ma Dai to lead troops across a shallow spot on the lower course of the Lu River and cut Menghuo's supply route. At the same time Ma Dai was told to gain the allegiance of the two chieftains Dongtuna and Ahuinan.

Ma Dai successfully carried out his first commission, capturing more than a hundred wagons bearing food for Menghuo's army. When the tribal chief learned of this, he sent a young officer out to do battle. Ma Dai defeated him easily. Next Menghuo sent out the chieftain Dongtuna to regain the enemy bridgehead on their side of the river. Some of Ma Dai's men recognized Dongtuna and told the officer that the man was one of those who had been captured and then released.

Ma Dai galloped toward Dongtuna and berated him for his ingratitude. This affected Dongtuna deeply. Without replying or lifting a weapon, he rode back in shame.

Menghuo was furious and screamed, "Traitor! Just because Zhuge Liang treated you well, you refuse to fight." And he ordered Dongtuna's execution. With great difficulty the other officers persuaded Menghuo to rescind the order. Instead, he had Dongtuna punished with a hundred blows of the cudgel. Inwardly, most chieftains sided with Dongtuna.

Later, the chieftains assembled in Dongtuna's camp and said, "Zhuge Liang is a master of stratagems. He is feared even by Cao Cao and Sun Quan, ruler of Wu. How much more, then, must we fear him! Moreover, he has treated us well. We owe him our lives. It is time we showed him our gratitude. Let's kill Menghuo and subordinate ourselves to Zhuge Liang. In that way we will spare our people greater misery."

Whereupon Dongtuna took his sword and, accompanied by about a hundred men, hastened to the main camp. It so happened that Menghuo was drunk at this time. He was taken prisoner by Dongtuna, brought to the Lu River, and turned over to Zhuge Liang. When Dongtuna had recounted the entire course of events to him, Zhuge Liang rewarded him handsomely and released him and the group of chieftains with him. Then he ordered the executioners to bring Menghuo out, and said to him, "The last time you said that if I took you captive again you'd surrender. Well?"

Menghuo replied, "My capture this time was not due to your abilities. My own people are responsible for my unfortunate position. Why should I surrender?"

"And what will happen if I release you again?"

"I am, it is true, only a member of the southern peoples. But do not think that I therefore know nothing about the arts of war. If you let me return to my glens, I will assemble another army to fight against you. If you capture me again, my heart will yield and I will acknowledge fealty to you."

Whereupon Zhuge Liang loosened his fetters and had food and drink brought for the prisoner. Then Zhuge Liang invited Menghuo to ride with him through his army camp, to see how well equipped and supplied his troops were. After the inspection Zhuge Liang turned to Menghuo.

"Consider my experienced troops, my capable officers and ample supplies. How can you hope to defeat me? If you yield, I will inform our sovereign. You will get to keep your kingdom, and your sons and grandsons will be the guardians of the southern territory forever. What do you say?"

Menghuo responded, "Even if I were to yield, the people in my glens would never agree. If you let me return home, I will call them together and convince them that we should accept your dominion."

Overjoyed at these words, Zhuge Liang took Menghuo back to his great tent, ate and drank with him until evening, and then personally accompanied him to the Lu River, where he had him transported to the opposite bank.

But upon returning home, Menghuo's first act was to have Dongtuna and Ahuinan executed. Then he took counsel with his brother Mengyou. "I'm now familiar with the situation in Zhuge Liang's camp," he said, and gave his brother certain instructions which the latter immediately began to carry out.

Mengyou loaded a hundred strong men with gold, jewels, pearls, and rhinoceros horn, crossed the Lu River, and headed for Zhuge Liang's camp. There he was stopped by soldiers under the command of Ma Dai, who asked what he wanted, listened to the reply, held Mengyou back, and sent a message to Zhuge Liang. When Zhuge Liang read the note, he asked Ma Su what he thought of its contents. Ma Su replied that he did not dare express his opinion aloud but would offer it in writing. When Zhuge Liang read what Ma Su had written, he was delighted, for Ma Su's view of Mengyou's mission coincided exactly with his own.

Zhuge Liang thereupon issued orders to a few officers, and when everything was ready he sent for the bringer of gifts.

Mengyou said, "My brother Menghuo wishes to express his gratitude for your benevolence. You spared his life, and so he has sent me with these gifts. Moreover, in future he will pay tribute to the ruler of Shu."

Zhuge Liang had Mengyou and his hundred fierce-looking men served a royal feast.

In the meantime Menghuo waited in his tent for news. Finally two scouts returned and reported on how well Mengyou and his gift-bearers had been received. Everything, they said, was ready for the attack that was to be made during the second watch of the following night.

Confidently, Menghuo now set out with thirty thousand soldiers. In the dusk he crossed the Lu River. Then, accompanied by a hundred picked men, the tribal chief stormed Zhuge Liang's main camp. Its gate stood open and he encountered no resistance. Menghuo rode through the camp to Zhuge Liang's great tent and swept the entrance curtain aside. The tent was brightly lit with torches—and there lay his brother and all his men, totally drunk. The wine they had been served had been drugged.

Menghuo realized that he had again fallen victim to one of

Zhuge Liang's stratagems. He loaded his brother on his shoulder and had the other unconscious men carried away to rejoin their main force.

But as he turned to go, torches suddenly sprang into life on all sides and drums began to beat. Fear gripped his men, who scattered in every direction, pursued by Zhuge Liang's warriors. Menghuo tried to escape, but his path was cut off everywhere. Finally, in a last desperate attempt, he reached the river. There he saw a boat that seemed to contain some of his own men. He called it over and jumped aboard. Suddenly an order was given, and several men grabbed Menghuo and took him prisoner. The boat had been prepared by Ma Dai and manned by Shu soldiers dressed like Menghuo's troops.

This time it was not only Menghuo but also his brother and numerous dignitaries who had been captured. But none of the prisoners was harmed in any way.

Once again Menghuo found himself brought before Zhuge Liang, who laughed. "Did you really think that I'd be fooled by that trick with your brother and his gifts? Well, I've captured you again. Will you yield now?" he asked.

Menghuo replied, "This time I was caught because of my brother's drinking and the effect of your drugs. If I had played my brother's role and he had given me outside troop support, I would certainly have won. It's rotten luck that has caught me, not my own inability. So why should I yield?" And Menghuo hung his head and remained silent.

Zhuge Liang smiled and said, "I'm going to let you go again."

Menghuo responded, "If you let me and my brother go, we'll gear up for another battle with your army. But if I'm captured again, I shall yield at last."

Zhuge Liang ordered Menghuo, his brother, and the other officers to be released. They thanked the minister for his mercy and hurried away.

Proud of having escaped three times running, Menghuo returned to his glen, from which he sent his friends out as emissaries to the eight hordes and ninety-three tribes. In due course he assembled an army of 100,000 men.

When Zhuge Liang heard about it, he said, "This is what I've been waiting for. Now we have a chance to demonstrate our full power." At first, however, he avoided an armed confrontation, since he wanted to dampen the opposing army's appetite for battle a bit. After a while, detecting signs of fatigue among Menghuo's troops, he instructed his unit commanders to lay certain traps. Then he pretended an overly hasty withdrawal, by leaving behind an empty camp full of supplies. Menghuo reasoned, "It must have been something urgent to cause Zhuge Liang to break camp so suddenly. Shu is probably being attacked either by Sun Quan, ruler of Wu, or by Cao Pi, Emperor of Wei. We must not miss this opportunity. We must give chase at once."

Arriving at the Erhe River, Menghuo immediately saw Zhuge Liang's camp pitched on the northern riverbank. He said to his men, "Zhuge Liang fears our pursuit. So he has dug in on the northern bank. He'll probably pull out in a few days."

Menghuo gave the order to cut down trees and prepare to ford the river. He had not noticed the Shu soldiers hidden on the southern bank of the river. That day, the wind blew strongly. Suddenly Menghuo's army found itself surrounded by a sea of torches, while drums beat on every side. The Shu troops had left their hiding places and swarmed toward Menghuo's positions. There was panic, and Menghuo fled with a few followers. He tried to return to his old camp, but Shu troops were already there. The only escape route open to him led along the edge of a dense forest. Suddenly he saw an escorted wagon, with Zhuge Liang seated on top in solitary splendor. Menghuo immediately ordered his men to take Zhuge Liang prisoner. They all ran toward the wagon, there was a shout—and they seemed to disappear. Zhuge Liang had had a ditch dug, and Menghuo and his men had fallen into it. Menghuo, his brother Mengyou, and their men were again prisoners of the Shu army.

Once again Zhuge Liang freed all the lower-ranking prisoners after offering them lavish hospitality and some encouraging words. Menghuo's men left the Shu camp filled with gratitude. Then Mengyou, Menghuo's brother, was brought forward. Zhuge Liang castigated him. "Your brother is a simple fool.

You should talk some sense into him. This is the fourth time I've captured him. Does he feel no shame?"

Mengyou blushed with disgrace. He threw himself to the ground and begged for clemency. Zhuge Liang said, "If I'm to kill you, it won't be today. I pardon you. But you must bring your brother to his senses!" And he ordered Mengyou's chains to be loosened and the man released. Mengyou thanked him tearfully and went on his way.

When Menghuo was brought out, Zhuge Liang feigned fury. "Well, I've caught you again today. What have you to say?"

Menghuo replied, "Again I've been a victim of your stratagems."

Zhuge Liang ordered his prisoner beheaded. But Menghuo showed not the slightest fear. He merely turned his head toward Zhuge Liang and said, "If you let me go again, I will avenge my four defeats."

Zhuge Liang laughed, ordered him released from his chains, invited him into the commander's tent, and served him lavishly. Later he asked, "Four times I've treated you with courtesy, and yet you won't yield. Why?"

To which Menghuo replied, "I am a man from outside the realm of Chinese culture. Unlike you, I do not rely on perfidious stratagems. Why should I yield?"

Asked Zhuge Liang, "Will you resume the struggle if I let you go a fourth time?"

Said Menghuo, "If you capture me again, I will pledge fealty to you with all my heart and give everything I have in my glen to your army. I will swear never to betray you."

Once again Zhuge Liang released him. Menghuo headed southward and finally met his brother Mengyou, who said to him, "We're not strong enough for this enemy. We've been beaten several times now. I think it'd be best if we hide in the mountains. The Shu army won't be able to stand the summer heat. They'll have to leave."

So the two men went to Tulong Gorge, which was ruled by Mengyou's friend King Duosi. This glen was highly inaccessible. One entrance was barricaded by King Duosi's men, and the

other was mortally dangerous to pass, infested with scorpions
and poisonous snakes. At night deadly fumes floated above the
earth; anyone who drank from the area's four wells was doomed
to die.

In this secure refuge, the two brothers and King Duosi gave
themselves over to a life of drink and revelry. With supernatural
help, however, Zhuge Liang managed to penetrate to their lair
and set up camp nearby. When Menghuo learned of this, he
gave a big feast to raise his troops' morale and decided to launch
an attack against the Shu army. Just at that moment Yangfeng,
chieftain of the Yixiyinye Gorge, appeared on the scene with
thirty thousand soldiers and offered his help to Menghuo. The
tribal king held a festive banquet for Yangfeng and his sons.
During the meal, Yangfeng brought in some sword dancers to
perform and had his sons pour wine for Menghuo and Mengyou.
As they were about to begin drinking, Yangfeng issued a sharp
command, and his two sons grabbed Menghuo and his brother
and bound them. The same thing happened to King Duosi.

"We were friends! Why are you doing this to me?" asked
Menghuo.

"My brother, my sons, and my nephews joined your rebellion.
They were captured along with you. But Zhuge Liang released
them. I've captured you today to repay his generosity. Now I'll
bring you to him."

Zhuge Liang asked Menghuo, "Will you yield this time?"

"It was not your cleverness," replied Menghuo, "but treach-
ery in my own ranks that put me in your hands. Kill me if you
wish. I'll not yield."

Zhuge Liang responded, "I will show mercy yet again. You
may lead your army into battle against me another time. But if
I get my hands on you again, I'll exterminate you and your
entire family." And he released Menghuo, Mengyou, and King
Duosi. Yangfeng and his men were rewarded with rich gifts and
high offices and sent home.

Menghuo, however, hurried to the Yinkang Gorge, where he
concluded an alliance with King Mulu. But Zhuge Liang was
victorious this time too. King Mulu was killed and the Yinkang

Gorge conquered. Zhuge Liang gave orders to search for Menghuo. Then a report reached him that, after fruitless attempts to persuade Menghuo to surrender, Menghuo's brother-in-law had taken him, his wife, and a hundred members of his clan prisoner and was bringing all of them to Zhuge Liang. Hearing this, Zhuge Liang instructed two of his commandants to hide with two thousand men near the great tent. Then he ordered that Menghuo and all the other prisoners be permitted to enter.

When the prisoners stopped in the entranceway of the tent to bow, Zhuge Liang gave a prearranged signal to the hidden troops. They pounced upon the new arrivals and searched them thoroughly, revealing that each and every one of them was carrying a sharp sword or dagger.

Zhuge Liang said, "You only pretended to surrender. In reality you wanted to murder me." And turning to Menghuo he added, "Did you not say last time that you would yield if I were to capture your family? What do you say now?"

"We came here voluntarily, risking our own lives. My capture is not a result of your skill. Why should I yield?"

Said Zhuge Liang, "This is the sixth time I've caught you, and still you won't give in. How long will this go on?"

"If you capture me a seventh time I shall give you my loyalty and never rebel again."

"Very well," replied Zhuge Liang. "Your last refuge is destroyed. What have I to fear?" And he loosened Menghuo's chains with the words "If I capture you again, I will not release you."

Menghuo and his people covered their heads with their hands and fled like rats.

Now the tribal king was left with only one possible ally: King Wutugu of Wuge, who was prepared to provide thirty thousand troops for a campaign of vengeance. The soldiers were clad in a kind of armor woven of vines that had been soaked in oil for half a year and then dried, the process being repeated several times, after which the vines were woven into helmets and body armor. Thus clad, the Wuge warriors could swim rivers without getting wet, and no blade was able to penetrate their armor.

In an initial clash at the Taohua River, Zhuge Liang suffered a setback. He spoke with the local people to find out about his new opponent, then climbed a mountain to examine the topography. On his way back down the mountain, he came upon a valley which was like a long snake, its stone walls to right and left barren of vegetation. A single path led through the valley. This discovery gave Zhuge Liang great satisfaction. He immediately issued secret orders to his officers and commanded Wei Yan to set up a camp at the ford of the Taohua River. If King Wutugu attacked, Wei Yan was to relinquish the camp, keep a lookout for a white flag, and march toward it. During a period of half a month he was to flee the Wuge troops fifteen times, leaving behind seven pitched camps and their tents.

In the meantime, Menghuo warned King Wutugu about Zhuge Liang's stratagems. He was especially dangerous, said Menghuo, when it came to ambushes, and Wutugu was to be particularly wary of big valleys. Wutugu took the warnings very seriously.

Then a report arrived about the establishment of a Shu camp on the Taohua River. Wutugu sent some of his armored troops across the river, and after just a few skirmishes the Shu soldiers fled. Fearing a trap, the Wuge troops refrained from pursuit. Similar clashes took place on the second and third days. Then Wei Yan saw a white flag waving in the distance. Leading his retreating troops there, he found an empty camp. Fifteen times Wei Yan accepted similar defeats, and he relinquished seven camps in the process. Wutugu's pursuit became increasingly reckless, yet he halted whenever he came to dense woods or undergrowth. Sometimes he sent scouts on ahead, and they spotted Shu flags in the trees.

Menghuo said with a laugh, "Zhuge Liang has run out of stratagems. We've finally figured him out. He's been forced to run fifteen times now, and we've conquered seven bases. One last effort and victory is ours."

Wutugu heard this with great joy. By this time he was not inclined to take the Shu army very seriously. On the sixteenth day there was another skirmish with Wei Yan's troops, who once again fled before any serious fighting had taken place. Wutugu's men followed hard on their heels. Wei Yan led his unit into the narrow, winding, stony valley which Zhuge Liang had discovered and where another white flag was waving. Seeing neither tree nor bush in the valley, Wutugu decided there was no ambush to be feared and continued his pursuit.

In the interior of the valley, several dozen wagons suddenly blocked the path. Believing them to be Shu supply wagons abandoned in the enemy army's flight, Wutugu pressed his men onward toward the valley's exit. Suddenly tree trunks and rubble came tumbling down the valley walls, blocking the narrow exit. At the same time Wutugu realized that the wagons were filled with straw and had started to burn. Hidden charges of powder were exploding, set off by burning torches tossed down the valley and lighting long fuses which led to the wagons. The whole valley was suddenly turned into a sea of flames. The oil-soaked armor of the Wuge troops quickly caught fire, and thirty thousand warriors died.

Watching the horrible bloodbath from his observation post, Zhuge Liang felt tears come to his eyes, and he said, "I've performed a great service for the imperial house, but at a terrible cost in human life."

Wuge soldiers reported to King Menghuo, who had not taken part in the pursuit, that his ally Wutugu had scored a great victory. Joyfully Menghuo hastened to the valley of his triumph, only to find that Wutugu and his army had been wiped out. Attempting to withdraw, Menghuo was taken prisoner by the same Wuge troops who had led him to the scene of the slaughter—they were actually Shu soldiers in disguise. Once again Menghuo and members of his family found themselves in Zhuge Liang's hands. They were brought to a tent and served food and drink. During the meal a messenger appeared in the doorway and turned to Menghuo. "Zhuge Liang would find it shameful to come before you again. He has commissioned me to release you. Mobilize another army against him, if you can, and try once more to defeat him. Now go!"

But instead of fleeing, Menghuo began to weep.

"Seven times captured and seven times released," he said. "Nothing like this has ever happened. Though I do not share your culture, I do not lack a sense of what is right and proper. How could I be so shameless!"

Now he and the members of his party fell on their knees, bared their torsos as a sign of penitence, and crawled to Zhuge Liang's great tent. "O Great Minister, yours is the majesty of Heaven. We men of the South will never again offer resistance to your rule."

"Do you now yield?" asked Zhuge Liang.

"I, my sons, and my grandsons are deeply moved by Your Honor's boundless, life-giving mercy. How could we not yield!"

Zhuge Liang invited Menghuo into his tent, offered him a seat, and had a festive banquet prepared. He confirmed Menghuo's kingship and restored all conquered territories to his rule. But two of his high officers objected to his generosity. "After such a difficult campaign, why do you not appoint our own officials?"

Zhuge Liang replied, "There are three obstacles to doing so. First, I would have to send contingents of troops to safeguard our own officials. Second, after their heavy losses in the fighting, the southern peoples would resist rule by Chinese officials. And third, the southern tribes would always remain mistrustful of foreign overlords. If I leave no one behind, moreover, I will also not have to supply food for anyone down there."

The compassion of the conquering Zhuge Liang was requited by the gratitude of the southern peoples. They even built a shrine in his honor. From then on there was peace along Shu's southern border. And so Zhuge Liang won the hearts of the defeated through the use of Stratagem No. 16.[2] (The authors of a book issued by the People's Liberation Army Press,[3] however, point out that Zhuge Liang's psychological warfare would not have succeeded if it had not been backed by great military might.)

16.3 MAO AND HIS PRISONERS OF WAR

According to a copy of the first stratagem book I ever bought[4]—I acquired it at a large book fair in Taipei—Mao Zedong too drew inspiration from No. 16 during the civil war (1945–49) between Communist troops and Chiang Kai-shek's Nationalist army.

In applying this stratagem to captured Guomindang troops, Mao first separated those officers and men who were considered specially loyal to Chiang Kai-shek. They were to be treated strictly as prisoners. The others received a more lenient treatment. The most effective tools in reorienting them in favor of the Communist cause were the so-called "complaint sessions" (*sukuhui*). At these meetings, carefully indoctrinated members of the lowest social class drastically compared their poverty and the misery of all their "class brothers and sisters" with the luxury of the wealthy, whose patron they alleged to be Chiang Kai-shek. Dramatic descriptions of events were offered at these sessions, sometimes reinforced by bloody props—such as the rope with which a youngster's father had hanged himself after being harassed by a big landowner. These techniques aroused hatred against the "exploiters" and their political and military representatives.

In his later writings, Mao praised the remarkable efficacy of these efforts at "reeducating" captured Guomindang soldiers. Those who did not opt to immediately join the Red Army after this treatment were given food and money and told to go home, with the following advice: "Next time you come up against our troops in the field, don't forget: Chinese don't fight against Chinese!"

Mao expected that the released soldiers would cause agitation and subversion in the enemy ranks and thus undermine Guomindang morale. They would also effectively counter enemy propaganda about alleged Communist brutality.

Of course, the released soldiers went about insisting they had escaped. Many of them told their comrades and superiors about the high morale and military discipline of the Communist army. Others committed acts of sabotage or deserted to the Communist side at critical moments. Even before the Red Army crossed the Yangtze River in 1949 for its decisive advance southward, the morale of the Guomindang troops had been severely shaken.

In this way, Mao succeeded in neutralizing the opposing army by releasing those of its members whom he had previously captured and indoctrinated. (But here too, as in the previous case, Mao's own military strength was a prerequisite for the stratagem's success.)

16.4   ESCAPE AS A TRAP

Beginning on June 30, 1947, five columns of the Shanxi-Hebei-Shandong-Henan Field Army, some 130,000 Communist troops under the command of Liu Bocheng and Deng Xiaoping, crossed the Yellow River and moved toward the Dabie Mountains in Shandong Province.

On July 14, two Red Army columns surrounded two enemy units near the hamlet of Liuyingji. In order not to force the enemy to fight with the desperation of doomed men, the Communist commanders decided to apply Stratagem No. 16 and opened the encirclement on one side. This led the enemy to attempt a breakout. The Communist commanders had naturally positioned their soldiers so that the escaping enemy troops fell right into the trap and were easily destroyed.

Sun Tzu wrote, "Do not drive a desperate enemy into a hopeless corner." This is confirmed by the original treatise on the 36 Stratagems as reproduced in the 1979 Jilin book, where it is written:

> If you drive an opponent into too tight a corner, he will mobilize his utmost energy to save himself. But if you open a way out for him, his tension and fighting energy slacken,

To Catch Something, First Let It Go

and in that state he becomes easy prey. This also helps avoid bloodshed on your own side.[5]

Taking its inspiration from the *I Ching,* the old treatise on the 36 Stratagems states in its chapter on No. 16, "Easing leads to subjugation—bright future."

16.5   RAFSANJANI AND THE AMERICAN GIFTS

On November 14, 1986, in its column *Shijie zhi chuang* (Window on the World), the Shanghai newspaper *Wenhui bao* opened a long report on the latest Iran affair with the following remarks:

> Exciting news has just been reported in the American press. The U.S. has been conducting secret negotiations with Iran for the past 18 months and has delivered arms to Iran in order to gain release of American hostages being held in Lebanon. According to the American revelations, these negotiations were carried out in circumvention of the State Department, the Department of Defense, and the CIA, with the personal approval of President Reagan. The latest issue of the American magazine *Newsweek,* whose newsstand date was moved forward, has a report on the background [of the affair]. The following paragraphs are an adapted translation of that report for our readers.

These introductory remarks by editors Ji Yun and Liang Ren were followed by an abridged translation of the article "Cloak and Dagger" from the November 17, 1986, issue of *Newsweek.*

On November 4, 1986, the article remarked, the seventeenth anniversary of the occupation of the U.S. Embassy in Teheran, Iranian Parliamentary President Rafsanjani was especially pleased, because an article in a Lebanese periodical had caused embarrassment to the "Great Satan."

Up to this point, the Chinese editors followed the *Newsweek* text closely. But here they inserted a subhead with an indirect reference to Stratagem No. 16:

> McFarlane came bearing gifts, but Iran's Parliamentary President first let go of the thing he wanted to catch.

The report then went on to describe how five U.S. officials, including the former head of the National Security Council, Robert McFarlane, had secretly flown to Teheran. The delegation had brought with it symbolic gifts, such as a cake in the shape of a key (a hint about the establishment of new relations) and a Bible with a dedication by Ronald Reagan. High Iranian officials had even been promised Colt pistols. According to another version of the story, a far more worrisome offer had been made: a planeload of U.S. weapons.

"Iran did not go for the bait," remarked Rafsanjani. "We told them that we did not accept the gift and that there was nothing for us to discuss." The Americans, he opined sarcastically, "wanted to borrow our influence in order to solve their problems in Lebanon."

This refusal of the initial American offer—i.e., the Colts, or a planeload of military equipment—was interpreted by the Chinese journalists in terms of Stratagem No. 16. The Iranians, they remarked, had first let something go in order to lure the Americans into making a better offer. The result of this application of No. 16 was, according to the *Newsweek* report, that Iran harvested more than $60 million worth of equipment, including antitank missiles, radar systems, and spare parts for their obsolete navy.

It is interesting to note the differences between the American and Chinese reports. The former was simply a rather dry presentation of the facts, without a deeper analysis of the possible Iranian tactics behind the episode. The Chinese, on the other hand, whether rightly or wrongly, described the Iranian behavior during the early phase of the American advances as arising from a specific stratagem. This is an excellent example of the

Chinese inclination to view international developments in tactical (or "stratagemical") terms.

16.6   SHANG YANG'S CONFUCIAN SLEEPING PILL

In the fourth century B.C., Duke Xiao of Qin issued a decree calling on China's most capable men to apply for positions in his service. Having learned of this in his homeland of Wei, Shang Yang traveled to Qin in 361 B.C. Thanks to a recommendation from Jing Jian, one of the Duke's confidants, he was received by the ruler personally.

At the first audience, Duke Xiao fell asleep during Shang Yang's presentation. Five days later, during a second audience, the Duke was equally unmoved by the theories that Shang Yang expounded. It was only during his third audience that Shang Yang's words seemed to catch the Duke's attention, and at the fourth audience the ruler's interest was sparked to such an extent that his conversation with Shang Yang went on for several days.

Jing Jian asked Shang Yang, "The Duke has completely changed his opinion about you. How did you manage it?"

Shang Yang replied, "During the first two audiences I spoke about the Confucian way of ancient rulers. The Duke thought these old Confucian methods of ruling too inefficient. To succeed with that technique requires a sustained effort over dozens or even hundreds of years. According to Confucian doctrine, the rulers of antiquity succeeded chiefly through the impact of their own virtue, and long stretches of time were required for that influence to spread throughout the land. What ruler these days possesses such patience? So Duke Xiao found this model of sovereignty inadequate.

"Then I began to expound to him the theory of the School of Legalism about how to create a wealthy nation with a strong army—a goal that can be achieved quickly through application of a strict system of rewards and punishments that favor farmers but are war-oriented and anchored in a code of law. Of course, the reputation of a ruler may suffer in implementing such a method. Nevertheless, suddenly the Duke was infused with a fiery enthusiasm."

One Taiwanese writer on the subject of stratagems points out that Shang Yang deliberately began by presenting a position— the Confucian doctrine—that was not his own. By not immediately trying to win the Duke to his own theories, those of the School of Legalism, he was first exposing him to "enemy concepts," so to speak. But apparently Shang Yang represented those concepts in such a manner that the Duke was bored to death. Once the ruler had turned away from a doctrine that he found boring, Shang Yang began to speak up for what was nearer his own heart, putting forward the theories of the School of Legalism. In short, Shang Yang's long-winded exposition of the other ideas was really only a ploy with which to intensify the Duke's interest in his own position.[6]

16.7 THROUGH SLOVENLY RULE TO STRICT MORALITY

Duke Jing of Qi appointed Yanzi as administrator over the city of Dong'e. After three years one heard nothing but ill of him throughout the land. Duke Jing was not pleased and summoned him to court to dismiss him. But instead of resigning, Yanzi said, "I admit my mistakes. I beg you to permit me to conduct the affairs of Dong'e for another three years, after which time you will surely hear nothing but good spoken of me throughout the land."

Duke Jing could not refuse this appeal and appointed him as administrator of Dong'e for another three years. After that period, indeed, nothing but good was heard of Yanzi. The Duke was delighted and again summoned him to his court, this time to reward him. But Yanzi refused any gifts. When Duke Jing asked him his reasons, he replied:

"When I first came to guide the affairs of Dong'e, I had roads built and I promoted measures favoring the poor farmers. This was resented by the wicked. I encouraged the thrifty and the industrious, as well as those who demonstrated filial piety and brotherly love. I punished the fraudulent and the lazy. This was resented by the good-for-nothings among the people. In criminal matters, I did not go out of my way to protect the wealthy and the powerful. This was resented by the wealthy and the powerful. What the people around me requested, I granted if it was compatible with the law but denied when it violated the law. This was resented by the people around me. When I attended my superiors, I never did more than was required by rite and custom. This was resented by my superiors. And so, all these people spread their slander about me, even here at court. After three years these slanders came to Your Excellency's attention.

"This time I wanted to be very careful and do things differently. So I had no roads built and postponed measures to benefit the poor farmers. This delighted the wicked. I discriminated against the thrifty and industrious and those who demonstrated filial piety and brotherly love. I let the fraudulent and the lazy go unpunished. This delighted the good-for-nothings among the people. In criminal matters, I favored the wealthy and the powerful. This delighted them. I approved of everything that the people around me requested. This delighted them. When I attended my superiors, I did more than custom required. This delighted my superiors. And so it was that all these people sang my praises everywhere, even here at court. After three years these hypocritical praises came to Your Excellency's ears. Three years ago, when you wanted to punish me, I really deserved a reward. And now that you wish to reward me, punishment would be more appropriate. These are the reasons why I cannot accept your gifts."

Recognizing Yanzi for the truly capable man he was, Duke Jing appointed him administrator of the entire country. And in just three years the land of Qi experienced a period of great growth.

In this anecdote from *Yanzi chunqiu* (The Springs and Autumns of Yanzi—see Section 3.3, "Two Peaches Kill Three Knights"), Yanzi wanted to gain the confidence of Duke Jing. He could not do so by following his own inner convictions and conducting an honest government. Instead, he eased off for three years. By temporarily relinquishing all his principles and thus generating positive gossip about himself, he regained the Duke's interest and goodwill. Then, by dint of a skillful presentation, he convinced the ruler of the value of his ethical position.

16.8 TENSION TO THE LAST

In Section 8.6, "The Match," we briefly reviewed part of Wenkang's nineteenth-century *Tale of the Gallant Maid,* in which the young scholar An Ji, traveling to visit his old father, was rescued by Thirteenth Sister from the clutches of a gang of criminals and thus from probable death. Later in the story he tells his father about his miraculous rescue.

Father An would like to express his gratitude to his son's rescuer, but An Ji knows nothing about her identity. As to where she lives, he recalls only a poem she had written on a wall of the monastery which the bandits had used as their headquarters. Its last lines were:

> *If you seek me,*
> *you will find me somewhere in the clouds.*

Father An sits lost in thought, endlessly chanting the poem's last lines and outlining with his finger on the table the three Chinese written characters for "Thirteenth Sister." Suddenly he pounds his fist on the table and shouts in gleeful relief, "I have it!"

His son naturally wants to know what it is his father has understood. The old man says, "I see clearly now. But it is not yet time to reveal it to you. Be patient for a while. Then I shall both speak and act."

For better or for worse, An Ji is forced to control his curiosity, while questions spin around in his head. The author writes:

It is not only the young An who is plagued by doubts. The reader of this book, too, must be experiencing impatience. But just as other authors write works in which they first let the reader go in order to catch him later, so am I constrained in this tale of mine to narrate things in their proper order, from head to toe. So have patience! You, dear Reader, shall know everything at the proper time.

Author Wenkang reveals the secret of Thirteenth Sister only near the end of his novel.[7]

In effect, Wenkang is using Stratagem No. 16 here as a kind of literary trick. What he wants to catch is the reader's attention, in order to hold it for the remainder of the novel. Shortly before revealing the secret and thus resolving the tension, he lets the reader drop back into uncertainty. In this way, the author piques the reader's curiosity about the solution to the mystery, which has been held out as a kind of bait.

16.9   FIRST FORBEARANCE, THEN ADMONITION

Someone who causes an auto accident is usually shocked and ashamed at first. If the guilty party is reproached harshly while in that state of mind, it is very likely that he will react negatively in self-defense, instead of realizing and admitting his fault. So the first thing to do with a person who is responsible for a traffic accident is to speak gently with him, sympathize, listen to his version of things, and wait until he has calmed down, before stating clearly that he is to blame.

To state the matter in more universal terms: At first, permit the feelings of the guilty party free rein, because in the initial stage he will not be open to accepting blame or admonitions. But once his excitement has abated, he may be receptive to a sense of responsibility and an awareness of his own mistaken behavior.

16.10 PRAISE UNTO DEATH

The foregoing observations are linked to the Confucian virtue of forbearance. In another variant of Stratagem No. 16, Lin Biao is reported to have jotted down this maxim in the margin of a page of Stalin's essay *On Questions of Leninism:*[8]

> When there is no other choice, resort to the method of base flattery and fulsome praise. Later, you can expose the praised one and bring him down.

At that time, Lin Biao was regarded as the crown prince, Mao's heir designate. But in 1971 it was reported that, after a failed coup attempt against Mao, he died in a plane crash while trying to escape to the Soviet Union. Afterwards, Lin Biao was branded as Mao's archenemy. The maxim quoted above was cited by some authorities as proof that Lin Biao hoped to "praise [Mao] to death."[9]

During that period, the ideas of Mao Zedong were firmly entrenched in Communist China. To openly oppose them would have been suicidal. An enemy such as Lin Biao—according to this analysis—had no other choice but to pretend to be an especially zealous follower of Mao. But in order to discredit Mao's ideas and the man himself, Lin Biao did everything possible to raise Mao to impossible heights, declaring him to be the kind of genius who is born only once every thousand years: "Mao is the genius of geniuses."—"Mao Zedong's ideas are greater than material forces, and can even replace them."—"The ideas of Mao Zedong are the pinnacle of human thought."—"Every sentence uttered by Mao Zedong is an ultimate truth."

By pushing the Mao cult to extremes, Lin Biao was trying to create the conditions under which Mao could be toppled from his exaggeratedly high position. This process may also be subsumed under Stratagem No. 16: You give your enemy total freedom, in fact encourage his vanity and inflate the reverence in which he is held, to the point where a reaction of resistance and disgust sets in and it becomes relatively easy to obtain popular support for his downfall.

16.11 THE TRAP OF ARROGANCE

One day in 1925, He Long,[10] the military commandant of Feng-zhou (Hunan Province), received a report that an English businessman had been caught trying to smuggle munitions and opium near the city of Jinshi and that the contraband had been impounded on the spot. A little later an official of the British Embassy, accompanied by an official from the Chinese provincial government, appeared in He Long's office. The Englishman was aggressive and arrogant.

He Long led his guests into the reception room and asked the Englishman what his problem was. "An English businessman who was going about his business near Jinshi was thoroughly robbed by one of your subordinates. I insist that you set the matter to rights."

Calmly, He Long replied, "I am aware of the incident. I have already ordered an investigation. As soon as it is concluded, I shall institute the appropriate measures."

Believing that He Long was intimidated, the Englishman responded, with even greater arrogance, "Each and every piece of stolen property must be replaced."

"In that case," said He Long, "be so kind as to list the lost items on this form."

By his seemingly naive and tame reaction, He Long made the Englishman think that all the contraband would be given back. The man did not realize that, in keeping with Stratagem No. 16, He Long was deliberately cultivating that impression. As the Englishman began listing the impounded goods, a soldier appeared and reported to He Long, "The investigation has been concluded. Our people did indeed confiscate the goods carried by an English merchant near the city of Jinshi. The goods consisted of rifles, ammunition, and opium."

"Very well," said He Long. Stepping over to the British official, he said, "Be sure to list everything."

The Englishman did so, and signed the list. He Long took the sheet and read it through. His expression darkened, and he pounded his fist on the table. "This is just the kind of arms peddler and drug smuggler I most want to get my hands on," he said emphatically. He ordered the contraband brought to him, compared it with the official's list, and said flatly, "Your compatriot has violated Chinese law."

Outmaneuvered, the British official was speechless.

16.12 ACCOMMODATING ILLUSIONS

The Chinese have a saying, *Qi yi qi fang,* which means "to deceive someone by means of his own attitude or cast of mind." This can be seen as a highly refined application of Stratagem No. 16: You let your opponent bask in his own preconceived ideas, prejudices, convictions, or wishful thinking rather than saying anything to disturb or contradict them, even when the truth in a particular instance may run contrary to those notions. In this way you leave your opponent "free" to remain, in reality, a prisoner of his own illusion. The writings of Mencius, the second most important advocate of Confucian doctrine, contain two apt examples of this technique.

1. Yao, a legendary sage-emperor of ancient China, named the virtuous Shun as his successor. This aroused the jealousy of Xiang, Shun's younger brother, who decided on fratricide. One day Shun was cleaning out a well. After his work was done, he came out of the well by way of a side shaft which tunneled into the basement of the palace. Believing his brother was still in the well, Xiang ordered his servant to seal up the mouth of the well so that Shun would drown. Then he returned to the palace, where he saw Shun seated on his bed playing the zither. Xiang feigned pleasure. "Brother," he said, "how I've been longing to see you!" When Shun saw Xiang he was truly delighted. "You've come at just the right time," he replied. "I'm thinking about some important affairs of state. Help me work things out."

Reading this anecdote, the student Wan Zhang was confused. He asked Mencius, "If things really happened as the book says, wasn't Shun's pleasure in seeing Xiang equally a pretense?"

Mencius replied, "No. Shun was a truly virtuous man. When he saw his younger brother's pleasure, he was happy too."

2. An official named Zichan once received a live fish as a gift. He couldn't bring himself to kill it for dinner, so he gave it to the pondkeeper and told him to throw it into the pond. But the pondkeeper killed the fish and ate it. Afterward he told Zichan that he had released the fish and that it had looked dead at first when it landed in the water but then had begun to move and had swum away.

Zichan was pleased. But the pondkeeper said to others, "How can people think Zichan is a wise man? I ate his fish, but he thinks the fish is still swimming around in the pond."

In a more active version of the same predicament, one may be put in the uncomfortable situation of having to lie in order to appear truthful, to "bend" the truth in such a way that the person one is dealing with will be able to fit it into his own fixed conception of reality. This is exemplified in the following short-short story:[11]

The host poured tea into the cups and placed them on a little table before his guests. Then he covered the cups, each cover making a sweet, tinkling sound as it went on. Seeing that something was missing, the host placed the thermos jug on the floor and hurried into the next room. The two visitors, a father and his ten-year-old daughter, heard the sound of pantry doors opening and things being moved around.

The daughter stood at the window looking at some flowers. The father's finger was approaching the delicate handle of his teacup, when suddenly there was a terrible bursting sound, like an explosion.

The thermos jug on the floor had fallen over. The girl started and looked around quickly. Everything seemed normal and yet somehow strange. Neither she nor her father had touched the jug. There could be no doubt of that. When their host had put it on the floor it had wobbled but had not fallen over right away.

The sound of the crash brought the host running to his guests. In his hand he held a box of sugar cubes. He looked at the steaming puddle on the floor and murmured, "It doesn't matter. It doesn't matter!"

The father seemed inclined to say something but held his tongue at first. Then he said, "I'm terribly sorry. I kicked it accidentally."

"It doesn't matter," repeated their host calmly.

On the way home, the girl asked her father, "Did you kick the thermos jug?"

"I was nearest to it," said her father.

"But you didn't touch it! I saw your reflection in the window just at that moment. You weren't moving at all."

Her father laughed. "Well, tell me then, what else could I have done?"

"The thermos fell by itself," insisted the girl, "because the floor was uneven. I saw it wobble when Uncle Li put it down. Father, why did you say . . . ?"

"Uncle Li didn't see what happened."

"But you could have explained it to him."

"No, my child" was the father's reply. "It was better to say that I had accidentally kicked it. That was much more believable. Sometimes you just don't know how something happens. And the more truthfully you tell about it, the less truthful it seems and the less you are believed."

The girl was silent for a while.

At last she asked, "Was that the only way?"

"The only way!"

16.13 THREE VISITS TO THE THATCHED HUT

The names of Liu Bei, founder of Shu, and his Chief Minister Zhuge Liang have come up several times in previous chapters.

How did those two men develop the unshakable mutual confidence which marked their relationship?

In his early years Zhuge Liang lived as a recluse in the Longzhong Mountains near the city of Xiangyang, observing political developments in China. Speaking with his intimate friends, he often compared himself to Guan Zhong and Yue Yi, the great old masters of statesmanship and military strategy in preimperial China. What he lacked, in order to emulate their example, was a personage in whose service he could prove himself. He saw no opportunity for rapid advancement in any of the established power groups. Liu Bei seemed to offer the only chance worth taking.

Although Liu Bei's high-flown plans to become China's supreme leader had thus far come to nothing, he nevertheless radiated a certain princely aura, since he was remotely related to the imperial house of Han. Hearing that Liu Bei was looking for an adviser, Zhuge Liang decided to do everything possible to gain his trust. So he prompted certain people to sing his praises to Liu Bei.

At that time Liu Bei, already tortured by his sense of approaching age, had recently suffered one setback after another. In a battle against Cao Cao he had lost almost his entire army. Then he had barely escaped two assassination attempts by Liu Biao, the governor of Jingzhou, a distant cousin with whom he had sought asylum. Everything seemed lost. Then, while fleeing from Xiangyang after the second attempt on his life, he encountered the hermit Sima Hui (also known as Master Water-Mirror).

"I chanced to pass this way," said Liu Bei, "and have been guided to you by a shepherd boy. I am grateful for the privilege of greeting you."

Sima Hui replied, "Your Excellency is clearly in flight. I conclude this from your wet clothing and your exhausted look. Your Excellency should not attempt to hide the truth."

Whereupon Liu Bei recounted what had happened to him in Xiangyang. Sima Hui gave him tea to drink and said, "Your fame has long preceded you. How have you come to this difficult pass?"

To which Liu Bei responded, "My fate is not a good one."

Said Master Water-Mirror, "It is not Your Excellency's fate that is lacking, but good men at your side."

Liu Bei did not agree. He enumerated all his helpers and declared that they were all loyal to him.

"Agreed, you have first-rate warriors," said Sima Hui. "However, the three advisers you have named are nothing but pallid scholars. They are not capable of bringing order out of chaos or help to a troubled world."

Said Liu Bei, "I have also been seeking one of those sages who live in seclusion, waiting for their day to come round. But in vain, alas."

Sima Hui replied, "The most capable men in the kingdom are assembled in this region. Seek them out!"

"Where may I find them?"

"If you could win the help of the Sleeping Dragon, the kingdom would be yours."

"Who is he?"

Sima Hui clapped his hands and said, laughing, "Well, well!"

When Liu Bei repeated his question, Sima Hui said, "It is late. Your Excellency may spend the night here. Tomorrow we will talk again."

After supper, Liu Bei lay awake for a long time, the words of Master Water-Mirror going round and round in his head. The next day he asked Sima Hui about the Sleeping Dragon. But the hermit only laughed and again said, "Well, well!"

Liu Bei asked Sima Hui to enter his service. But the hermit refused, saying, "There are others ten times more qualified than I to lend you their support. Your Excellency must only seek them out."

Liu Bei took his leave of Sima Hui and rode to Xinye, where he again joined his boon companions Guan Yu and Zhang Fei.

At a later point a friend of Zhuge Liang, known as Dan Fu, entered Liu Bei's service as a military adviser. Compelled by family affairs to quit his service, Dan Fu in parting strongly recommended Zhuge Liang to Liu Bei in these words: "His father died young, and he was raised by his uncle in Nanyang. He took the name 'Sleeping Dragon' after a nearby mountain.

Following the death of his uncle, he went to live in the Long-zhong Mountains with his younger brother. If Your Excellency succeeds in obtaining his assistance, you need have no more worries about pacifying the kingdom."

Liu Bei's attention was thus focused on Zhuge Liang by both Sima Hui and Dan Fu. From then on, obtaining Zhuge Liang's services as adviser became Liu Bei's main goal. With his two companions, and laden with costly gifts, he set out to find this mysterious personage.

According to the version of the tale recorded in a Taipei stratagem book, Zhuge Liang had also taken other steps to increase his prestige in Liu Bei's eyes. When the Prince approached the Longzhong Mountains, he heard peasants in the fields singing a song the lyrics of which contained hints about a wise hermit in the area. When asked who had composed the song, the peasants named Zhuge Liang. They also pointed out the way to the thatched hut in which he lived.

Now Zhuge Liang was very eager to enter Liu Bei's service. But he made sure not to be at home when the Prince called. Making himself scarce was yet another device for piquing Liu Bei's interest.

Disappointed, the Prince returned to Xinye. En route he "chanced" to meet Cui Zhouping, yet another of Zhuge Liang's friends, who, in the course of a brief conversation, struck Liu Bei as a profoundly wise man. From Xinye, Liu Bei sent scouts to the Longzhong Mountains to look for Zhuge Liang. They returned with the report that he had now gone back to his hut, whereupon Liu Bei set out for another visit. His confidant Zhang Fei first suggested that, since Zhuge Liang was simply an ordinary man of the countryside, it would be more appropriate to bid him come to them. But Liu Bei replied, "How could I order the wisest man of our time to come before me?"

So Liu Bei, accompanied by his good companions, rode for a second time into the Longzhong Mountains. It was midwinter and very cold. Suddenly a blizzard struck. His friends advised turning back, but Liu Bei said, "By braving the snow, I may demonstrate my respect to Zhuge Liang."

But once again Zhuge Liang was absent. From his younger

brother, whom he met in the hut, Liu Bei learned that the man he sought had set out with Cui Zhouping on a long hike. Their destination, however, was unknown to the brother. For a second time, Liu Bei was forced to leave Zhuge Liang's dwelling without having encountered the man himself. This time, though, he left a message behind, in which he expressed his profound disappointment at having missed him again and the hope that Zhuge Liang would lend him his support in pacifying the realm. He also promised to come again, after having purified himself through fasting and cleansing herbal baths.

This time Liu Bei waited for the spring and consulted the oracle of the *I Ching* to select a favorable day for his visit. On that day he traveled to Zhuge Liang's thatched hut for the third time. To show his respect, he dismounted early and went the last few miles on foot. The young boy who guarded Zhuge Liang's house informed him that his Master had returned the previous day.

"Please inform him that I have come to visit him."

"My Master is at home, but just now he is sleeping."

"Then do not tell him now," said Liu Bei.

He told his two companions to wait outside the hut. He himself went in cautiously and found Zhuge Liang deeply asleep on straw mats. Liu Bei folded his hands breast-high in greeting and waited silently at the foot of the bed. A long while passed, and still Zhuge Liang did not awake. Finally he moved but only to turn over on his other side, with his face to the wall. The young servant boy wanted to wake him, but Liu Bei did not permit it. He stood there for another hour, waiting. Finally the Sleeping Dragon opened his eyes. He turned to the boy and said, "Have guests come?"

"It is Liu Bei, the Emperor's uncle," said the boy. "He has been standing here waiting a long time."

"Why did you not tell me sooner? First let me change my clothes." And Zhuge Liang disappeared into an adjacent apartment, to reappear after a lengthy interval, carefully clothed.

During the subsequent conversation, Zhuge Liang explained how Liu Bei might gain the kingdom. He proposed that Liu Bei first secure the territory of what is now Sichuan Province as his power base, then establish good relations with Sun Quan, the ruler of Wu to the east, win the allegiance of the alien peoples to the west and south, and finally, with massed forces, move against Cao Cao, ruler of the kingdom of Wei to the north.

Liu Bei's heart could not have been more open to Zhuge Liang's ideas. Their strategic talks in the Longzhong Mountains ended with Liu Bei jumping up, crossing his hands across his breast in greeting, and exclaiming, "Having listened to you, it is as if a light has suddenly appeared, as if dark clouds have blown away and I see the blue sky. I have no great name and am a man of but little virtue. Yet I dare hope that you, O Master, do not despise me, that you will deign to come out of your seclusion and lend me your support. I shall follow your instructions with the greatest respect."

To which Zhuge Liang replied, "For a long time now I have been tilling my fields here and have been happy in doing so. I have no desire to conform to the demands of the outside world and therefore cannot grant Your Excellency's request."

Liu Bei began to weep. "If you, O Master, do not choose to step out into the world, what will become of the poor people?"

When he saw that the other man's sleeves were wet with his tears, Zhuge Liang was convinced of Liu Bei's firm intention to rely upon his advice. Liu Bei, so urgently in search of a wise counsellor, had placed his heart firmly in Zhuge Liang's hands. Zhuge Liang hesitated no longer. And thus began his meteoric rise as chief to Liu Bei, who gave him his absolute trust.

Although the historicity of this episode, as depicted in *The Romance of the Three Kingdoms*, has not been proven beyond all doubt, many historians place these events in the year A.D. 207. In any case, they are regarded as the basis for the relationship of rockbound confidence between Liu Bei and Zhuge Liang. As noted in stratagem books from Hong Kong and Beijing, Zhuge Liang made clever use of No. 16, twice letting Liu Bei go, so to speak, in order to bind him more firmly the third time.

This episode lives on today in the Chinese saying *San gu mao lu*—"Make three calls at the thatched cottage."

16.14 THE DEATHBED WISH

Through his own carelessness, and because he had failed to follow Zhuge Liang's advice, Liu Bei suffered a serious defeat during a campaign against the kingdom of Wei to the north. Plagued by grief and self-accusation, he fell ill and was brought to White Emperor City. When his sickness took a dramatic turn for the worse, he employed Stratagem No. 16 against Zhuge Liang.

Deeply fearful that his dynasty might fall, as the hour of his death approached he called his faithful minister to him and said tearfully, "Thanks to your counsel, I was able to gain an empire. But my own abilities were too poor. Thus I ignored your advice and brought this defeat upon myself. Now I am ill from worry and shame. I find myself facing death. My own son is weak and inept. Yet I have no choice but to give the empire into his hands."

As he spoke these words, his tears fell copiously. Zhuge Liang, deeply moved, could not help crying as well. Later, brushing his tears away with his hand, the dying Liu Bei said, "My end draws near. I will reveal to you my innermost thoughts. You are greatly superior to the ruler of Wei. You have the capacity to pacify China and complete the great task. If you can bring yourself to support my son, please help him. Should he prove himself unfit for the crown, assume the throne yourself!"

Hearing these words, Zhuge Liang was beside himself. He broke out in a cold sweat, wept, then knelt by Liu Bei's deathbed and swore, "Never would I presume to do anything other than serve your son loyally, with all the strength at my command, even unto death!''

By offering him the empire and virtually encouraging him to mount a coup against his own son, the dying ruler Liu Bei cemented Zhuge Liang's loyalty and thus secured the future of his endangered family dynasty.

16.15   PATIENCE BRINGS SUCCESS

Hexagram No. 5 of the *I Ching* is *Hsü* (or *Xu*), which is given the two meanings of ''Waiting'' and ''Nourishment.'' There is a commentary on this hexagram which explains the relation between those two meanings and elevates the contents of Stratagem No. 16 to a higher plane in the art of living:

> We should not worry and seek to shape the future by interfering in things before the time is ripe. We should quietly fortify the body with food and drink and the mind with gladness and good cheer. Fate comes when it will, and thus we are ready.[12]

Toss Out a Brick to Attract Jade

The Chinese characters	抛	砖	引	玉
Modern Mandarin pronunciation	*pāo*	*zhuān*	*yǐn*	*yù*
Meaning of each character	throw (toss)	brick	attract	jade

Applications

Much like the English expression "Throw a sprat to catch a herring."

Give someone something of lesser value in order to obtain something precious in exchange; derive great benefit from an insignificant gift or favor; give your opponent something expendable now in order to gain something more valuable later. The "give-take" stratagem; the "worm-fish" stratagem.

Since ancient times, jade has been China's favorite gemstone. It is a compact mineral that, depending on its iron content, appears in a wide variety of colors from red to black, blue, green, and even white (though it's best known in its green form, of course). In ancient China, jade was used for imperial and ritual symbols, as well as for decoration and jewelry. The "Jade Emperor" is the highest divinity in Chinese folk religion.

Just as the phrase "Let a hundred flowers bloom" does not refer to real flowers but to a broad range of artistic and literary forms and styles, so Stratagem No. 17 does not refer to actual bricks and jade. The goal of No. 17 is to obtain something of value (the "jade") by giving something of lesser worth (the "brick") or using it as bait. The images may stand for many different things, which is why Li Zongwu, a Hong Kong expert on stratagems, has declared that No. 17 has the broadest range of application among the 36.

17.1 COMPLETING THE POEM

The famous Tang poet Zhao Gu was about to pay a visit to Suzhou. A local poet by the name of Chang Jian wanted to make sure that Zhao would produce at least a few lines of poetry while he was there. Chang Jian was certain that Zhao Gu would pay a visit to the Lingyansi, the Temple of the Spirit Cliff. So, on one wall of the temple, Chang Jian deliberately wrote just two undistinguished lines of a Chinese verse form that really calls for four lines, each with five or seven characters.

When Zhao Gu visited the temple, he was disturbed by the incomplete poem and finished it by adding the final two lines. Zhao's lines were far more skillfully composed than the two contributed by Chang Jian, and so subsequent generations referred to Chang's ruse as "tossing out a brick to attract jade."[1]

17.2 THE HALF-BAKED NOVICE

During the Tang period, the Buddhist monk Congshen used to assemble his novices in a room where they meditated together. With eyes closed, they had to sit very still and purge their minds of all worldly thoughts in an effort to approach a state of genuine withdrawal from self. Before one of these sessions, the monk announced, "This evening there are questions to be answered. Any of you who has achieved profound insight into Buddhist doctrine, please step forward."

Most of the novices reacted correctly, by assuming the proper seated position and sinking into silent, unmoving meditation. But one young novice, very taken with himself, arose, stepped forward, and bowed. The monk Congshen said slowly, "Just now I tossed out a brick, hoping to attract a piece of jade. And what did I get back? A half-baked brick."

This anecdote is taken from a Buddhist anthology dating from the Song period. The monk Congshen's challenge before the meditation period is the "brick" with which he hoped to discover the "jade" of a novice who had truly gone far along the path of enlightenment. But his ploy failed.

17.3 SOVIET WOODCUTS FOR CHINESE PAPER

In modern China, No. 17 is still often used as a rhetorical ploy involving self-deprecation. For example, in the first section of Mao Zedong's 1940 essay on the *New Democracy* he wrote:

> As to cultural matters, I am a layman. . . . For the cause of progressive culture in our country, what I have to say should be regarded merely as a brick tossed out in expectation of a piece of jade.

Chinese authors often refer, ironically or self-effacingly, to their own works as "bricks." For example, a long essay on the study of the English language, published in the Beijing newspaper *Guangming Daily,* begins its final paragraph this way:

> Our ideas and proposals are still tentative. We have merely raised a series of questions, tossing out a brick in hope of attracting a piece of jade.

In a note to his 1985 detective novel, *Dark Shadows over the Villa of Autumn Fragrance,* which deals with the Chinese Communist Party's political norms for private home ownership, author Cao Zhengwen writes:

> The Chinese detective story . . . is only in its infancy. By offering this slender volume to the Reader, I have tossed out a brick in order to attract jade.

In this rather lighthearted spirit, Communist China's best-known twentieth-century author, Lu Xun, gave the title *Yin yu ji* (Collection of Attracted Jades) to a 1934 collection of Russian woodcuts which he edited. In 1931, when Lu Xun wanted to publish the novel *The Iron Stream,* by Alexander S. Serafimovitch, he read in a magazine about the existence of Russian woodcuts made for this work and very much wanted to acquire them. A friend of Lu Xun who was visiting the Soviet Union at the time sent him a few of the woodcuts, remarking that they were very expensive. But, he wrote, Russian printmakers were very partial to Chinese paper for making their prints, and if Lu Xun could send paper he would get the woodcuts gratis. Examining the woodcuts, Lu found that they had indeed been printed on Chinese paper, the kind used in China merely for bookkeeping and bills. So Lu Xun sent a supply of cheap Chinese and Japanese paper (the "bricks") in exchange for which he received thirty-six valuable woodcuts (the "jade pieces").

17.4   THE GRAVESIDE PROMISE

The maiden Cai was lovely of feature, with a strong, healthy body. She found favor in the eyes of King Gong of Chu, who chose her for his wife. One day the courtier Jiang Yi visited Lady Cai and asked her, "Did your ancestors perform outstanding military service for the dynasty?"

"No," replied Lady Cai.

"Have you yourself performed any special services for the crown?"

"No."

"How then," asked Jiang Yi, "have you come to enjoy such a lofty position?"

"I do not know the reason," answered Lady Cai.

Jiang Yi remarked, "I have heard it said that, if you attract a person with money, he will withdraw his favor as soon as the money is gone. And if you attract a person with beauty, he will withdraw his favor when the beauty pales. Today you are in the full bloom of your womanhood, but one day your beauty will fade. How will you insure that the King will continue to grant you his favor and not turn away from you?"

Lady Cai replied, "I am young and ignorant. Therefore I entreat you, give me your sage advice."

Said Jiang Yi, "It will suffice for you to let His Majesty know that you propose to be buried with him."

"I shall follow your advice," said the young woman.

Jiang Yi took his leave. A year later he met Lady Cai again and asked her whether she had conveyed to the King her intention to be buried with him. She replied, "I have found no opportunity of doing so."

A year later, Jiang Yi once again visited Lady Cai and asked, "Have you told our ruler?"

"No. I have found no suitable opportunity."

To which Jiang Yi responded, "You ride with His Majesty in the same carriage. Two years have gone by, and yet you maintain that you have not been able to speak with the King about this. Presumably you regard my advice as of little value." And he went away grumbling.

Later that year the King held a great hunt. Torches smoked like fiery clouds; the howling of wolves and roaring of tigers were like peals of thunder. A frenzied rhinoceros broke out of the forest and headed for the side of the royal carriage. The King raised high his standard of command and ordered his best marksman to kill the beast. One arrow, and the rhino sank to the ground. The King clapped his hands in delight, laughed, turned to his wife, and said, "With whom will you share such pleasures after my life has ended?"

Lady Cai hesitated a moment, then shed a few tears, threw her arms around the King, and said, "After Your Majesty has lived for ten thousand years, his humble subject will accompany him into his tomb. How, then, shall I know who will enjoy these pleasures as the next king?"

Hearing these gratifying words, on the spot King Gong awarded Lady Cai a fiefdom of three hundred households. This is why it is said, "Jiang Yi is an expert in stratagems, and Lady Cai is an expert at picking the most opportune moment."[2]

In this instance, of course, the "brick" is Lady Cai's promise, while the "jade" is the gift which made her secure for the rest of her life.

17.5 ODE TO A FART

"Flowering talent"—*Xiucai*—was the designation for a certain rank of scholar in imperial China. One such scholar had just died and made his appearance before Yama, the Prince of Hell. At that moment Yama broke wind mightily. And immediately the "flowering talent" improvised this "Ode to a Fart":

> *The golden-shimmering rump arches high,*
> *Releasing an expansive zone of savory aspiration.*
> *The sound is like that of strings and brass,*
> *The aroma that of musk and fragrant marjoram.*

The Prince of Hell was greatly pleased, gave the "flowering talent" a gift of ten additional years of life, and sent him back to the world of mankind.[3]

Here the "brick" is the totally worthless "ode," a piece of unbridled, bootlicking flattery. The "jade" that it brings in, of course, is the extra ten years of life granted by the Prince of Hell. A blatant case of "I give you a little, you give me a lot."

17.6 SCHOPENHAUER'S 36TH STRATAGEM

In "The Art of Controversy," the philosopher Arthur Schopenhauer explains the following tactic:

> You may also puzzle and bewilder your opponent by mere bombast, and the trick is possible, because a person generally supposes that there must be some meaning in words

[*gewöhnlich glaubt der Mensch, wenn er nur Worte hört, es müsse sich dabei doch auch was denken lassen*]. If he is secretly conscious of his own weakness, and accustomed to hear much that he does not understand, and to make as though he did, you can easily impose upon him by some serious fooling that sounds very deep and learned, and deprives him of hearing, sight, and thought; and by giving out that it is the most indisputable proof of what you assert.[4]

17.7 ANGLING FOR A KING

Meaningless but attention-provoking actions are another way of getting high returns on small investments. According to legend, this was the technique used by Jiang Ziya toward the end of the Shang Dynasty to enter the service of King Wu of Zhou.

Disgusted by conditions at the Shang court, Jiang Ziya left the capital and withdrew to live a hermit's life on the bank of the Wei, an important tributary of the Yellow River. At that time this area was ruled by Prince Ji Chang of the Zhou clan, an enemy of the Shang. Jiang Ziya was aware of Ji Chang's far-reaching political plans and his search for capable advisers.

In order to attract Ji Chang's attention, Jiang Ziya began to fish in the Wei River—but in a most unusual manner. His hook was straight instead of bent, he had no bait on it, and he kept the hook at least three feet above the water. He sat there, his fishing pole pointing up toward the sky, and repeated this sentence over and over: "All fish that are tired of living should come up and bite my hook."

This odd angling technique naturally was soon reported to Ji Chang. He thought the fisherman must be a very unusual fellow and sent a soldier to bring him to the court. Jiang Ziya, however, paid no attention at all to the soldier. Instead he muttered to himself, "Hook! Hook! Hook! But instead of a fish, there's a little shrimp out to make mischief!"

The soldier went back to the palace and reported the failure of his mission to Ji Chang, who became more than ever convinced that the fisherman must be a strange but extraordinary person. Whereupon he sent a government official to invite the man to the court. When Jiang Ziya spotted the arriving official, he ignored him completely and spoke to himself, "Hook! Hook! Hook! The big fish won't bite, but a smaller one is hanging around."

The official went straight back and reported to Ji Chang, who said to himself, "That's really a very intriguing fellow."

Prince Ji Chang now loaded himself up with precious gifts and personally went to invite the fisherman to the palace for a conversation. This proved to Jiang Ziya that Ji Chang was sincere in his search for capable advisers, and he entered the service of the Zhou. According to all reports he was of material help to the Zhou in toppling the Shang Dynasty.

In terms of this stratagem, Jiang's strange fishing technique was the "brick," and the growing interest of the Zhou ruler was the "jade."

17.8 A FRAGRANT NAME FOR A HUNDRED GENERATIONS

"A fish sees only the bait, not the hook," writes Wang Zhihua in the *Chinese Youth Journal*. Because of this the fish bites and lands on the fisherman's dinner plate. Society too offers plenty of "bait," observes Wang, and as an example he cites some advertising copy for a commercially published *Who's Who* of the Chinese business world:

> This *Who's Who* is an absolute must for every factory director and manager. Keep a copy handy at all times. From this book you can learn about the experiences and ideas of others and, with the help of its data, can make contact with other people in situations similar to yours. The book also helps spread glory and honor over your own family, down to your grandchildren and great-grandchildren, by

d opens his pointy beak full wide
give forth song—but the cheese he drops,
d into the fox's mouth it pops.
s Fox, "Each flatterer, Old Bird,
ds off those who swallow his words.
s lesson—which I hope will please—
ertainly worth a ripe old cheese."

(from La Fontaine's *Fables*)[5]

rds of greeting clearly are the "brick" through
ains the cheesy "jade."

17.10 A GIFT OF FIVE CITIES

States period, the state of Qin wanted to conquer
Vei. To that end it allied itself with the state of
mised that, in the event of a victorious campaign,
Ye (in what is today Henan Province) would be

by a two-front war, the King of Wei was terrified
ministers together for a council. No one knew
nally the monarch asked General Mang Mao,
ially prized for his cunning. The General said
eally no cause for alarm, since relations between
had never been good.

e of the present military alliance," continued
Mao, "is only to divide up our land and expand
the other two kingdoms. Though the strength
ems overwhelming, in fact each partner is pur-
als. Qin sets the tone, while Zhao serves only
. All we need do is offer Zhao a tangible ad-
hould be easy to shatter its alliance with Qin."
en spun out his own plan. The King of Wei
carried it out. He sent an emissary to Zhao
ng communication for that realm's ruler: "In

showing how you ha
ily's history. Your na
of Chinese factory ar
in history and spr
generations.

The price of being liste
and Managers is a reg
more for layout and
total of twenty-six yι
at the 1988 rate), wh
The publishers try t
officials by issuing a s
promises.

Irving M. Copi, a
this kind of propaga
he cites the examp
rounded by a bevy
prove that it's the b
their products and
dreams.

17.9 THɪ

Master
holds i
Master
speaks
"*God*
hands
Your
and e
A ve
in al
Our

---

an
to
anι
Sa)
fee
Th
is c

The fox's w
which he obt

In the Warring
the state of W
Zhao. Qin pro
the Wei city o
ceded to Zhao

Threatened
and called his
what to do. Fi
who was espec
that there was r
Qin and Zhao
"The purpos
General Mang
the territory of
of the alliance s
suing his own g
a subsidiary rol
vantage, and it s
Mang Mao th
approved it and
with the followi

the present situation we can no longer hold the city of Ye. Sooner or later it will fall. You are attacking our land along with the kingdom of Qin for no other reason than to obtain that city. To avoid a war the King of Wei has decided to hand over the city of Ye without a fight. Do you accept our offer?"

Delighted, the King of Zhao said, "Why should the King of Wei deign to make us a gift of the city even before the battle is joined?"

The emissary replied, "That is quite simple. War is a terrible thing; it costs human lives and devastates entire areas. His Majesty the King of Wei is being guided by humanitarian considerations and loving care for his people, whom he wishes to spare misery and destruction. Therefore he has chosen the path of peace."

The ruler of Zhao inquired, "But what does the King of Wei expect of me, should I accept his offer?"

To which the emissary responded, "Naturally, His Majesty does have certain expectations, since he is offering a peaceful settlement, not an unconditional surrender. Wei and Zhao used to enjoy friendly relations and a working alliance. On the other hand, profound hostility has always characterized relations between Wei and Qin. Qin is a predator; the Qin warriors are like wild beasts. We would prefer to entrust our territory to old friends rather than let it become the prey of barbarians. That is surely comprehensible. If you are prepared to conclude a treaty of friendship with the King of Wei, he expects you to break off relations with Qin. Then you shall receive the city of Ye as a token of that friendship. However, should you refuse this offer, our state will pursue a scorched-earth policy and fight to the last drop of blood."

That night the King of Zhao conferred with his minister, who suggested accepting the offer. After all, he reasoned, if they could gain the real objective of the war—the city of Ye—without fighting, why conduct a war at all? Moreover, after annexing the kingdom of Wei, Qin would become even more powerful and might then turn its spears against Zhao. So it made sense, concluded the minister, to exploit the excellent opportunity offered them by Wei, secure Wei's support, and in so doing, to contain Qin's expansionism and thus strengthen Zhao's own security.

The King of Zhao therefore accepted the conditions laid down by Wei, immediately broke off relations with Qin, and closed the border crossings to that country. This news so infuriated the King of Qin that he immediately broke off his preparations for an attack against Wei and instead laid plans to move against Zhao.

In the meantime, thinking to translate into action the terms of the pact he had concluded with the emissary from Wei, the King of Zhao sent an army marching toward the city of Ye with the intention of occupying it. Ye was held by troops under the command of General Mang Mao, who blocked the path of the Zhao army at the frontier and asked its commandant whether they came in peace or in war. The Zhao commander explained about the Wei-Zhao pact and the ceding of Ye to his army.

"Damn it!" roared Mang Mao, "I've been put in charge of safeguarding this city. Do you expect me to just hand it over without a fight?"

"We're talking about a secret diplomatic agreement," replied the Zhao General. "The King of Wei has given his approval."

"What d'you mean, secret agreement?" responded Mang Mao. "Has my King personally put his seal to this business? Has he signed that pact you're talking about? If so, kindly show me the document."

"What?" said the Zhao commander. "Are the words of a royal emissary from Wei worth nothing?"

"What emissary?" replied Mang Mao gruffly. "If you're relying on the words of an emissary, you'd better apply to him for further instructions. Our King has given me no new orders. I'm not empowered to hand over the city. If you want to take over the city, ask my commander in chief for permission. Now I'm warning you: if you don't withdraw immediately, I'll cut off your retreat and attack you!"

The Zhao General had no choice but to withdraw and report back to his ruler. Only then did the King of Zhao realize that he had been tricked by the King of Wei. Just then he heard reports that Qin was trying to conclude a military alliance with Wei against Zhao, which made him even more fearful. After an emergency meeting with his advisers, he voluntarily ceded five cities to Wei to persuade that kingdom to join with Zhao in an alliance against Qin.[6]

The "brick" here is Wei's deceptive promise to cede the city of Ye; the deterrence of the planned Qin attack and the five cities ceded by Zhao constitute the "jade."

17.11 STALIN'S WAR AGAINST JAPAN

The anonymous author of a Taipei stratagem book[7] refers to the Yalta Conference of February 1945 as "the secret division of spoils." According to that writer, Stalin applied Stratagem No. 17 at Yalta. In order to end the war as quickly as possible, Roosevelt (at that time "a very sick man," according to Lord Moran, Churchill's personal physician) and Churchill (who, according to the same source, had "feelings of friendship and respect" for Stalin) requested Stalin to declare war on Japan. The Soviet leader agreed to enter the war against Japan after Germany's capitulation. This was Stalin's "brick," in exchange for which he elicited various Western concessions in East Asia, among them the annexation of the Japanese Kuriles and the southern part of Sakhalin Island.

According to the Yalta agreements Stalin should have declared war on Japan in May 1945. But he permitted the date to pass without taking any action, leaving the Japanese a free hand in their war with the Allies.

It was only on August 8, after the atomic bomb had been dropped on Hiroshima—in other words, at a time when Japan was already ripe for capitulation—that Stalin formally declared war on Japan and effortlessly harvested the profits that Roosevelt and Churchill had promised him. Among other things, the Kremlin was able to impose its influence on northeastern

China, which helped the Communist Chinese army gain control of the entire country.

According to the Taiwanese stratagem book referred to above, Stalin's behavior is a perfect example of No. 17. At the Yalta Conference he exploited the Allies' thirst for victory, mobilized their sympathies with a few well-chosen words, and thus assured himself of gaining power in East Asia.

Similarly, according to another Taiwanese author, the Soviet government under Stalin signed an agreement with Chiang Kai-shek in Moscow on August 14, 1945, in which the Kremlin recognized Chiang's regime as the sole legal representative of the Chinese people and promised it help against the advance of the Chinese Communists. In exchange, the Soviet government gained three important concessions: recognition of the old Chinese territory of Outer Mongolia as an independent state (which quickly fell under Soviet influence), joint administration of the Changchun railway line in northeastern China for thirty years, and a thirty-year lease on the harbors at Port Arthur and Dalian. The author notes that, through this application of No. 17 (the "brick" being Stalin's fraudulent promise to treat the Guomindang as China's legitimate government and help it against the Chinese Communists), Russia gratified its imperialist ambitions and secured a bridgehead in the Far East.

17.12 ALL THE KINGDOMS OF THE WORLD

Chapter 4 of the Gospel According to Matthew recounts:

> The devil took him to a very high mountain, and showed him all the kingdoms of the world in their glory. "All these," he said, "I will give you, if you will only fall down and do me homage." But Jesus said, "Begone, Satan! Scripture says, 'You shall do homage to the Lord your God and worship him alone.' "
>
> Then the devil left him; and angels appeared and waited on him.[8]

Satan's offer—"all the kingdoms of the world"—is obviously a worthless illusion, nothing but the "brick" with which Satan hopes to obtain what is of real value to him, Jesus' abandonment of God and worship of himself. Here Jesus provides the model for an appropriate reaction to the malicious use of No. 17: he throws the "brick" back at the one who offered it.

17.13 QUENCHING THIRST WITH A PROMISE OF PLUMS

One time Cao Cao lost his way during a battle campaign and led his men into an area without water. The soldiers became very thirsty, whereupon Cao Cao had the following proclamation made: "Up ahead there is a large grove of plum trees. Much of the fruit is ripe. It has a sweet-sour taste and is very thirst-quenching." When the troops heard this, their mouths watered. In this way Cao Cao kept them marching until at last they really did find a source of water.[9]

Today this incident lives on in the Chinese expression "to quench the thirst with a promise of plums"—that is, to console or sustain someone with an illusion.

17.14 SATISFYING HUNGER WITH A PAINTED CAKE

In his search for Buddhist enlightenment, the monk Zhixian left his family, renounced the world, and went to the Dhyana monastery on Mount Guishan. There the monk known as Master You, who liked Zhixian for his dedication to the Buddhist path and hoped to bring him further enlightenment, said to him, "I do not ask you to speak of what you have learned in your lifetime of study or of what is written in the great classics. Instead, I beg you, tell me something of what it was like while you were still in your mother's womb and had not yet learned to differentiate anything. Tell me of that primal state untouched by learned wisdom and experience with the external world."

Somewhat taken aback, Zhixian was silent for a while, then muttered to himself for a long time, and finally uttered a few sentences in an effort to meet the Master's request. But You was not satisfied with the answer. Finally Zhixian said, "I beg you to say something about this matter."

Master You replied, "Anything I could say would be my own view. How could that possibly enrich your perceptions?"

Zhixian then returned to his cell and searched all his books and manuscripts for an appropriate response. But he found none. Finally he said to himself with a mighty sigh, "One cannot satisfy hunger with a painting of a cake." Whereupon he burned all his books, saying, "I shall study the Buddhist way no longer in this life. Instead I shall become a wandering beggar and thus plague my spirit no more."

Tearfully he left Mount Guishan and went out into the world. Zhixian had suddenly found Buddhist doctrine to be like the mere painting of a cake, the consumption of which had only seemed to offer profound insights. The painted cake was the "brick," the presumed knowledge the "jade." But in this case even the jade turned out to be only a brick.

17.15 THE UNGUARDED WOODGATHERERS

In the military sphere, says a Beijing stratagem expert, "tossing out a brick" often means executing a tactical dissimulation designed to mislead the enemy in specific ways. The dissimulation may involve sham troop movements or sham attacks. The main ingredient insuring that your side obtains its "piece of jade," however, is the psychological state of the enemy. If you judge the enemy's state of mind properly, you can induce him to take the pretense for the real thing.

In the year 700 B.C. the state of Chu attacked the state of Jiao and laid siege to its capital city, which was stoutly defended by the Jiao army. Finally an official by the name of Qu Xia came to the King of Chu and said, "The state of Jiao is small, and its ruler can therefore be easily disconcerted. He who is easily disconcerted does not think things through carefully. Let us therefore send our troop of woodgatherers out to do their work unguarded, in order to lure the Jiao defenders into a trap."

In ancient times, a Chinese army out in the field took with it a troop of men responsible for gathering firewood and preparing meals. Usually, these men were protected by soldiers when they went out searching for firewood. Qu Xia was proposing to send them out unguarded this time.

The King of Chu approved the plan. The first time the wood-gatherers went out unprotected, thirty of them were captured by Jiao troops. The next day the entire Jiao army was on the alert to capture the woodgatherers when they were again sent out unguarded. In the meantime, the Chu army had sent some of its forces to set an ambush in the mountains and others to lay in wait outside the city gates. When the Jiao army, concentrating on hunting for the woodgatherers, was solidly encircled, the Chu army attacked and defeated its opponents, eventually forcing Jiao to capitulate.

The woodgatherers captured on the first day by the Jiao troops served as the "brick," and Jiao's surrender was the "jade."

17.16   MISLEADING THE ENEMY

In March 1947, a 230,000-man army of the Guomindang regime advanced toward the Communist stronghold in the Shaanxi-Gansu-Ningxia border area. Mao Zedong ordered that, instead of trying to hold any particular positions, the Communist forces were to operate in a hit-and-run mode and inflict the heaviest possible losses on the enemy. He then pulled out of the Red headquarters at Yan'an, which was promptly occupied by twelve Guomindang brigades. The fall of the Communists' symbolic capital was naturally celebrated by Chiang

Kai-shek's Nationalist regime as a great victory, and a large part of the Guomindang army dug itself in at Panlong near Yan'an.

The Communist Northwest Field Army wanted to attack the base at Panlong, but it was very strongly fortified. To overrun it, they must lure away the forces guarding the base. So the Red Army concentrated a large number of boats at certain crossing points of the Wuding and Dali rivers, in the area of Suide and Mizhi, and sent small detachments of troops marching by diverse routes, apparently heading for Suide. Observing these movements through its aerial reconnaissance, the Guomindang mistakenly believed that the Red Army's main force was trying to pull back eastward to an area around the Yellow River. In consequence, it sent nine regiments marching northward.

The Red Army now applied Stratagem No. 17. It ordered various units to mount constant attacks against the enemy forces moving northward. At the same time it deliberately left substantial objects behind it, in order to clearly mark the route for the enemy and awaken the impression that the presumed main force of the Red Army intended to veer northward. In this way the Guomindang regiments were misled into constantly chasing what they believed to be the main force of the Northwest Field Army, in the hope of joining forces with a Guomindang force stationed in Yulin and catching the fleeing Red Army in a pincers movement.

When the main Guomindang force had thus been lured northward, the main Red Army force came out of its hiding place near Yongping, marched to Panlong, surrounded the fortified base on April 29, 1947, began its attack on May 2, and took the base on May 4, killing all 6,700 troops left behind to defend it. By that time the main enemy force was much too far away to be able to relieve Panlong.

17.17   WOMEN INSTEAD OF WEAPONS

At the end of the third century B.C. the Xiongnu, sometimes known as the "Huns of East Asia," founded a large federation of nomadic tribes. Their empire stretched from Lake Baikal (in southern Siberia) to Lake Balkhash (in what is now Soviet Kazakhstan) and southward to the areas of today's Inner Mongolia, Gansu, and Xinjiang. The Xiongnu mounted many attacks against Chinese territory,[10] in the course of which they captured much booty and made slaves of the prisoners they took. The Han Emperor dared not go to war against these fierce barbarians. What was he to do?

In the year 198 B.C., Emperor Gaozu summoned Prince Liu Jing to come to the palace and discuss the situation. Liu Jing began by observing that the Xiongnu could not be defeated by force of arms. "Surely you don't think," replied the Emperor, "that we could tame them through cultural influence?"

To which Liu Jing countered, "The nature of Mo Du, King of the Xiongnu, is like a smoldering fire. His actions are those of a wolf. To try and speak with him about such matters as humanity, duty, and virtue would be futile. But there is another way of taming him, and not only him but his descendants as well. It is a long-term strategy. But I do not know what Your Majesty will think of it."

The Emperor wanted to hear more. Liu Jing continued: "The only way to tame the Xiongnu is by political marriage, which turns the enemy into a relative. I propose that you offer a princess to Mo Du as his wife. That will fill him with gratitude. The Chinese woman will be his queen, and the sons she bears him will be Mo Du's successors. You can use the relationship of father-in-law to son-in-law as a vehicle by which to cultivate regular contacts, supported by frequent precious gifts. Such treatment will turn even the wildest tiger into a tame one on which you can ride. As your son-in-law, Mo Du will no longer dare to plague your empire, and his successors, your grandsons, will most certainly behave peaceably. In this way you can subjugate the enemy's soldiers by peaceful means, without war. This is a scheme that offers long-term security."

The Emperor's first reaction was an angry one. "How could an honorable Chinese Emperor give a wild barbarian a Chinese princess for a wife? I would earn scorn and derision."

Liu Jing replied, "Your Majesty might also sacrifice a plum

tree in place of a peach tree, by pretending that the most beautiful lady-in-waiting at your court is a princess and marrying her to Mo Du."

The Han Emperor followed this advice. And indeed, Mo Du gleefully accepted the proffered bride and declared himself willing to assume a family tie with Emperor Gaozu. Chinese women were also married to Xiongnu rulers after Mo Du's death. Although the peace between the Xiongnu and China was of relatively brief duration and the barbarian attacks never ceased entirely, the Chinese ruler's action certainly ranks as an application of Stratagem No. 17. The Chinese brides, with all due respect, were the "bricks" in this instance, and the "jade" was the peace (however temporary) won by the ploy of political marriage.

17.18 THE HELPFUL TELEGRAM

During World War II, American forces in the Pacific became aware that the letters *AF* were cropping up frequently in Japanese wireless communications they were monitoring. The Americans assumed that this was a code designation for the Midway Islands. In order to confirm their suspicion, the U.S. Marine commandant on Midway was ordered to send a telegram, in readily comprehensible English, stating that there was a problem with the drinking water supply on the islands. Soon afterward the Americans intercepted a Japanese telegram containing the message that "*AF* would probably run out of drinking water soon." This confirmed the American suspicions that *AF* was the code name for the Midway Islands, and from then on the U.S. forces were able to anticipate all Japanese actions against the islands.

17.19   THE EMPTY CASE

Bi Ai, a resident of Lanxi District in Zhejiang Province, was a man wise in the ways of the stratagems. One day he received a visit from a friend who worked in the *yamen*, the district's government building. The man asked Bi Ai to please come to the *yamen*. There he met Huang, the new prefect, who was widely regarded as a thoroughly honest official and was now in a state of extreme agitation.

After an elaborate greeting, Prefect Huang told Bi Ai of his problem. It seems that the official district seal had suddenly disappeared. Huang suspected the prison guard Hu, a greedy fellow who did not always place the law above his own material advantage. District chief Huang had already reprimanded him several times on that account, which had earned him the prison guard's enmity. To get revenge, Hu had befriended the keeper of the seals and apparently had taken advantage of the keeper's brief absence to purloin the district seal.

Having discovered the theft, Huang had called a meeting of those officials loyal to him. The situation was complicated. There was no proof of Hu's guilt. Were he to be arrested, he would doubtless deny everything. If he felt driven to desperate measures, there was even a danger of his destroying the seal. Then Hu could not be arrested, the seal would be gone forever, and Prefect Huang, who bore overall responsibility, might lose his position and even be punished. Friendly admonition would not persuade Hu to confess either, since he would fear a harsh reaction from the prefect. The officials at the meeting had turned matters this way and that but arrived at no solution. Finally they had hit upon the idea of consulting Bi Ai.

After thinking for a while, Bi Ai said to Huang, "Do not trouble yourself any longer. Report yourself sick immediately. Receive no visitors for three days, do no official business, and issue no documents. You can be certain that, by the fourth day, the seal will be in your possession once again." Whereupon Bi Ai recounted the details of his plan to the district chief.

On the night of the third day, a fire suddenly broke out in the *yamen*. The news shocked the whole city. Gongs sounded and people shouted. Prefect Huang ordered all town employees to fall to and help put out the fire. The prison guard Hu naturally had to obey the order too. When he came running up, Huang called him aside and said, "Many people are helping to put out the fire. I've taken charge of the operation myself. You need not involve yourself. Instead I want you to take care of the official seal of the district. Here is the case. If you take good care of it, I shall regard it as your contribution toward fighting the fire."

With those words, the prefect hurried away. Hu had accepted the case without much thought and now found that it was locked, so that he could not simply open it on the spot, show everyone that it was empty, and give it back to Huang. Suddenly the prison guard realized that he had been tricked. As soon as he handed the case back to the prefect, Huang would open it in front of all those present and, should it be empty, would accuse him of theft. Hu could see no alternative but to take the empty case home and return the seal to it in the same way that he had removed it.

The fire was extinguished that same night. The next day Prefect Huang assembled his employees in order to reward them for their good work. Prison guard Hu appeared with the case. Huang opened it immediately—and there was the official seal, nestled within as it should have been. Naturally, Prefect Huang pretended to be unaware that anything had happened and gave Hu his reward along with everyone else.

In this way Prefect Huang averted the danger of losing his position and being punished for loss of the seal, by applying Stratagem No. 17.

17.20 LAO-TZE—PHILOSOPHER OF INTRIGUE?

What you wish to limit, you must first expand.
What you wish to weaken, you must first strengthen.

What you wish to topple, you must first erect.
To him from whom you would take, you must first give.[11]

Because of this passage in the *Daodejing,* the main scripture of
Daoism, its reputed author Lao-tze is sometimes accused of
propounding a philosophy of intrigue. In some commentaries
these lines are said to apply to the military realm.

Gao Heng, a historian of philosophy who died in China in
1986, rejected such an interpretation. In defense of Lao-tze, he
rendered the lines quoted above as follows:

What will shrink, must surely first expand.
What will become weak, must surely first be strong.
What will decline, must surely first rise.
What is to be taken, must surely first be given.

In his *Readily Comprehensible Interpretation of the Lao-tze
Text* (Beijing, 1987), Lu Yuanchi tries for a compromise between the first and second renderings. In his view, both readings
are linguistically correct; Gao Heng's version applies to natural
phenomena and the earlier one to human society. Lao-tze himself, says Lu Yuanchi, was primarily describing certain "dialectical laws" in nature but at the same time sought to provide
metaphors for specific social processes and thus warn people
about them.

Be that as it may: In the *Han Feizi,* a book ascribed to Han
Fei and containing the oldest collection of examples elucidating
Lao-tze citations, the passage in question is unmistakably treated
in terms of stratagems and tactics.

17.21   A Bell as a Vanguard

Marquis Zhi, the most powerful of the six nobles in the kingdom
of Jin in the mid-fifth century B.C., was thinking of attacking
the kingdom of Chouyou. But its terrain was very difficult. So

he had a great bell cast and offered it as a gift to the ruler of Chouyou. That worthy was delighted and proposed making his country more accessible so that the bell could be brought to him. His adviser Chizhang Manzhi said, "You must not! Marquis Zhi is acting like the ruler of a small state paying his respects to the ruler of a larger one. But Marquis Zhi rules a powerful state. The bell will surely be followed by soldiers. Do not accept the gift!" But the ruler of Chouyou did not take this advice. He accepted the bell—and seven months later Chouyou was destroyed. Marquis Zhi's troops had indeed followed the bell.

The *Han Feizi* uses this anecdote to illustrate the relevant ideas in the *Daodejing*. After citing the incident, the *Han Feizi* states, "That is why it is said: 'To him from whom you would take, you must first give.' "

17.22   THE DEADLY GIFT

Another time, Marquis Zhi demanded a piece of land from Prince Xuan of Wei. The Prince refused. His adviser Ren Zhang asked, "Why do you not give him the land?"

"Marquis Zhi is demanding land from me without so much as giving a reason. Why should I let him have it?"

To which his adviser replied, "If you give the Marquis some land now, his arrogance will increase, as will his greed for yet more land. This will make the rulers of neighboring states nervous and they will join forces against him. When this happens, Marquis Zhi's life will be over. As it is said, 'To him from whom you would take, you must first give.' Your Excellency would do well to let the Marquis have the land and thus increase his arrogance."

"Very well," said the Prince. And he gave Marquis Zhi a fiefdom of ten thousand households. Zhi was delighted. Later he demanded land from the kingdom of Zhao, which refused. Thereupon Marquis Zhi launched a war against Zhao. The kingdoms of Han and Wei hurried to Zhao's aid—and Marquis Zhi lost his life.

Here the "brick" is the fiefdom, while the "jade" is the ultimate destruction of Marquis Zhi.

17.23 DOWNFALL OF A DYNASTY

In the eighth century B.C., with the Western Zhou Dynasty seemingly nearing its downfall, Duke Huan said to his adviser Shi Bo, "Our dynasty is endangered. I fear that its imminent collapse will affect me as well. Where can I flee to escape death?"

Shi Bo replied, "The foreign peoples to the west and north will surely gain strength from our decline. There are many other states around Zhou, but none of them offers a true haven. Hao and Kuai are among the larger royal fiefdoms. Because of their strategic locations, the rulers of Hao and Kuai are proud and arrogant. They are also greedy. If you offer to entrust your wife, children, and fortune to the care of those two rulers, they will not dare refuse your request. But if the Zhou Dynasty then collapses, their arrogance and greed will prompt them to break their word. They will turn against you in order to get their hands on your wealth. You will then have good reason to mobilize your loyal Zhou vassals, march against Hao and Kuai because they betrayed you, and conquer their territory."

The Duke found this advice very attractive. So he sent his wife and children to the rulers of Hao and Kuai, who took them under their care. In this way Duke Huan lured the other rulers into a trap. The "brick" was his family and his wealth, which the others' greed would tempt them to try and hold onto. The "jade" was the secure haven which Duke Huan obtained for himself by creating an excuse to go to war.[12]

17.24 MORE THAN A HORSE

The Donghu began settling in eastern China during the Spring and Autumn period and had repeated friction with neighboring peoples. In the year 209 B.C., the ruler of the nearby Xiongnu (see Section 17.17, "Women Instead of Weapons") was murdered by his son Mo Du, who then ascended the throne. Wishing to feel Mo Du out, the Donghu ruler sent an emissary to him with a request that Mo Du give him a gift of a "thousand-mile horse"—a horse of great speed and endurance.

Mo Du saw the intention behind the request. He called his ministers together and held council. The ministers noted that there was only one thousand-mile horse in the entire land, inherited from the late king. How could it simply be given away to another realm?

But Mo Du decided differently. "We cannot possibly risk our good neighborly relations for the sake of a horse." And so he gave away the thousand-mile horse.

The Donghu ruler now believed that Mo Du feared him. After a while he sent another emissary, this time demanding that Mo Du's wife be given to him. Once again Mo Du took council with his advisers. Indignant, they called out, "Scandalous, the arrogance of that Donghu chieftain. Now he wants our queen for his wife! We suggest that you punish him by declaring war."

Again Mo Du took a different tack. "Why should we endanger our friendship with our neighbors for the sake of a woman?" And he had his wife delivered to the Donghu ruler.

Having received from Mo Du not only his finest horse but also his beautiful wife, the Donghu chief's success went to his head. A short time later he sent yet another messenger to the Xiongnu court. This time he demanded a thousand-mile strip of land in the frontier territory between the two states.

Once again Mo Du met with his advisers. Some of them advocated yielding the land, others were opposed. Suddenly Mo Du stood up and thundered, "Land is the foundation of the state. How could we ever give it away!" And he commanded that all those advisers who had proposed giving up the land be executed. Then he drew on his armor, mobilized the army, and struck with lightning speed against the Donghu.

The enemy's troops were so surprised by the attack and by this first refusal that they were unable to mount any defense.

In no time, Mo Du had destroyed the entire Donghu state and penetrated to the ruler's palace, where he killed the Donghu chief.

The "bricks," the princely gifts to the Donghu ruler, yielded the "jade" of greater power and territory.

17.25   GOLD AND SILKS FOR THE TURKS

In the mid-sixth century A.D., Turkic-speaking peoples established a large empire in the territory of what is now Mongolia and stretching far to the west. In the year 582 the empire split into a western and an eastern part. Though held in check to some extent by China's Sui Dynasty, the Eastern Turks were encouraged by the chaos and palace intrigues early in the succeeding Tang Dynasty to mount repeated incursions into Chinese territory.

In the year A.D. 622, Xieli, the Khan of the Eastern Turks, led an army of 100,000 men in an attack against the area that is now the Chinese province of Shanxi. By promising annual tribute, an emissary of the Tang Emperor persuaded Xieli to withdraw. Then, in 624, Xieli joined forces with Tuli, another Turk leader, and again attacked China. That threat was likewise averted, this time thanks to the courage of Li Shimin, a son of the Chinese Emperor, who succeeded in sowing discord between the two Turkic leaders.

In the year 626, Xieli attacked China yet again with 100,000 troops and advanced to within a few miles of the Chinese capital of Chang'an. At that time the recently founded Tang Dynasty was still weak. The youthful Li Shimin, now Emperor of China, rejected the suggestion by one of his advisers that he fortify his position inside the capital, fearing that if he did so the Turks would lay waste to the Chinese provinces. "I must show them that I am not afraid," he declared. He mobilized his small army and rode ahead with a few warriors to the bank of the Wei River, where the Turks were waiting on the opposite bank for the battle to begin. His voice ringing with outrage, Li Shimin hurled an accusation against the Khan: "You are violating earlier agreements!"

At the sight of the Chinese Emperor, the Turk leaders lost their courage, dismounted from their horses, and made reverent obeisance to him. Suddenly, the well-ordered Chinese force appeared on the scene—a majestic sight, with banners flying and armor glittering in the sun. The Turks were overcome with naked fear. At a sign from the Emperor, the Chinese troops fell into battle order in the background. Then the Emperor rode alone onto the Bian Bridge and challenged the Khan to single combat.

Intimidated by his opponent's boldness, Xieli did not dare accept the challenge. Instead, he offered peace. Having achieved his objective of averting the immediate Turkish threat, the Tang Emperor accepted the offer and gave generous gifts of gold and silks to Xieli.

According to a chronicle known as the *Old History of the Tang* (compiled A.D. 940–945), the following conversation subsequently took place between the Tang Emperor and one of his subjects:

> Said Xiao Yu, ". . . Your advisers and brave generals wanted war, but Your Majesty avoided it. I have some doubts about that."
>
> To which the Emperor replied, "Had I engaged the Turks in battle, there would have been many dead and wounded. And had I been victorious, the Turks would no doubt have reorganized their government in the coming years for fear of further defeats. Filled with hatred against me, they would eventually cause us much misery. Today I laid down my armor and weapons. I lured them with jade and fine silks. In this way I have nourished the arrogance of our intractable enemy—and that is undoubtedly the beginning of their eventual total defeat. That is what is meant by the words 'To him from whom you would take, you must first give.' "

In the year A.D. 630 the time was ripe. In a single campaign, the Tang Emperor destroyed the Eastern Turkish state. Khan

Xieli was at that time totally isolated, a hopeless position to which he had been brought by discord in his own ranks, some of which had been skillfully sown by the Chinese.

The rich gifts which the Tang Emperor had given the Turkish ruler in 626 were the "brick." They played their part in easing relations between China and the Eastern Turk state. As the conflict with China grew less acute, internal conflicts within the Turkic realm became worse, and China was able to exploit them to eliminate its enemy. This was the "jade."

17.26   THE VANISHING HORSE

Once there was an old man who lived in a Chinese frontier area. He was known as the Old Man of the Border. One day he found that his splendid horse had disappeared without a trace. Neighbors and friends came running to console the old man over his loss. But he showed no sign of being upset. Smiling gently, he said, "Yes, the horse has vanished, but who knows if that may not be a fortunate thing?"

Some time went by. And lo and behold! The lost horse returned to the Old Man of the Border. Unexpectedly, it brought another horse with it, an even more valuable one. The entire village was wild with excitement over this turn of events. Crowds of people came along to congratulate the old fellow. But he showed no sign of happiness. Said he, "What is there to congratulate me about? Who knows if this may not really be a misfortune?"

A few days later the old man's only son mounted the second horse. The animal, unfamiliar with its new rider, ran wild and finally threw the young man, who was crippled for life.

When the villagers heard about it, they came by to console the old man, who showed no sadness and said, "Who knows if this may not be a fortunate mishap?"

Some time later, war broke out in the frontier region. Many young men were conscripted into the army and sent to the front.

All of them were killed. Only the invalid son of the Old Man of the Border remained at home and survived.[13]

The *Liberation Daily,* the newspaper of the Party Committee of the Chinese Communist Party in Shanghai, alluded to this story in a sports report. It related how, during a European basketball tournament, the Bulgarians were matched against the Czechs in the semifinals. With only eight seconds to the final whistle, the Bulgarians were ahead by two points. But the rules called for a five-point lead to qualify for the finals. At that decisive moment the Bulgarian coach called a time-out and gave special instructions to two players. When the game resumed, the Bulgarian team took the ball toward the opposing basket at first. But the Bulgarian player who had the ball suddenly turned around and sank it in his own team's basket. At that moment the whistle blew, leaving the game with a tied score. The Czech players and the spectators were totally surprised by the home basket, which also puzzled some members of the Bulgarian team. But the rule book stipulated that a tied score permitted the game to go into five minutes of overtime. The Bulgarians pulled themselves together, summoned all their energies, and won the game by six points, which got them into the finals.

The Chinese commentator writing about this incident points out that the final result revealed the cleverness of the Bulgarian coach. The remaining eight seconds of playing time would not have enabled the Bulgarians to gain the necessary five-point lead. So their coach ordered his players to risk a deliberate loss by scoring two points for the Czech side. This was the "brick" that they threw out, and it gained the Bulgarian team a precious extra five minutes in which to score extra points; those minutes were a "piece of jade," which led to the even more valuable prize of qualifying them for the finals. The Bulgarian coach's cleverness lay in properly weighing loss and gain on the spur of the moment and in resolutely accepting a momentary setback for the sake of ultimate victory.

"To him from whom you would take, you must first give," says the Chinese author of the article, Chu Zhang, pointing out that matters often develop in accordance with the dialectic of "taking one step back in order to take two steps forward."

17.27 COPPER FOR CUSTOMERS

A comic-strip magazine published in Beijing in 1987 tells the story of a small food company that participated in a Chicago trade fair in 1975. When John, the owner of the company, arrived at the exhibition hall, he found that he had been assigned a remote corner for his display. Many people visited the trade fair, but hardly any found their way to John's booth. He did not give up, however. On the third day, early arrivals at the fair found the floor strewn with little copper plaques, on which was written, "The bearer of this plaque is entitled to a souvenir at the booth of John's Food Company, Inc." Suddenly the once-obscure corner which housed John's display was flooded with visitors. Even when the supply of copper plaques was exhausted, people kept coming.

17.28 TRAINING AS CONTRACT BAIT?

The title of this section was used back in 1985 in a report by the Tokyo correspondent of the prominent Swiss daily *Neue Zürcher Zeitung*—an inadvertent but apt allusion to Stratagem No. 17. The report dealt with a Sino-Japanese agreement on cooperation in the nuclear energy field. The relevant part of the text reads:

> As soon as the nuclear treaty between Japan and China was signed in August 1985, a negotiating team from Mitsubishi Heavy Industries traveled to Beijing bearing offers

of cooperation designed to give Japanese suppliers access to the presumably lucrative market for nuclear power stations in China. The leading Japanese business newspaper, *Nihon Keizai,* reported that Mitsubishi Heavy Industries had come to terms with the Chinese on a broad technical cooperation agreement. The report states that Mitsubishi has offered its Chinese counterparts know-how for the construction and operation of an atomic power station south of Shanghai. . . . [The] first Japanese technicians are expected to travel to China next year.

Also proposed is a special study program for Chinese engineers and technicians in Japan, to give them practical experience in the construction and operational stages. According to *Nihon Keizai,* this training program could begin next month.

The Japanese business journal reports that Mitsubishi expects the cooperation agreement to give it an excellent starting position in the competition with American and European suppliers, when it comes to securing contracts for construction of additional nuclear power stations in China.

Clearly, Mitsubishi was offering the "brick" of a training program in hope of securing the "jade" of advantage against its competitors for access to the Chinese nuclear business.[14]

17.29 COOPERATION AS DIVISIVENESS

In his book *View of Japan* (Beijing, 1985), Wu Xuewen offers this tactical analysis:

In the spring of 1979 the Soviets tried to turn Stratagem No. 17 against the Japanese by offering certain Japanese fishing companies the right to fish in the territorial waters surrounding those formerly northern Japanese islands which the USSR has occupied since the end of World War II. The Soviets also proposed forming some joint-venture fishing companies with the Japanese. These offers were the "brick." By making them, the Soviets hoped to weaken the Japanese demand for the return of those northern territories to Japan. If Japanese fishing companies had accepted the offer of cooperation, they would have been tacitly accepting Russian sovereignty over the islands. That was the "jade" the Kremlin was trying to gain.

17.30 A GIFT OF MELONS YOU GAVE ME

We end the chapter on Stratagem No. 17 with a poem that is more than twenty-five hundred years old, from the classic Confucian *Book of Songs,* the oldest collection of Chinese poetry. Its verses deal essentially with the exchange of gifts between a man and a woman, and in a broader sense with how a modest gift may be reciprocated by a more valuable one. If a gift of fruit brings a jewel in return, what would the gift of a jewel bring? But perhaps the deeper sense of the poem is that friendship is greater than any gift:

> *A gift of melons you gave me,*
> *I give you a ruby in its place.*
> *Mine does not requite your gift,*
> *But my love is eternally yours.*
>
> *A gift of peaches you gave me,*
> *I give you a jade in their place.*
> *Mine does not requite your gift,*
> *But my love is eternally yours.*
>
> *A gift of plums you gave me,*
> *I give you a sapphire in their place.*
> *Mine does not requite your gift,*
> *But my love is eternally yours.*

To Catch the Bandits, First Capture Their Leader

The Chinese characters	擒	賊	擒	王
Modern Mandarin pronunciation	*qín*	*zéi*	*qín*	*wáng*
Meaning of each character	catch	thieves (bandits)	catch	leader
Applications	Neutralize your enemy by first eliminating his elite (thinkers, leaders, etc.); eliminate your opponent's head, or leadership, or headquarters, in order to more easily checkmate the opponent himself. "Catch-the-leader" stratagem; "blow-to-the-head" stratagem; the stratagem of the Archimedean point.			

18.1 THE ORIGINAL POEM

The phrase that describes Stratagem No. 18 is more than twelve hundred years old. It was coined by Du Fu, one of the most prominent poets of the Tang period, an age when Chinese literature flourished, producing more than twenty-three hundred poets and an outpouring of some fifty thousand poems. Feng Zhi, himself a poet and translator, wrote in 1962 that Du Fu's work "shines down the centuries like an inextinguishable lamp." Du Fu suffered a great deal of privation during his lifetime; one of his children actually starved to death. But posterity elevated him to the highest pinnacle of fame. He is known in China as *shisheng*, literally the "poet-sage," with the "sage" to be understood not in a religious sense but rather as someone who has achieved the height of poetic perfection. His works, sometimes termed "history in verse," provide a colorful picture of his times. They tell of a bitterly harsh rural life, and also of political and military events. Of the approximately fourteen hundred poems by Du Fu that have come down to us, one from the cycle "Into the Borderlands" is especially famous:

> *If you draw a bow, draw the strongest.*
> *If you use an arrow, use the longest.*
> *To shoot a rider, first shoot his horse.*
> *To catch a gang of bandits, first capture its leader.*
> *Just as a country has its borders,*
> *So the killing of men has its limits.*
> *If the enemy's attack can be stopped,*
> *why have any more dead and wounded than necessary?*[1]

In the year A.D. 730, the Tufan Empire in Tibet, having suffered a number of defeats, put out peace feelers to the Chinese imperial court. Heeding his advisers, Chinese Emperor Xuanzong reluctantly agreed. Peace came to the border areas, and the Tufans withdrew all their troops. Seven years later, the Chinese Emperor wanted to exploit the opportunity presented by the unguarded Tufan frontier, and in a period of peace he ordered an attack against the Tibetans. The Chinese General Cui Xiyi penetrated far into Tufan territory and inflicted a grievous defeat on the Tibetans. Once again, China and the Tufans were at war. In the year 740, when the Chinese princess married to a Tufan ruler died, a Tibetan delegation traveled to the Chinese imperial court to convey the sad news and sue for peace. Emperor Xuanzong refused their suit. A year later the Tibetans captured Shibaocheng, an important border fortification. The Chinese Emperor ordered it retaken. But the military commander charged with the task refused to obey, for which he was nearly executed. In 749, the Emperor ordered Geshu Han, a Turk in the service of the Chinese throne, to retake Shibaocheng. With an army of thirty-three thousand men, Geshu Han carried out the order. The fortified position was again in Chinese hands, but more than ten thousand men were killed in the process. It is this wanton policy of conducting war that Du Fu is attacking in his poem.[2]

The main message of the poem is this: In every situation,

concentrate first on the central point, the driving force; limit your action initially to that, and only then deal with the secondary issues. Du Fu uses a number of colorful images to make his point: If you want to use a bow, choose the strongest bow available and don't waste time and effort with a weaker one. The same applies to the choice of arrow. In aiming at a mounted soldier, the main thing is to rob him of his driving power, his mobility. So do not aim at the slender silhouette of the rider and risk missing the mark; instead, aim for the horse, which gives you a better chance of stopping your enemy with a single stroke. Instead of hunting down the individual members of a band of outlaws, capture its leader or leaders; deprived of their leadership, the remaining bandits will be easy marks. Along similar lines, war with foreign enemies should be confined to effective defense against their attacks; once that objective has been achieved, hostilities should cease. The best-known of the poem's images is "To catch a gang of bandits, first capture its leader."

Shu Han, a Taiwanese writer on stratagems, points out that, while the phrase "To catch a gang of bandits . . ." must be regarded first and foremost as a verse from a famous poem, "it is also the key to victory in many kinds of conflicts."

18.2 MONKEYS WITHOUT A TREE

Not only in war but also in life's everyday struggles, one should concentrate on discovering the "leader" of the "bandits," figuratively speaking. This may be an individual or a group of people, perhaps an object or a particular problem.

Once you have figured out who or what is the "leader," or the main support of the opponent, you must concentrate your efforts on eliminating it. Success in doing so will set off a chain reaction affecting the overall situation. To borrow a colorful image from the *I Ching*, when the "leader" has been neutralized or knocked out of the battle, "the horde of dragons loses its head." The enemy organization becomes a headless creature. As one commentary on Stratagem No. 18 puts it: When you capture the enemy leader, you can bring down the entire enemy force; if its main support has been destroyed, the enemy will collapse. This is reminiscent of another pithy Chinese saying: "When the tree falls, the monkeys scatter."

According to revelations published in the Chinese press, during China's Cultural Revolution the so-called Gang of Four (Shanghai leader Wang Hongwen, chief ideologist Zhang Chunqiao, propagandist Yao Wenyuan, and Mao Zedong's wife Jiang Qing) headed a countrywide network of supporters. It also exercised virtually total control over China's mass media. And yet the Gang of Four and its nationwide network were neutralized almost overnight. How? In October 1976, a few weeks after the death of Mao Zedong had deprived the Gang of its main support, its four leaders were arrested. And, as the *People's Daily* put it some years later, "When the Gang of Four was smashed, the tree fell and the monkeys scattered."

Naturally, there are many methods of "neutralizing" the "leaders of the gang." Sometimes other stratagems are used; the choice of these depends on the nature of the "leader" and the general circumstances of his central function. If the "leader" is a person, there are two basic choices: hard or soft means. The use of violence is among the possible hard means, involving the physical elimination of the leader. Soft means often aim at "capturing" the leader's thoughts and feelings, changing his mind or corrupting him. One prominent "soft" technique is the use of a "flesh bomb"—the Chinese equivalent of the Western term "sex bomb"—which, according to a Hong Kong stratagem book, is often more effective than a real bomb.

18.3 WHEN A MAN DIES HIS POLICY DIES WITH HIM

Basic to Stratagem No. 18 is a powerful belief in the overarching power of a single ruler or an elite class. In this sense it reflects the hierarchical thinking and personalistic regimes of China's imperial period. Just as the emperor reigned supreme in the empire as a whole, so within each family the father's authority was unquestioned. Most social groups in traditional China were organized along similar lines. The importance of one powerful leader remains largely true in China today, where there is still often talk of *renzhi,* "personal rule." The essence of *renzhi,* basically advocated by all the philosophers of ancient China, is reflected in the following sentence from a classic Confucian work: "As long as the man [i.e., the leader] lives, his policy is carried out; if he dies, his policy dies with him."

This sentence also alludes to the chain reaction triggered by the life or death of a central authority figure. In a 1980 speech officially titled "On the Reform of the System of Party and State Leadership," which dealt with the traumas of the Cultural Revolution, Deng Xiaoping (China's strongman after the death of Mao Zedong) said:

> During the "Cultural Revolution," when someone got to the top, even his dogs and chickens got there too; likewise, when someone got into trouble, even his distant relatives were dragged down with him.

None of this has changed much. "Personal rule" and its ramifications remain essentially the same today. The West's "institutional rule," which limits the power of individual leaders to a certain extent through division of power and systems of checks and balances, has not yet taken firm hold in contemporary China.

18.4 THE ABANDONED EMPEROR

Every rule has its exceptions. Even in China, the capture of a central leader has not always had the desired effect.

During the Ming Dynasty, the powerful palace eunuch Wang

Zhen (d. A.D. 1449) forced the twenty-three-year-old Yingzhong Emperor to personally lead a field campaign against the Oirats, who were attacking from eastern Mongolia under their leader Esen Khan (d. 1454). Yingzhong was defeated and taken prisoner near Tumu, a fortification in the north of what is now Hebei Province. Infuriated Chinese soldiers thereupon killed the eunuch Wang Zhen. The Oirat army continued its advance toward Beijing, in the course of which 100,000 Chinese men and women were killed or taken prisoner. The Oirats took the Chinese Emperor with them as they advanced. The further course of events is described by Wolfram Eberhard in his book on Chinese history:

> The Oirats had no intention of killing the emperor. They wanted him as a hostage, for whom they hoped to obtain a rich ransom. But the various cliques at the imperial court had little loyalty to their Emperor. With the decline of the clique around [the palace eunuch] Wang, there were two cliques left. The group centered on General Yu enjoyed special power, because he had managed to fend off the Oirat attack against Beijing itself. The general appointed a new Emperor—not the infant son of the captured Emperor, as should have been the case, but his brother. Another clique, however, insisted that the infant become the new ruler. All of which convinced the Oirats that the Chinese were not inclined to give much for their former Emperor. So they reduced their ransom demand enormously and virtually forced the former Emperor on the Chinese again, hoping that his reappearance in Beijing would create new political unrest advantageous to the Oirats—which is exactly what soon happened.[3]

This example illustrates that the capture of the "leader" does not invariably result in paralyzing the entire "gang of bandits."

18.5   Drowning in Superstition

In the fifth century B.C., during the reign of Duke Wen of Wei, an official by the name of Ximen Bao was appointed chief officer of Ye District. Arriving there, he paid visits to the town elders and asked them what the local people found most oppressive in their lives. The elders replied, "We are plagued by the obligation to supply brides for the river god. This is what keeps us in poverty."

Requesting more details, Ximen Bao was told, "Each year our three education officials and the district clerk levy taxes on the people. The revenues they collect amount to a hundred times ten thousand. Between twenty and thirty times ten thousand are used for the wedding of the river god. The remainder the officials divide with the old sorceress and keep for themselves. When the time comes, the sorceress roams the district looking for beautiful girls. When she proclaims, 'This maiden shall be the bride of the river god,' a wedding ceremony is arranged. New silken garments are prepared for the maiden. She is made to live a secluded life and may consume neither alcohol nor meat. On the riverbank, a special hut for the ceremony is erected, its four sides hung with gold and red silk curtains. The maiden is quartered there. The meat of oxen and other foods are prepared for the ceremony. After about ten days the girl is bedecked with jewelry, then ordered to lie down on a mat, which is tossed into the river. It floats for a few miles, then sinks with the river god's bride. Families in which there is a beautiful young daughter live in fear that, when she reaches the right age, she may be chosen by the sorceress as the river god's bride. Hence most families with daughters flee to remote areas. As a result, our city is being steadily depopulated, and its poverty increases. This has been going on for a long time. There is a saying among the people: 'If no bride is given to the river god, the waters will rise, destroy our property, and drown us all.' So they say."

After this recitation, Ximen Bao said, "The next time the river god takes a bride, I want the three education officials, the sorceress, and the town elders to be present and bid farewell to the maiden when she is sent out upon the river. I shall be there as well." Everyone agreed.

When the day came, Ximen Bao went to the riverside. The three education officials, magistrates and other officials, the town elders, and all the prominent people of the community were assembled. About three thousand townsfolk also gathered to witness the spectacle. The sorceress was a woman of about seventy years, and she arrived with an entourage of ten other women, all robed in silk and following closely behind the priestess of magic.

Ximen Bao said, "Call the bride of the river god to me. I wish to see if she is truly beautiful."

The chosen one was brought from the ceremonial hut. Ximen Bao gazed at her. Then he turned to the three education officials, the sorceress, and the town elders, and said, "This maiden is not beautiful. I therefore request that the great sorceress go down into the river and report to the river god. Should he wish a more beautiful bride, tell him that she shall be sent down to him another day." Whereupon he ordered his bailiffs to toss the old woman into the river.

After a while Ximen Bao said, "Why does the old sorceress remain so long beneath the water? Send one of her women followers to hurry her up." So one of the women was thrown into the river.

After a while Ximen Bao said, "What's keeping them so long? Send another woman after them." And another of the sorceress's followers was tossed into the river. After some time, the same thing happened to a third woman.

Finally Ximen Bao said, "The sorceress and her followers are women; they are incapable of giving a clear report to the river god. I request that the three education officials go into the river and report to the god." And he had the three officials tossed into the water.

Now Ximen Bao bent forward and gazed into the river for a long time. The town elders, the other officials, and even the common spectators were filled with fear. Finally Ximen Bao turned around and said, "The old sorceress, her followers, and the three education officials have not returned. What shall we do next?"

He was about to have the town clerk and another local dignitary thrown into the river as well, in order to hasten the earlier emissaries along. But these worthies suddenly sank to their knees, bowed to the ground, turned toward Ximen Bao, and beat their heads against the earth until their foreheads bled. Their faces were as pale as cold ashes. "Very well," said Ximen Bao, "we'll wait awhile."

After a short time he said, "Stand up! I assume that the river god will keep his guests with him for quite a long time. You needn't join them. Go home!"

All the people, the officials and the common folk of Ye, were horrified by what they had witnessed. After that, no one dared even speak of the river god's wedding, much less ever try to hold such a ceremony again.

An attempt at mere verbal explanation by Ximen Bao would doubtless have failed to shake the popular superstition. Yet that superstition was the basis for chicanery through which a small clique enriched itself at the people's expense. Once the leader of that clique, the sorceress, had been thrown into the river along with several of her accomplices, the superstition was drowned forever, so to speak, along with the villains of the piece.[4]

18.6 ARROWS OF RUE

During the An Lushan rebellion (A.D. 755–63), a battle developed between Zhang Xun, governor of Zhenyuan District (Henan Province), and the rebel General Yin Ziqi. Zhang Xun's troops stormed the opposing army's position, taking some five thousand lives. But victory was not yet won. Zhang Xun wanted to eliminate the leader of the enemy force, but in the confusion that prevailed among the opposing troops he could not identify

General Yin Ziqi. So Zhang Xun commanded his own soldiers to shoot off arrows made of rue branches. Finding such powerless projectiles raining down on them, the opposing soldiers were delighted, for they assumed that Zhang Xun's men had run out of proper arrows.

The enemy troops crowded around one particular warrior, obviously their leader, to whom they showed the useless arrows. Observing this, Zhang Xun now knew which man on the opposite side was Yin Ziqi. He immediately ordered his troop leader to shoot a real arrow at the rebel general. The arrow hit Yin Ziqi in the left eye, whereupon he instantly gave up the battle and withdrew in defeat.

In this case it was only the elimination of the opposing leader that brought final victory. The Jilin book on the stratagems warns, "To believe that one can gain total victory without eliminating the enemy leader and without destroying the main enemy force is as foolish as letting a tiger escape back into the mountains."

18.7 SNOWY NIGHT MARCH

The rebellion of An Lushan and Shi Siming dealt a harsh and lasting blow to the power of the Chinese imperial court. The weakening of the empire's top leadership prompted numerous regional military governors to set up their own little kingdoms. During the rule of Emperor Xianzong (A.D. 805–20), there were two secession-minded brothers, Wu Shaocheng and Wu Shaoyang, who served successively as military governors of Huaixi Region. But Wu Shaoyang's son, Wu Yuanji, openly rebelled against the Emperor in 814. He established himself in Caizhou and steadily expanded his power. Various attempts to tame this rebel failed. Finally, at his own request, Li Su was appointed military governor of the region adjacent to the area under Wu Yuanji's rule and was assigned the task of beating down the uprising.

By initially assuming a low profile, Li Su led Wu Yuanji to believe that he was faced with a weak opponent. At the same time, Li Su quietly prepared for battle. He studied the topography of his enemy's territory, sent out spies, and drilled his troops. Most particularly, he made sure that captured rebels were treated well. Even high-ranking deserters who fell into his hands were pardoned and accepted into his own army. Thus he built up a core of warriors who were intimately familiar with Wu Yuanji's territory. In this way Li Su learned that Wu Yuanji had set up his main base not in Caizhou but in nearby Huiqu and that Caizhou itself was virtually unprotected.

In planning his campaign, Li Su concentrated on these considerations: All his predecessors had failed to make any headway against Wu Yuanji, who had never suffered a defeat. As a result, his prestige had risen tremendously. He had two important friends, Li Shidao, military governor of Yunzhou, and Wang Chengzong, military governor of Hengzhou. Those two had not yet openly broken with the Emperor, but if there were to be a long, drawn-out campaign against Wu Yuanji there was a danger that the two military governors would ally themselves with the rebel. There was only one way to prevent such an unwelcome development: a devastating surprise blow against Wu Yuanji—in other words, an application of Stratagem No. 18.[5]

On a wintry night late in the year A.D. 817, Li Su set out for his surprise attack against Caizhou. No imperial soldiers had put in an appearance there for the past thirty years, so that no one in the city expected an attack, especially on such a night. It was snowing, and the flags of the marching army snapped in an icy wind. But Li Su's troops forged ahead. Toward morning they reached the walls of Caizhou. The watchmen on the ramparts were sound asleep. Li Su's soldiers quickly cleared a way and marched into the city.

News of the fall of Caizhou took the rebel Wu Yuanji totally by surprise. He was soon captured and deported to the imperial court at Chang'an. Thus the years-long secession of Huaixi Region was ended with a single blow.

More than eleven hundred years later, during China's civil

war, Chen Yi, who after 1949 held several important posts in the People's Republic, wrote a poem titled "Snowy Night March," which seems to evoke the scene from the year 817:

> *Mount Taishan is shrouded in deep snow.*
> *The River Yi is covered in thick ice.*
> *A quick march*
> *through the black night.*
> *Army morale is high*
> *and hearts are united.*
> *To catch the gang of bandits, we will first*
> *capture its leader.*
> *Then together we will celebrate*
> *the Festival of Spring.*

18.8   Grabbing the Enemy by the Throat

The advent of parachute troops gave a new dimension to Stratagem No. 18. Paratroopers make it possible to mount a large-scale, lightning attack against the enemy's nerve center. Under cover of diplomatic smoke screens and political maneuvering, the enemy's capital or crucial strategic positions can suddenly be occupied by airborne troops; the enemy is thus "grabbed by the throat," his central command positions put out of action, and the way cleared for ground-based units to march in. According to one Chinese writer on the stratagems, the occupation of the Afghan capital of Kabul by Soviet airborne troops in 1979 provided a perfect example of this technique.

18.9   Posthumous Glory through Brush and Ink

Many Chinese deeply long "to exude fragrance for a hundred generations"—that is, to stand high in the world's regard long after their death. And they profoundly fear "to leave behind a stench for myriad years"—that is, to be sullied by scandal and shame for generations to come.

The following dialogue between high imperial official Zhuang Xiaoyan and his son Zhuang Zhiyan is taken from the novel *Blossom in a Sea of Sin,* by Zeng Pu. First published in 1907, the novel was issued in a French translation by Isabelle Bijon in 1983, as *Fleur sur l'Ocean des Péchés.*

Zhuang Xiaoyan: "I have something important to tell you. Leave the city quickly, go to Ai Yun, and tell him I said he is to wait on old Master Li in the garden of His Excellency Cheng this afternoon. Now hurry, lose no more time!"

Zhuang Zhiyan, surprised: "Who is old Master Li?"

Zhuang Xiaoyan, laughing: "You've no way of knowing that, of course. Master Li is none other than Li Chunke, the most important literary figure of our time. His disciples are to be found everywhere. Anyone who wants to have our leading literary men on his side must first win the favor of Li Chunke. As the old saying goes: 'To catch a gang of bandits, first capture its leader.' "

Zhuang Zhiyan: "But what influence has this old gentleman, that you're so eager for his favor?"

Zhuang Xiaoyan: "His influence is enormous! Don't you realize? The axe and lance of rulers may have effects lasting a hundred years. But the brush and ink of the literary artist leave impressions for a thousand years. Posterity's judgment as to whether we have acted properly or falsely, indeed the question of whether we will be remembered or forgotten by posterity, depends entirely on the writings of these literary men."

Zhuang Xiaoyan is acting on the assumption that, if he wins the sympathy of the man he considers the leading literary light of his time, his own posthumous fame will be secure forever. One is reminded here of the poem "Euphrosyne," by Goethe, which the poet dedicated to his early love, Christiane Neumann, who died at a young age. In the poem he talks of seeing her ghostly form in the mountains at night and hearing her words of farewell, in which she begs him to immortalize her in a poem, since only those praised by the poets live on after death; the others fade to insubstantial shadows:[6]

> *Do not let me go unsung down to the Shades!*
> *Only the Muse can grant Life in Death.*[7]

18.10 THE INSPIRED MIND

In the early thirteenth century A.D. Wang Mai, a government official and literary figure, wrote the following poetic guidelines for an aspiring young writer, Zhang Jingshan. In them he uses "capturing the leader of the robber band" as a metaphor for the writer cultivating "the breath of spirit" in himself.

> *Heavy of heart I bid you farewell,*
> *I take you by the hand and reveal to you the secret chamber*
>   *of my heart.*
> *The foundation of a literary education is the assimilation*
>   *of the greatest works;*
> *That is a principle never to be forgotten!*
> *It is like preparing for a journey of a thousand miles, for*
>   *which you must take provisions enough to last three*
>   *months.*
> *There is yet another key to literary success, one that is*
>   *forever valid, and that is the unfolding of one's own*
>   *spirit.*
> *Our concern with this may be likened to an attack against*
>   *enemy fortifications:*
> *It is essential to capture the leader of the robber band.* . . .
> *Once the foundation of literary creativity, the knowledge*
>   *and assimilation of literary works, is firmly rooted, it*
>   *grows ever stronger.*

Once the breath of one's spirit unfolds fully, its inspiring
power grows ever stronger.

After a time of ripening, the assimilated literary knowledge
broadens and deepens, and the spirit's ability to take
wing increases.

When a profoundly educated man takes up his brush to
write, it is like a wealthy man who can conjure endless
gold from his pocket.

He who has cultivated the breath of his spirit has a broad
horizon, unlike the common man who, attempting to
create literary works, sinks into profound emptiness and
never grasps the essence.

One day, when you are famous, we shall meet again and
I shall be only an insignificant scribbler in comparison
to you.[8]

It is the "breath of the spirit," Wang Mai tells us, that gives soul and inner fire to a literary work. Cultivation of the spirit is the central key to success in literary endeavor, and without that inspiration a literary man's book learning, no matter how broad, remains lifeless raw material. In light of this, Wang Mai regards cultivation of the spirit as comparable in importance to capturing the opposing leader when storming enemy fortifications.

18.11   SHOOTING DOWN A PING-PONG ACE

During the Twenty-sixth Table Tennis World Championships held in Beijing in 1961, the Chinese men's team won the world title in their category for the first time. Previously, Japan had won the team title five times running. But the Chinese success could not mask the fact that some of the Chinese players, who specialized in the speed-attack method, had not found an effective way of dealing with the Japanese topspin technique. The

Chinese had a very difficult time holding their own whenever they came up against Japanese players using this technique.

Zhang Xielin, a member of the Chinese team, was a specialist in defensive tactics, a superb player, and knowledgeable about the use of stratagems. Secretly he planned to concentrate on the outstanding Japanese specialist in the topspin, study his methods, and devise adequate defenses.

In the Twenty-seventh Table Tennis World Championships, held in Belgrade in 1963, Japan hoped to regain the team title. But the Chinese team sent Zhang Xielin in for the decisive game, equipped with his newly developed moves to counter the topspin. Almost as soon as the match began, the Japanese player found himself totally outclassed, with nothing in his bag of tricks to handle Zhang Xielin's mercurial, varied defensive technique and sharply cut serves. Hardly knowing what hit him, he lost the game. Zhang Xielin's victory had a miraculous effect. Once he had defeated the strongest member of the Japanese team, the Chinese were firmly in control and successfully defended their title.[9]

The strongest Japanese player may here be regarded as the "leader." Zhang Xielin's concentration on the best player of the opposing team and his victory over him dealt a mortal blow to the morale of the Japanese team (the "gang of bandits").

18.12 THE FOUR MAIN CONTRADICTIONS

In the very first sentence of his 1981 remarks on No. 18, Beijing stratagem specialist Li Bingyan uses the phrase "main contradiction."[10] The fundamental importance of No. 18 in wartime, he writes, is to focus on the main contradiction, resolve it, and thus achieve total victory.

The "main contradiction" is a central concept in the teachings of Mao Zedong dating from the 1930s. As I have shown elsewhere,[11] these teachings long constituted the guiding doctrine for the leadership of this nation of more than one billion people (and may still do so to a considerable degree). According to Mao, the whole world is a tangle of conflicts, dilemmas, polarities, and paradoxes, for all of which the Chinese use the single generic term "contradiction." In each phase of development it is the task of China's political leadership to select one of the currently existing conflicts and proclaim it the "main contradiction." All the energies of the Chinese people must then be concentrated on dealing with that issue—until such time as the Chinese leadership defines some other phenomenon as the "main contradiction." It is this "dialectic" that results in the tremendous changes, the radical shifts in course, which have so astonished the world in recent Chinese history.

Four times since the mid-1930s, the Chinese leadership has redefined the main contradiction:

1. In the period 1937–45, the main contradiction was China vs. Japan. At that time, in the view of the Chinese Communist Party, "China" included the Guomindang headed by Mao's archenemy Chiang Kai-shek. The primary task was to defeat Japan.

2. During 1946–49, the main contradiction was the Chinese Communist Party under Mao vs. the Guomindang regime under Chiang. The primary task was to defeat Chiang Kai-shek.

3. From 1949 to 1976, the main contradiction was the proletariat vs. the bourgeoisie. The primary task was the "class struggle" of the Chinese proletariat to defeat the bourgeoisie.

4. Since 1976 (or 1978, by some reckonings), the main contradiction as officially defined by the Chinese Communist Party has been (and still remains) modernization vs. backwardness. The new primary task is to overcome China's backwardness through the "four Socialist modernizations"—i.e., by modernizing China's industry, agriculture, national defense, and science and technology, under the unshakable leadership of the Chinese Communist Party.[12]

To most Western observers, the link between the "main contradiction" and "secondary contradictions" may often seem
puzzling. But, in its essence, the logic of the theory of contradictions is quite clear. For instance, once it has been established
that the main contradiction facing China in recent years is that
between the need for modernization and the country's long-
standing backwardness, the conceptual path is more or less
cleared for dealing with all secondary conflicts or tensions. It is
logical, for example, that everything within reason be undertaken to encourage modernization. Since the industrial West
seems to be in the vanguard of modernity, the resolution of the
"secondary contradiction" represented by the question "Should
Chinese students be sent to the West to study modern Western
science and other important fields?" appears self-evident. The
same holds true for the secondary contradiction stated as
"Should China increase its imports of Western technology and
foreign capital?" For instance, to the extent that the Coca-Cola
Company can contribute to modernizing China's soft-drink industry, from the standpoint of orthodox Maoist Sino-dialectics
there is little fundamental problem about resolving the question
"Cooperation with Coca-Cola: yes or no?"

Of course, in China as elsewhere, "the devil is in the details."
Developing concrete solutions to secondary contradictions can
sometimes give rise to serious disagreements on basic policy
issues. For example: "In addition to Western technology and
management methods, should China also adopt Western social
and/or political institutions?"[13]

At any rate, in terms of Stratagem No. 18, whatever has been
declared the "main contradiction" by the Chinese leadership in
effect takes the role of "leader," with all secondary issues con-
stituting the "robber band." In singling out such a main contradiction, China's Party and government unleash a kind of
windstorm which sweeps across the countryside, blowing all
grasses in the same direction. Every individual problem area—
whether in the economy, in sports, literature, etc.—may be defined in terms of the main contradiction, and pursuing the
resolution of that main issue is the equivalent of trying to capture

the leader of the robber band. Although it would be an exaggeration to see the Chinese version of Marxist dialectical materialism entirely in terms of stratagems, Mao's doctrine of the "main contradiction"—which still exerts a fundamental influence on China's leaders—certainly is related to the essential idea behind Stratagem No. 18.

The following remarks appear in a previously cited university textbook on the principles of Marxist philosophy:

> The main contradiction occupies a leading, indeed a dominant position among all contradictions. . . . Its resolution has a decisive influence on the overall situation. The diverse other contradictions are subordinate to this main contradiction. If the main contradiction is resolved, all others can be more easily resolved. During the Chinese civil war [1945–49], for example, the battle for Jinzhou was the main contradiction with respect to all operations in West Liaoning-Shenyang [September 12 to November 2, 1948]. Once Jinzhou was conquered, the enemy was transformed into "a turtle caught in a jug"—that is, it was possible to cut off the enemy's path of retreat and to defeat him. This ultimately accomplished the strategic goal of destroying the enemy in the entire northeastern region.
>
> This example shows how the main contradiction determines and influences the other contradictions. . . . If the other contradictions are to be moved toward resolution, one's energies must be concentrated on resolving the main contradiction. Some common expressions [which describe] this method are: . . . "If you beat a snake, beat him on the head" [or] "If you lead an ox, lead him by the nose-ring" [or] "To catch a gang of bandits, first capture its leader."[14]

Jiang, Henan Province.

Jiangling, county in Hubei Province.

Jianning, city in the old Shu empire; today known as Puning, in Yunnan Province.

Jiao, pre-Qin state, in Hubei Province.

Jinggangshan Mountains, in Jiangxi Province.

Lam Son, in province of Thanh–hoa, central Vietnam.

Liaodong, region in eastern and southern Liaoning Province (formerly southern Manchuria).

Lin'an, now city of Hangzhou, Zhejiang Province (provisional capital of the Southern Song Dynasty in the twelfth century).

Lu, pre-Qin state, in southern Shandong Province and northern Jiangsu Province.

Lukou, town in Chongyang County, Hubei Province.

Nanjing (Nanking), imperial capital during the Three Kingdoms and Southern Dynasties periods (third to sixth century) and again in the early Ming (1368–1421); in 1928–37, capital of the Republic of China.

Pengcheng, now city of Xuzhou, Jiangsu Province.

Puban, former town in western Yongji County, Shaanxi Province.

Qi, pre-Qin state, in northern and central Shandong Province and northeastern Hebei Province.

Shibaocheng, former city southwest of Xining, Qinghai Province.

Shu, third-century state, in Sichuan Province.

Taocheng, now town of Taoyangcheng, Gansu Province.

White River, in northeastern Songpan County, Sichuan Province.

Wu, pre-Qin state, in Jiangsu Province, eastern Anhui Province, and northern Zhejiang Province.

Xiayang, now Hancheng County, in Shaanxi Province.

Xiangyang, prefecture in Hubei Province, with Longzhong Mountains to the west.

Xingyang, city in Henan Province.

Yaoshan (Mount Yao), in Henan Province.

Ye, former Wei city, now in Henan Province.
Yue, pre-Qin state, in Zhejiang.
Yunzhou, city in what is now Shandong Province.
Zheng, now Zhengzhou, capital of Henan Province, south of
　　the Yellow River.

Appendix B

CHINESE STRATAGEM BOOKS

Jilin:

Wu Gu. *Sanshiliu ji* (The 36 Stratagems). *Jilin Renmin Chubanshe* (Jilin People's Press). 1st edition, Changchun, 1979; 3rd ed. 1982.

Wu Gu. *Huitu sanshiliu ji* (The Illustrated 36 Stratagems). *Jilin Wenshi Chubanshe* (Jilin Literary-Historical Press). Changchun, 1987.

Beijing:

Li Bingyan. *Sanshiliu ji xin bian* (The 36 Stratagems: A Modern Version). *Zhanshi Chubanshe* (Soldiers' Press). 1st edition. Beijing, 1981. The publishing house changed its name, so reprints and subsequent editions (varying only in minor details) appear under the imprint of *Jiefangjun Chubanshe* (People's Liberation Army Press); the latest edition consulted by the author was the 9th printing, dated March 1991.

Taiwan:

Shu Han. *Sanshiliu ji miben jijie* (The Secret Book of the 36 Stratagems, with Explanations). *Guojia Chubanshe* (National Press). 1st edition, Taipei, 1982; 2d edition, 1984; 3d edition, 1986. (The 2d and 3d editions are each listed simply as *zaiban* [new edition], so it is uncertain whether other "new editions" may not have appeared between 1982 and 1986. The 1986 edition does not differ from that of 1982.)

Douzhi—sanshiliu ji (Wisdom in Struggle: The 36 Stratagems). *Xingguang Chubanshe* (Starlight Press). 19th edition, Taipei, 1985. (This is a pamphlet—no author given.)

Hong Kong:

Ma Senliang and Zhang Laiping. *Sanshiliu ji gu jin yin li* (The 36 Stratagems, with Examples from Times Past and Present). *Yuzhou Chubanshe* (Universe Press). Hong Kong, 1969.

Appendix C

HISTORICAL FIGURES

An Lushan (d. A.D. 757), Turkish-Sogdian military governor
in the service of Emperor Xuanzong, who launched a
disastrous rebellion against the Tang in 755. [Sections
7.1, 18.6, 18.7]

Bai Juyi (A.D. 772–846), popular mid-Tang poet. [Section
10.1]

Bao (d. 204 B.C.), Prince of Wei. [Section 6.2]

Cao Cao (A.D. 155–220), warlord, politician, and leading
literary figure; founder of the Wei Dynasty. [Sections
3.11, 9.1, 9.2, 13.12, 14.10, 16.1, 16.2, 16.13, 17.13]

Chen Sheng (d. 208 B.C.), peasant rebel leader during the Qin
Dynasty. [Section 14.2]

Chen Yi (1901–72), Communist official who held numerous
posts after 1949, including mayor of Shanghai and
foreign minister of the People's Republic. [Section 18.7]

Chiang Kai-shek (1887–1975), statesman and general; leader
of the Guomindang (Nationalist) regime on mainland
China 1943–49, then of the Nationalist government on
Taiwan until his death. [Sections 2.4, 6.6, 9.3, 9.5, 11.5,
16.3, 17.11, 17.16, 18.12]

Chou En-lai (1898–1976), now generally spelled Zhou Enlai; prominent Communist and Chinese foreign minister and long-time premier of the People's Republic. [Sections 8.7, 11.5]

Confucius (551–479 B.C.), Chinese sage from the state of Lu; taught humanistic philosophy canonized as Confucianism. [Sections 3.6, 7.15, 10.5]

Deng Ai (A.D. 197–264), a Wei general during the Three Kingdoms period. [Section 8.2]

Deng Xiaoping (b. 1904), early member and official of Chinese Communist Party; comrade-in-arms of Mao Zedong; political official who has held many offices (e.g., vice-premier, member of Presidium and Central Committee, etc.); out of favor with Mao Zedong for some years, later restored to favor; became heir apparent, de facto leader of the country after Mao's death; now officially retired from public office but still regarded as China's strongman. [Sections 1.6, 2.4, 7.9, 16.4, 18.3]

Di Qing (A.D. 1008–57), prominent general of the Northern Song Dynasty. [Section 11.3]

Du Fu (A.D. 712–70), one of the best-known poets of the Tang Dynasty; sometimes considered China's greatest poet. [Section 18.1]

Fuchai (d. 473 B.C.), ruler of Wu. [Section 10.3]

Gaozong (A.D. 649–83), Tang Emperor. [Section 10.1]

Gaozu [See under Liu Bang]

Goujian (d. 465 B.C.), King of Yue. [Section 10.3]

Guan Zhong (d. 645 B.C.), politician and political philosopher; considered the founder of the School of Legalism. [Intro. to No. 15, 16.13]

Han Fei (ca. 280–223 B.C.), leading representative of the School of Legalism. [Section 10.2; Intro. to No. 15, 17.20]

Han Shizhong (A.D. 1089–1151), general under the Southern Song Dynasty. [Section 7.12]

Han Xin (d. 196 B.C.), general under Liu Bang; instrumental in launching the Han Dynasty. [Section 6.2, 8.1, 8.4]

He Long (1896–1969), a founder of the People's Liberation Army. [Section 16.11]

Huai (d. 299 B.C.), King of Chu. [Sections 8.1, 14.2]

Huan, Duke (r. 806–771 B.C.), ruler of Zheng, in the Western Zhou Dynasty. [Sections 3.5, 17.23]

Hui (369–319 B.C.), King of Wei. [Section 12.2]

Hui (r. 337–311 B.C.), King of Qin. [Section 9.5]

Hui [the Jianwen Emperor] (r. A.D. 1399–1403), Ming Dynasty ruler. [Section 12.6]

Jiang Wei (A.D. 202–64), a Shu general during the Three Kingdoms period. [Sections 8.2, 14.6]

Jianwen Emperor—see third entry for Hui, above.

Jing, Duke (d. 490 B.C.), ruler of Qi. [Sections 3.3, 16.7]

Kong Rong (A.D. 153–208), twentieth-generation descendant of Confucius; Han statesman and loyalist executed for opposition to Cao Cao. [Sections 1.4, 3.11]

Lao-tze (b. 604 B.C.?), now usually spelled Laozi, Chinese philosopher, possibly apocryphal; reputedly the founder of Daoism and author of its central book, the *Daodejing* (or *Tao-te-ching*). [Intro. to No. 7, Sections 10.4, 13.11, 17.20]

Laozi—see Lao-tze.

Lê Loi (d. A.D. 1433), once a wealthy Vietnamese farmer, then leader of the uprising at Lam Son. [Sections 7.5, 11.4]

Li Boyuan (1867–1906), author. [Section 13.3]

Li Linfu (d. A.D. 752), Chief Minister to Tang Emperor Xuanzong. [Section 10.1]

Li Shimin (seventh century A.D.), Tang Emperor. [Section 17.25]

Li Su (ninth century, A.D.), military governor under Emperor Xianzong. [Section 18.7]

Li Yifu (A.D. 614–66), courtier and official at the court of Tang Emperor Gaozong. [Section 10.1]

Lin Biao (1907–71), Chinese Communist leader, earmarked

as Mao Zedong's successor, then accused of an attempted coup and reported killed in a plane crash while trying to escape to the Soviet Union. [Sections 7.9, 7.10, 16.10]

Liu Bang (ca. 250–195 B.C.), also known as Peigong, also as Emperor Gaozu of the Han; rebel leader against the Qin and founder of the Han Dynasty, China's longest-lived imperial dynasty (206 B.C.–A.D. 220). [Sections 6.2, 8.1, 12.1, 13.7, 14.8, 15.7]

Liu Bei (A.D. 161–223), founder and ruler of the kingdom of Shu (or Shu Han) in the area of Sichuan Province. [Sections 1.3, Intro. to No. 9, 9.1, 13.7, 13.12, 14.10, 16.1, 16.2, 16.13, 16.14]

Liu Xun (second century A.D.), warlord governor of Lujiang during the last decades of the Han Dynasty. [Section 15.3]

Luo Guanzhong (ca. A.D. 1330–1400), author active in early Ming period, to whom several novels and dramas are attributed, including the novel *Sanguozhi yanyi* (The Romance of the Three Kingdoms). [Section 2.1]

Lu Xun (A.D. 183–245), strategist in the kingdom of Wu. [Section 10.6]

Lu Xun (1881–1936), author, greatly revered in the People's Republic. [Sections 9.4, 17.3]

Lü Hou (241–180 B.C.), wife of Liu Bang, his helper, and, after his death, faithful executrix of his wishes. [Section 14.8]

Lü Meng (A.D. 178–219), strategist for the kingdom of Wu during the Three Kingdoms period. [Section 10.6]

Mao Zedong (1893–1976), founder of the People's Republic of China; initially a member of the Guomindang; after Guomindang-Communist split, led disastrous "Autumn Harvest Uprising" in Hunan; led the Red Army's "Long March" (1934–35); continued to fight Guomindang even during anti-Japanese war (1934–45) and after it; in 1949, with Communists in command of most Chinese territory, Mao became Chairman of the central government and the Party; led the country through various waves of upheaval, such as the Great Leap Forward (began 1958) and the Cultural Revolution (1966–76); one of the Communist world's leading theoreticians, his ideas became highly influential in the Third World. [Sections 1.6, 2.2, 4.3, 7.9, 9.5, 10.1, 14.5, 14.8, 16.3, 16.10, 17.3, 17.16, 18.2, 18.3, 18.12]

Mencius (390–305 B.C.), or Mengzi in Mandarin; great Confucian philosopher. [Section 16.12]

Mo Du (d. 174 B.C.), leader of the Xiongnu, founder of a large federation of nomadic tribes that launched many attacks against Chinese territory. [Sections 17.17, 17.24]

Nguyen Trai (A.D. 1380–1442), leading adviser to Lê Loi; Vietnamese scholar, author, strategist, and statesman. [Section 7.5]

Pang Juan (fourth century B.C.), Wei army commander. [Sections 4.2, 12.2]

Pu Songling (A.D. 1640–1715), prominent story writer of early Qing period; author of the collection *Liaozhai zhiyi* (Strange Stories from the Leisure Studio). [Section 11.6]

Pu Yi (1906–67), last emperor of China. [Section 14.2]

Qu Bo (twentieth century A.D.), author of the novel *The Forest in the Snow*. [Sections 12.4, 15.5]

Shang Yang (fourth century B.C.), government official of Qin; proponent of the School of Legalism. [Section 16.6]

Sima Guang (A.D. 1019–86), Song historian; compiler of the *Zizhi tong jian* (Comprehensive Mirror to Aid in Government), recounting the history of China from the end of the fifth century B.C. to the tenth century A.D. [Sections 10.1, 14.10]

Sima Qian (b. ca. 145 B.C.), historian; author of the *Shi ji* (Records of the Historian). [Sections 2.1, 9.5, 13.6]

Sima Yi (A.D. 179–251), commander of the Wei army and a frequent opponent of Zhuge Liang. [Prologue, Sections 13.7, 14.6]

Song Xiang (A.D. 1756–1826), poet. [Section 3.11]

Sun Bin (fourth century B.C.), strategist and military adviser to General Tian Ji during the Warring States period. [Sections 2.1, 4.1, 4.2, 11.9, 11.10]

Sun Ce (r. A.D. 175–200), Governor of Guiji. [Sections 13.12, 15.3]

Sun Quan (A.D. 182–252), King of Wu during the Three Kingdoms period. [Sections 9.1, 10.6, 14.10, 16.2, 16.13]

Sun Tzu (sixth century B.C.), now properly transcribed as Sunzi; general and military theorist; author of the treatise *The Art of War*. [Introduction, Sections 2.1, 2.2, Intro. to No. 4, Intro. to No. 5, Intro. to No. 6, 8.4, 10.5, 11.9, 13.7, 16.4]

Sun Yat-sen (1866–1925), Chinese revolutionary and statesman; founder and leader of the Guomindang; twice chosen president of China. [Section 14.5]

Sunzi—see Sun Tzu.

Taizong (A.D. 627–49), Tang Dynasty Emperor. [Intro. to No. 1, Section 11.11]

Tan Daoji (d. A.D. 436), general in the Southern Song Dynasty. [Introduction]

Tian Ji (fourth century B.C.), Qin army commander during the Warring States period; worked closely with Sun Bin. [Sections 2.1, 4.2, 11.9, 11.10, 11.11]

Wang Mai (thirteenth century A.D.), government official and literary figure. [Section 18.10]

Wang Mang (r. A.D. 8–23), Han emperor. [Section 14.3]

Wang Zhen (d. A.D. 1449), powerful palace eunuch during the Ming Dynasty. [Section 18.4]

Wen, Duke (445–396 B.C.), ruler of Wei. [Section 18.5]

Wenkang (nineteenth century A.D.), Manchurian author. [Section 8.6, 16.8]

Wu, Duke (r. 770–744 B.C.), ruler of Zheng. [Sections 10.2, 15.1]

Wu Cheng'en (ca. A.D. 1500–1582), author of the novel *Journey to the West*, which recounts some of the adventures of the mythological Monkey King. [Section 5.1, Intro. to No. 12]

Wu of the Han (140–87 B.C.), Emperor. [Sections 11.1, 14.3]

Wu Zetian (A.D. 624–705), Tang Empress and founder of the Zhou Dynasty. [Section 14.8]

Xiang Yu (third to second century B.C.), rebel leader against the Qin Dynasty, later "Hegemon of Western Chu." [Sections 8.1, 12.1]

Xiao, Duke (r. 388–361 B.C.), ruler of Qin. [Section 16.6]

Xieli (seventh century A.D.), Khan of the Eastern Turks. [Section 17.25]

Ximen Bao (fifth century B.C.), government official of Wei. [Section 18.5]

Xuan, Duke (r. 718–700 B.C.), ruler of Wei. [Section 11.2]

Xuanhui (r. 332–312 B.C.), a ruler of the Han state during the Warring States period. [Section 11.8]

Xuanzong (A.D. 712–56), Tang Emperor. [Section 18.1]

Xunzi (ca. 313–238 B.C.), philosopher. [Section 7.15]

Yanzi (fifth century B.C.), highly ethical administrator of the city of Dong'e under Duke Jing of Qi; later promoted to Chief Minister of Qi. [Sections 3.3, 16.7]

Yongle Emperor (r. A.D. 1403–24), Ming ruler. [Section 12.6]

Yuan (74–49 B.C.), Han Emperor. [Section 13.2]

Yue Bochuan (A.D. 1271–1368), Yuan period dramatist. [Section 14.1]

Yue Fei (A.D. 1101–42), military leader and patriotic hero of the Southern Song Dynasty. [Section 7.12]

Zeng Pu (1872–1935), Chinese author. [Section 18.9]

Zhang Xun (A.D. 709–57), loyalist Tang Dynasty general; governor of Zhenyuan District during the An Lushan rebellion. [Sections 7.1, 18.6]

Zhang Yi (d. 310 B.C.), famed rhetorician and political figure of the Warring States period; won greatest renown as minister of Qin. [Sections 7.6, 11.8]

Zheng He (fourteenth to fifteenth century A.D.), Muslim eunuch who, under the Ming Dynasty's Yongle Emperor, headed numerous naval expeditions in the early fifteenth century A.D. to remote parts of Asia. [Section 12.6]

Zhi, Marquis (midfifth century B.C.), powerful nobleman in kingdom of Jin. [Sections 17.21, 17.22]

Zhou Enlai—see Chou En-lai.

Zhou Yu (A.D. 175–210), general, commander of Wu forces. [Sections 9.1, 13.12, 15.3]

Zhuang, Duke (743–701 B.C.), ruler of Zheng. [Section 15.1]

Zhuge Liang (A.D. 181–234), also known as Kongming; legendary prime minister of Shu under Liu Bei during the Three Kingdoms period. [Prologue, Sections 1.3, 3 (Note 3), 9.1, 13.7, 13.12, 14.6, 14.10, 16.1, 16.2, 16.13, 16.14]

Zigong (b. 520 B.C.), disciple of Confucius. [Section 3.6]

Appendix D

MAJOR CHINESE DYNASTIES AND PERIODS

Xia	*c.* 2100 B.C.–*c.* 1600
Shang	*c.* 1600–*c.* 1028
Zhou	*c.* 1027–256
Western Zhou	*c.* 1027–771
Eastern Zhou	*c.* 770–256
Spring and Autumn	722–468
Warring States	403–221
Qin	221–207
Han	206 B.C.–A.D. 220
Former Han	206–8
Later Han	25–220
Xin	9–25
Three Kingdoms	220–265
Wei	220–265
Shu	221–263
Wu	222–280
Six Dynasties (Wu, Eastern Jin, Liu Song, Southern Qi, Southern Liang, and Southern Chen)	222–589

JIN	265–420
Western Jin	265–317
Eastern Jin	317–420
SOUTHERN DYNASTIES	420–589
Former (Liu) Song	420–479
Southern Qi	479–502
Southern Liang	502–557
Southern Chen	557–589
NORTHERN DYNASTIES	386–581
Northern Wei	386–534
Eastern Wei	534–550
Western Wei	535–577
Northern Qi	550– 577
Northern Zhou	557–581
SUI	581–618
TANG	618–907
FIVE DYNASTIES	907–960
LIAO	916–1125
SONG	960–1279
Northern Song	960–1126
Southern Song	1127–1279
JIN (Jurchen)	1115– 1234
YUAN	1260–1368
MING	1368–1644
CHING	1644–1911

Appendix E

THE 36 STRATAGEMS

(based on the oldest-known stratagem treatise, *Sanshiliu ji miben bingfa*)

1. Fool the Emperor and Cross the Sea.
2. Besiege Wei to Rescue Zhao.
3. Kill with a Borrowed Knife.
4. Await the Exhausted Enemy at Your Ease.
5. Loot a Burning House.
6. Clamor in the East, Attack in the West.
7. Create Something from Nothing.
8. Openly Repair the Walkway, Secretly March to Chencang.
9. Observe the Fire on the Opposite Shore.
10. Hide Your Dagger Behind a Smile.
11. Let the Plum Tree Wither in Place of the Peach.
12. Seize the Opportunity to Lead the Sheep Away.
13. Beat the Grass to Startle the Snake.
14. Borrow a Corpse for the Soul's Return.
15. Lure the Tiger Down from the Mountain.
16. To Catch Something, First Let It Go.

17. Toss Out a Brick to Attract Jade.
18. To Catch the Bandits, First Capture Their Leader.
19. Steal the Firewood from Under the Pot.
20. Trouble the Water to Catch the Fish.
21. Shed Your Skin Like the Golden Cicada.
22. Shut the Door to Catch the Thief.
23. Befriend a Distant Enemy to Attack One Nearby.
24. Borrow the Road to Conquer Guo.
25. Replace the Beams with Rotten Timbers.
26. Point at the Mulberry, But Curse the Locust Tree.
27. Feign Madness But Keep Your Balance.
28. Lure the Enemy onto the Roof, Then Take Away the Ladder.
29. Deck the Dead Tree with Bogus Blossoms.
30. Exchange the Role of Guest for That of Host.
31. The Stratagem of the Beautiful Woman.
32. The Stratagem of the Open City Gates.
33. The Stratagem of Sowing Discord.
34. The Stratagem of Injuring Yourself.
35. The Stratagem of Linking Stratagems.
36. [When the Situation Is Growing Hopeless] Running Away Is the Best Stratagem.

[Translator's note: In the original Chinese, the phrases depicting the 36 Stratagems are not couched in the imperative form used here for most of the English renditions. Chinese sentences often do not specify the subject of the verb, especially when the subject is clearly implied or readily understood by both speaker and hearer. Most of the stratagem formulas could equally have been rendered in the -ing form (e.g., No. 3: "Killing with a Borrowed Knife," or No. 22: "Shutting the Door to Catch the Thief"). But I felt that, in English, the imperative form most aptly captures the spirit and conciseness of the original.]

NOTES

STRATAGEM 1

1. *Shehui kexue zhanxian* (Social Science Front), publ. 1978 in Changchun, People's Republic of China (PRC).
2. This tale is taken from the photo comic strip *Zhuge Liang zhao qin* (Zhuge Liang Searches for a Bride), (Beijing: Chinese Theatre Press, 1985). The modern text, written by Zhao Kuihua, is certainly not historically accurate. But some of the same details, including people's scorn of the homely Huang Zhengying and Zhuge Liang's marriage to her, are recorded in the twenty-volume collection *Wall of Writings,* by the fourteenth-century literary figure and government official Tao Zongyi. That work, in turn, is a kind of extended anthology compiled from more than six hundred earlier books, some of which have since been lost. The story of Zhuge Liang and Huang Zhengying is recounted in the section "Reports from Xiangyang." Tao Zongyi's way of describing Huang Zhengying's homeliness is to refer to her "golden hair and dark skin."
3. This tale is even older than the preceding ones. It is cited to illustrate Stratagem No. 1 in the Jilin and Taiwan books mentioned in the Introduction and listed in Appendix B.
4. This additional tale from ancient Chinese history, illustrating Stratagem No. 1, is taken from the *Sanshiliu ji xin bian* (The 36

Stratagems: A Modern Version), 7th edition (Beijing, 1989). See Appendix B.

STRATAGEM 2

1. Cf. the story "Sun Bin wei Wei jiu Zhao" (Sun Bin Besieges Wei to Rescue Zhao), which appeared in the largest Chinese children's magazine, *Ertong shidai* (Children's Epoch), No. 18 (Sept. 16, 1981), Shanghai.
2. *Sunzi bingfa* (Sunzi's Art of War) has appeared in several English translations. Unless otherwise noted, all quotes from that work cited in this book are taken from: Sun Tzu, *The Art of War,* trans. Thomas Cleary (Boston & Shaftesbury: Chambala Publications, 1988).
3. *The Art of War,* op. cit., pp. 102, 105.
4. Su Ruozhou and Ke Li, *Junshi chengyu* (Military Idioms), *Shaanxi Renmin Chubanshe* (Shaanxi Province People's Press), (Taiyuan, 1983), p. 486.
5. *Zhongguo gudai zhexue yuyan gushi xuan* (A Selection of Philosophical Parables and Tales from Ancient China), (Shanghai, 1980).
6. Translator's note: Unless otherwise noted, all citations from the writings of Mao Zedong are translated into English from the author's German rendition of the original Chinese text: *Mao Zedong xuanji* (Selected Works of Mao Zedong), (Beijing, 1969). This quote is from vol. 2, p. 398.
7. This event was graphically depicted in a widely circulated comic strip published in Shanghai in 1981.
8. *Sanshiliu ji xin bian* (The 36 Stratagems: A Modern Version), op. cit. See Appendix B.
9. Shu Han, *Sanshiliu ji miben jijie* (The Secret Book of the 36 Stratagems, with Explanations), 3d edition (Taipei, 1986). See Appendix B.
10. *The Art of War,* op. cit., pp. 112–13.

STRATAGEM 3

1. Translator's note: This and subsequent biblical quotations are from *The New English Bible with Apocrypha* (Oxford & Cambridge University Press, 1970).
2. Translator's note: Sir James George Frazer, *The Golden Bough,* 8th printing (New York: Macmillan Paperbacks, 1975), p. 704.
3. The text of this story comes from *Yanzi chunqiu* (The Springs

and Autumns of Yanzi), a collection of anecdotes about Yanzi (d. 500 B.C.), who served three successive rulers of Qi. The book contains a great deal of poetry, some of it clearly influenced by the thinking of Chinese philosopher Mozi (ca. 468–376 B.C.). There is an excellent German translation of this work: *Die Frühlinge und Herbste des Yan Zi*, trans. R. Holzer (Würzburger Sino-Japonica, 1983, vol. 10).

I found a modern Chinese version of this story in a book on Chinese idioms published in Jilin in 1982 (Chen Ripeng and Jin Shijie, *Chengyu gushi sanbai pian* [Three Hundred Tales Built on Chinese Idioms], p. 99ff).

The poem at the end of the anecdote was composed by Zhuge Liang (A.D. 181–234), Prime Minister of Shu, himself an outstanding expert on stratagems. In it he glorifies the dead men and vilifies Yanzi for his use of Stratagem No. 3 and for not daring to openly call for the execution of the disrespectful knights. Instead, exploiting the well-known fact that heroic people are often irritable and oversensitive about their honor, pride, and dignity, Yanzi sowed discord among them and caused them to commit suicide.

4. Andrew Lang, ed., *The Blue Fairy Book* (New York: Dover Publications, 1965), pp. 304–12.

5. This application of Stratagem No. 3 is described in the *Han Feizi* (Book of Han Fei).

6. *Sanshiliu ji xin bian*, op. cit., p. 11ff. See Appendix B.

7. Participation of the German secret service in Tukhachevsky's liquidation by means of forged documents is still regarded as questionable in the West. But the Chinese version of the affair is confirmed by and large in Victor Alexandrov's historical work *L'affaire Toukhatchevsky* [Verviers/Belgium, 1978] and in Gustav Adolf Pourroy's *Das Prinzip Intrige* [Zürich/Osnabrück, 1986].

8. Ma Senliang and Zhang Laiping, *Sanshiliu ji gu jin yin li* (The 36 Stratagems, with Examples from Times Past and Present). (Hong Kong, 1969), op. cit., p. 32ff. See Appendix B.

9. In the People's Republic this stratagem tale has been staged by the Beijing Opera as *Wang Xifeng da nao Ningguofu* (Wang Xifeng Creates Great Tumult in the Ningguo Residence), which was well received by the public and praised by a critic in the *Beijing Evening News*. It was also reproduced in a sixteen-part comic-strip version of the *Dream of the Red Chamber* published in 1984 in Shanghai.

10. *The 36 Stratagems: A Modern Version*, op. cit., p. 10. See Appendix B.

11. *Sanshiliu ji miben jijie*, op. cit., p. 25. See Appendix B.

STRATAGEM 4

1. *The Art of War,* op. cit., p. 122.
2. *Ibid.,* p. 100.
3. Qin Shihuang (the first Emperor of the Qin), who founded the first centralized Chinese empire in 221 B.C., also employed Stratagem No. 4 in the year 223 B.C. to defeat Chu, one of the two remaining rival states standing in the way of his unification of China. During the Cultural Revolution (1966–76), Qin Shihuang was greatly lauded in the People's Republic for his historic accomplishments.
4. *Mao Zedong xuanji,* op. cit., vol. 1, p. 192.
5. Ibid., p. 188.
6. *Sanshiliu ji* (The 36 Stratagems), 1st edition (Changchun, 1979), p. 15. See Appendix B.

STRATAGEM 5

1. *The Art of War,* op. cit., p. 51. [This is an unclear rendition. It might better read: "When the enemy is in chaos, exploit the opportunity to overpower him."—ED.]
2. Translator's note: *Xi you ji* (Journey to the West), by Wu Cheng'en (ca. 1500–1582), is a classic of Chinese legend and has been published in several versions in the West. One of the more colorful is *The Monkey King,* translated from the Czech by George Theiner [London: Paul Hamlyn, 1964]. Probably the most popular is *Monkey,* translated by Arthur Waley [New York: Grove Press, 1958]. The complete *Journey to the West* (in 4 vols.) has been translated into English by Anthony C. Yu [Chicago: University of Chicago Press, 1977–83].
3. These details are related by Gu Yun in a pamphlet titled *Zhongguo jindaishishang de bupingdeng tiaoyue* (The Unequal Treaties in China's Modern History), (Beijing, 1973).
4. *The New English Bible with Apocrypha,* op. cit., Genesis 25: 29–33.

STRATAGEM 6

1. The statement serves as the title of a chapter on the nature of war in Du You's work *Tong dian* (A General History of Institutions).
2. *The Art of War,* op. cit., p. 103.

3. This historical incident is recounted, with an explicit reference to Stratagem No. 6, in a book for young people titled *Zhongguo gudai zhanzheng gushi* (War Stories from Ancient China) (Beijing, 1978).
4. *The New English Bible with Apocrypha,* op. cit., Joshua 6:8–20.
5. Cited in: Daniel Reichel, *Beweglichkeit und Ungewissheit* (Flexibility and Uncertainty), vol. 5 of *Studien und Dokumente* (Studies and Documents), Federal Military Dept. (Berne, Switzerland, 1986).
6. *Shuihu zhuan* (Water Margin, sometimes translated as On the Water's Edge) dates from the end of the Yuan and beginning of the Ming period (thirteenth to fourteenth century A.D.). An early translation of the work by novelist Pearl S. Buck was titled *All Men Are Brothers.*
7. This passage has been rendered into English from the excellent German version *Die Räuber vom Liangshan-Moor* (The Robbers of Liangshan Moor), translated from the Chinese into German by Johanna Herzfeldt (Leipzig, 1968).

STRATAGEM 7

1. *Sanshiliu ji xin bian,* op. cit., p. 24. See Appendix B.
2. The Lindenhof is a handsome, elevated square in Zurich's Old Town, still a favorite gathering place for lunchtime breaks, outdoor concerts, etc.
3. "If it be not true, 'tis a charming invention."
4. Gottfried Schädlich, *Kriegslist gestern und heute* (Tricks of War, Yesterday and Today), 2nd edition (Herford/Bonn, 1979).
5. Vu Can, "Un grand stratège du peuple," *Europe, Revue littéraire mensuelle,* No. 613 (May 1980), Paris, p. 71.
6. This example is drawn from the book *Zhanguo ce* (Stratagems of the Warring States), probably dating from the early 2nd century B.C., the largest anthology of fables, historical anecdotes, and stories about famous personalities from the time before the Han Dynasty (i.e., prior to 206 B.C.).
7. This is the title of a drama from the Yuan period (A.D. 1271–1368), the plot of which is summarized in these paragraphs.
8. The original title of the short story recounted here is "Kuang qi ji" (Stratagem for Fooling the Wife). Written by Yu Hengxiang, the story appeared in the anthology *Yibaige chengxin* (A Hundred Satisfactions) (Shanghai, 1983).
9. In: Gao Mingxuan, ed., *Xingfaxue* (Theory of Criminal Law), *Falü Chubanshe* (Legal Press) (Beijing, 1982), p. 421.

STRATAGEM 8

1.   The play is titled *The Great Emperor of the Han Washes His Own Feet and Thus Angers General Ying Bu.*
2.   *The Art of War,* op. cit., pp. 93–95.
3.   Publ. 1978 in Inner Mongolia, People's Republic of China.

STRATAGEM 9

1.   See, for example, *Makesizhuyi zhexue yuanli* (Principles of Marxist Philosophy), *Jilin Renmin Chubanshe* (Jilin People's Press), 4th edition, 5th printing (Changchun, 1983), p. 150.
2.   *Mao Zedong xuanji,* op. cit., vol. 2, p. 536.
3.   Ibid., p. 543f.
4.   Translated from the German-language edition: Mao Tse–tung, *Ausgewählte Werke* (Selected Works) (Beijing, 1969), vol. 2, p. 320f.
5.   *Mao Zedong xuanji,* op. cit., vol. 3, p. 943.
6.   Zhang Jian's analysis was published in the *Zhongguo qingnian bao* (Chinese Youth Journal), the official newspaper of the Chinese Communist Youth Federation (Jan. 24, 1981).
7.   *Sanshiliu ji xin bian,* op. cit., p. 30. See Appendix B.

STRATAGEM 10

1.   *Sanshiliu ji gu jin yin li,* op. cit., p. 221.
2.   Su Ruozhou and Ke Li, *Junshi chengyu* (Military Idioms), *Shaanxi Renmin Chubanshe* (Shaanxi Province People's Press) (Taiyuan, 1983), p. 486.
3.   In 1984, the Chinese press reported that a sword belonging to Fuchai of Wu had been unearthed in the course of excavations.
4.   *Sanshiliu ji miben jijie,* op. cit., p. 64f.
5.   *Sanshiliu ji gu jin yin li,* op. cit., p. 215.
6.   *The Art of War,* op. cit., p. 135.
7.   *Sanshiliu ji xin bian,* op cit.
8.   Ibid.

STRATAGEM 11

1. The *Yuefu shi ji* (Collection of Yuefu Poems) was compiled during the Song Dynasty.

2. *Sanshiliu ji gu jin yin li,* op. cit., p. 232.

3. Titled "Di Qing Saves His Elder Brother with a Stratagem," this story was recounted in the April 1986 issue of *Ertong shidai* (Children's Epoch), the leading Chinese magazine for children. In China most reading matter tends to have a didactic function. In this case the young readers are being taught the use of a stratagem in the service of brotherly love.

4. *Viêt-Nam Su-Luoc* (Outline of Vietnamese History), Ministry of Education, Republic of South Vietnam (Saigon, 1971), vol. 1, p. 219.

5. *Sanshiliu ji gu jin yin li,* op. cit., p. 239.

6. This story, recounted in the 1969 Hong Kong stratagem book, may be found in *Records of the Historian,* by Sima Qian, mentioned several times in the present work. During the Yuan period (A.D. 1271–1368) it was used by Ji Junxiang as the basis for his play *The Orphan of Zhao.* This was one of the first Chinese plays to be translated into a Western language. The French version, *L'orphelin de Tchao,* by P. Prémare, is found in *Description géographique, historique, chronologique, politique et physique de l'empire de la Chine et de la Tartarie chinoise,* vol. 3 (Paris, 1735), edited by the Jesuit father Jean Baptiste Du Halde (1674–1743). It inspired Voltaire's tragedy *L'orphelin de la Chine.*

7. This tale comes originally from *Stratagems of the Warring States* (see Note 6 to Stratagem No. 7). Our recounting of the story, however, was drawn not from the original text but from a modern version issued as a comic strip in 1982 in the Guangxi Zhuang Autonomous Region.

8. Fan Wenlan, *Zhongguo tongshi* (An Overview of Chinese History), 2nd edition (Beijing, 1978), vol. 3, p. 344.

9. This game has been highly prized in China for millennia, and eventually reached Japan. In it, the two opponents use white and black stones on a board to try and win as much territory as possible. The important thing is to concentrate on the decisive battle(s), even at the risk of being weak in secondary areas or accepting some small, partial defeats. This process is based on the Chinese understanding that the main concern is not to win each individual battle but to win the war as a whole.

10. This and subsequent citations from the writings of Lenin are translated into English from the German-language edition of Lenin's

writings: W. I. Lenin, *Werke* (Works), Dietz-Verlag (Berlin, 1974). This quote is from vol. 31, p. 476.
11.   Ibid., vol. 32, p. 480.
12.   Ibid., vol. 32, p. 359.

STRATAGEM 12

1.   This example is taken from: Kai Werhahn-Mees, ed., *Ch'i Chikuang—Praxis der chinesischen Kriegführung* (The Practice of Chinese Warfare) (Munich, 1980).
2.   See Section 11.13 and Note 9 to Stratagem No. 11.
3.   *Sanshiliu ji yin li* (The 36 Stratagems, with Examples) *Jinri Taiwan She* (Society for Modern Taiwan) (Taipei, 1973), p. 86.
4.   Ibid., p. 85.
5.   *Sanshiliu ji gu jin yin li,* op. cit., p. 85.

STRATAGEM 13

1.   This information has been drawn from the book *Chengyu gushi wubai pian* (Three Hundred Tales About Chinese Idioms), by Zhou Jinhua (Chongqing, 1982); see the chapter devoted to the phrase *"cheng yi jing bai"* (Punish one to intimidate a hundred).
2.   The version given here is based on a Chinese comic strip dealing with the 36 Stratagems, in which No. 13 is illustrated with this incident.
3.   *The Art of War,* op. cit., p. 133.
4.   *Sanshiliu ji xin bian,* p. 41. See Appendix B.
5.   This use of Stratagem No. 13 during the 1956 Suez crisis, however, is confirmed neither by Col. Trevor N. Dupuy in his book *Elusive Victory—The Arab-Israeli Wars, 1947–74* (London, 1978), nor by Jacques Massu in his work *La Vérité sur Suez 1956* (Paris, 1978).
6.   For detailed information on the Chinese Communist Party's three categories of party norms, see my essay "Recent Developments in the Relations between State and Party Norms in the People's Republic of China," in *The Scope of State Power in China,* ed. Stuart R. Schram (New York, London, Hong Kong: St. Martin's Press, 1985), pp. 171ff.
7.   See Section 16.13.
8.   This is a slightly abridged version of a folktale widespread in East Africa, taken from the book *L'enfant rusé et autres contes bambara —Mali et Sénégal oriental* (The Tricked Child and Other Bambara Tales from Mali and Eastern Senegal), collected, translated, and edited

by G. Meyer and V. Görög-Karady (Paris, 1984). The folk figure of the Trickster–Hare is also familiar in the Sudan and in South Africa; it is equivalent to the Black Antelope or the Turtle in Central Africa and Cameroon, and to the Spider Woman in the Atlantic zones of Africa.

9. The relationship between the Divinity and trickery in various cultures is illuminated by studies of the Trickster in mythology and folklore. Among the best-known trickster figures are the Norse god Loki (see Section 3.2) and the Greek god Hermes. This figure's appearance in Indian mythology is investigated by Paul Radin in his book *The Trickster*, with a commentary by C. G. Jung on the psychology of the trickster (3rd edition, New York: Greenwood Press, 1969). Another worthwhile study is Paul V. A. Williams's *The Fool and the Trickster* (Totowa, N.J.: Rowman & Littlefield, 1979).

10. *Sanshiliu ji miben jijie*, op. cit., p. 80.

11. "The Art of Controversy," Section 3, "Stratagems," XXIII, in *The Complete Essays of Schopenhauer*, trans. T. Bailey Saunders, Willey Book Co. (New York, 1942), pp. 26–7.

12. Ibid.

STRATAGEM 14

1. A German translation of this play, by Alfred Forke, was published in *Chinesische Dramen der Yüan-Dynastie* (Chinese Dramas of the Yuan Dynasty) (Wiesbaden, 1978).

2. Additional details are available in the *Lexikon chinesischer Symbole* (Lexicon of Chinese Symbols), by Wolfram Eberhard (Cologne, 1987).

3. This example was drawn from the chapter on No. 14 in a comic-strip series on the 36 Stratagems published in Jilin.

4. Wolfram Eberhard, *Geschichte Chinas* (History of China), 3rd edition (Stuttgart: Kröner Verlag, 1980), p. 109.

5. *Sanshiliu ji yin li*, op. cit. (see Note 3 to No. 12), p. 83.

6. A comic-strip series on the 36 Stratagems published in Lijiang used this tale in its chapter on Stratagem No. 14. The story's original source is chapter 104 of the novel *The Romance of the Three Kingdoms*, which is cited numerous times in the present work.

7. *Sanshiliu ji miben jijie*, op. cit., p. 85.

8. *Sanshiliu ji xin bian*, op. cit., p. 45.

STRATAGEM 15

1. This incident was described in the novel *The History of the Eastern Zhou States*, dating from the Ming period (fourteenth to seventeenth century A.D.). The novel was given its present form during the Qing period (seventeenth to twentieth century), and contains tales from the eighth to the third century B.C. Though based on historical fact, the stories are often imaginatively embellished. The events related here, for example, are also recounted in the Confucian classic the *Zuo Commentary*, but much more simply and without the addition of stratagem details. The version told in these pages is based on stratagem books published in Taiwan and Hong Kong.

2. This example of the application of Stratagem No. 15 is taken from the chronicle *Sanguo zhi* (The History of the Three Kingdoms) by Chen Shou (A.D. 233–97). It has often been retold, one recent version appearing in a series of comics about the stratagems published in the People's Republic of China.

3. This incident from the war of the Chinese Communists against the Japanese invaders appears in a comic strip published in 1982 in Shenyang, People's Republic of China, with a printing of 920,000 copies.

4. Cf. *Beweglichkeit und Ungewissheit*, op. cit.

5. Cf. Abraham Malamat, "Conquest of Canaan: Israelite Conduct of War According to Biblical Tradition," in *Encyclopaedia Judaica Yearbook 1975–76* (Jerusalem, 1977).

6. See Gottfried Schädlich, *Kriegslist gestern und heute* (Tricks of War, Yesterday and Today), 2nd edition (Herford/Bonn, 1979).

STRATAGEM 16

1. See Appendix E. Stratagems 19–36 will be treated in Vol. 2 of this work, scheduled for future publication.

2. The first mention of the seven releases of King Menghuo appears in the chronicle by Xi Zuochi (d. A.D. 384). Nowadays the historicity of the report is doubted by some scholars. Nevertheless, Zhuge Liang's heroic handling of this particular episode is often cited to young Chinese, especially in comic strips and books for young people.

3. Li Bingyan and Sun Jing, *Shuo san guo hua quanmou* (Explaining Stratagems Through the Novel "Romance of the Three Kingdoms"), *Jiefangjun Chubanshe* (People's Liberation Army Press), 5th ed. (Beijing, 1989), p. 208.

4. *Sanshiliu ji yin li,* op. cit., p. 118.

5. *Miben bingfa sanshiliu ji* (The 36 Stratagems: The Secret Book of the Art of War), as reproduced in: Wu Gu, *Sanshiliu ji* (The 36 Stratagems) (Jilin, 1982), op. cit. See Appendix B.

6. Historian Sima Qian, who wrote the earliest biography of Shang Yang, remarks, "On closer examination we see that Shang Yang, in first trying to persuade Duke Xiao of the value of the ways of the old kings and emperors, was operating with mere shadow arguments. This was not his true intention."

7. The German translation of the book, by Franz Kuhn, is titled *Die Schwarze Reiterin* (The Black Rider).

8. The German-language edition is: J. W. Stalin, *Werke* (Works), Red Morning Press (Dortmund, 1976). The specific reference is: vol. 8, p. 12ff.

9. This analysis by Wang Yunqiao appeared in the Beijing periodical *Lishi yanjiu* (Historical Research).

10. He Long (1896–1969) was one of the founders of the People's Liberation Army. After 1949 he served as vice-premier of the People's Republic of China and a leading sports official. I found this anecdote in the *Chinese Youth Journal.*

11. This short-short story is translated from the *Chinese Youth Journal.* The tale was written by Bai Xiaoyi and won first prize out of 30,000 entries in a 1985 all-China contest for short-shorts written by young people.

12. *I Ching,* trans. [German] Richard Wilhelm, [English] Cary F. Baynes, Princeton University Press, 3rd edition, Bollingen Series XIX (Princeton, N.J., 1967), p. 25.

STRATAGEM 17

1. This anecdote has been repeated in hundreds of books since the Song era. Yet it cannot be correct. Chang Jian lived during the first half of the eighth century, Zhao Gu in the first half of the ninth. Could an incomplete four-line poem painted on the wall of the Lingyansi Temple have evoked the two missing verses from Zhao Gu a century later? Perhaps. But even if that were true, the story as it is traditionally told would still be inaccurate.

2. This episode was recounted by Liu Xiang (77–6 B.C.) in the chapter on stratagems in his book *Shuo yuan* (Garden of Anecdotes).

3. This "ode" was composed by Zhao Nanxing (A.D. 1550–1627), a political and literary figure who rose in the Ming government to become Director of the Secretariat. He tried with little success to

combat corruption among the palace eunuchs under Wei Zhongxian. The "Ode to a Fart" is found in his book *Xiao zan* (In Praise of Laughter), in which he satirizes many abuses of the time.

4. "The Art of Controversy," in *The Complete Essays of Schopenhauer,* op. cit., p. 39.

5. Retranslated from the German by Myron B. Gubitz. The German rendition of the French original, which appears in the original edition of *Stratagems,* is by Hanno Helbling.

6. This incident was originally drawn from the book *Stratagems of the Warring States,* dating from around 200 B.C. That entertaining work uses anecdotes, political speeches, and aphorisms to depict in a most delightful way the political intrigues of the two centuries preceding the unification of the kingdoms under Qin. The elaborated version recounted here was taken from a modern stratagem book published in Taipei.

7. *Sanshiliu ji yin li,* op. cit., p. 246.

8. *The New English Bible with Apocrypha,* op. cit., Matthew 4:8–11.

9. This tale is taken from the chapter "Falsehood and Trickery" in *Shi shuo xin yu* (New Tales of the World), ascribed to Liu Yiqing (A.D. 403–44).

10. Although its history goes back to the seventh century B.C., the Great Wall of China was built largely in response to these attacks by the "barbarians from the north."

11. These lines have been retranslated from the German rendition.

12. I discovered this story in a popular edition of the *Guoyu* (Conversations of the States), published in China in 1985, a collection of reports and anecdotes purportedly dating from the tenth to fifth centuries B.C. To the Chinese, the *Guoyu* is the oldest historical work divided according to individual Chinese principalities; to a Western sinologist, however, the boundary between serious history and literary invention in this work seems rather blurred. The 1985 edition from which I drew this account contains a selection of passages from the original work, which is still regarded in Mainland China as instructive and stimulating.

13. This parable is found in the *Huainanzi,* a collection of enigmatic texts drawn from Daoist and Confucian sources and from the ancient Chinese School of Legalism. The work was written by learned men whom Liu An, Prince of Huainan (179–122 B.C.), gathered around him at the end of the second century B.C. The parable is reminiscent of the aphorism in Laozi's *Daodejing*: "Fortune rests on misfortune, misfortune is hidden in fortune."

I found this episode recounted in *Stories About Idioms* [Beijing:

Chinese Youth Press, 1982]. That book explains the significance of the tale as follows: "The saying 'Wasn't it fortunate that the Old Man of the Border's horse ran away?' indicates that something bad can turn into something good, or a temporary loss into a later gain."
14.   In September 1987, while in Tokyo, I learned that Mitsubishi's use of this stratagem had not worked so far.

STRATAGEM 18

1.   Retranslated from the author's German rendition.
2.   The historical background to the poem is given in Cao Mufan's work *Du shi zashuo* (Observations on Du Fu's Poems) (Chengdu, 1981).
3.   Wolfram Eberhard, *Geschichte Chinas* (History of China), op. cit., p. 318f; Jacques Gernet, *Die chinesische Welt* (The Chinese World), (Frankfurt a.M.: Insel Verlag, 1983), p. 341.
4.   This recounting of an event which took place more than twenty-four hundred years ago is drawn from Sima Qian's *Records of the Historian*—to be precise, from a supplement to that work, written by Chu Shaosun in the first century B.C. The story is known to almost every schoolchild in China. (Today the figure of Ximen Bao lives on in the People's Republic mainly in comic strips.) I found the tale in vol. 4 of the official series of school textbooks for Chinese language instruction in Taiwan's junior middle schools. It is also cited as a fine example of No. 18 in Hong Kong and Taipei books on the stratagems.
5.   That this in fact constitutes an application of Stratagem No. 18 is pointed out by Jiang Guowei and Jiang Yongkang, authors of a book on the stratagems published in Guizhou, 1983.
6.   This interpretation was taken from the article "Lob der Gegenwart" (In Praise of the Present) by Ernst Leisi, which appeared in the Swiss newspaper *Neue Zürcher Zeitung*, Aug. 29–30, 1987, p. 66.
7.   These lines translated from the German by Myron B. Gubitz.
8.   Retranslated from the author's German rendition.
9.   This incident was taken from the chapter on Stratagem No. 18 in: Zhuang Zedong and Niu Chen, *Chuang yu jian* (Battle and Sword) (Beijing, 1985), p. 141. Author Zhuang Zedong himself won the table tennis championships several times and also played some part in the 1971 "Ping-Pong diplomacy" between the USA and China during the Nixon administration.
10.   *Sanshiliu ji xin bian*, op. cit., 1st edition, p. 56.
11.   See my book *Partei, Ideologie und Gesetz in der Volksrepublik China* (Party, Ideology, and Law in the People's Republic of China),

Verlag Peter Lang (Berne, 1982), and my essay "Recent Developments in the Relations between State and Party Norms in the People's Republic of China" in *The Scope of State Power in China,* op. cit.

12.   This is the official definition of the "main contradiction" as laid down by the Third Plenum of the Eleventh Party Congress of the Chinese Communist Party in December 1978. The definition was not changed even after the June 1989 violence at Tiananmen Square, and it continues to dominate all official activities of the Party and government of the People's Republic. American (and many other Western) China experts, however, tend to ignore the Sino-Marxist theory of contradictions and the pervasive influence of the "main contradiction" in all aspects of China's official politics, internal and external.

[Some observers, however, see today's "main contradiction" as that between the need for social and political change on the one hand, and an aging, conservative leadership's determination to cling to power on the other.—ED.]

13.   Despite the violent suppression of the democracy movement in China and the subsequent clampdown on open dissent, the opportunities for Chinese university students to study abroad have continued more or less as before. This is because the official definition of the "main contradiction" has not changed. Chinese students continue to be sent abroad mainly to absorb the West's advanced technology, management methods, and social engineering techniques. During the Deng period of socialist modernization (1978–90), the number of Chinese students officially sent abroad to study the humanities and social sciences never exceeded 5 to 10 percent of all the Chinese students sent abroad.

14.   *Makesizhuyi zhexue yuanli,* op. cit., p. 162.

INDEX

NOTE: Chinese names are generally alphabetized under the Pinyin system. Exceptions occur for famous persons familiar to Westerners, which are in the Wade-Giles form. Titles of Chinese works are found under their English translation.